THE BEST OF
AFGHAN
COOKING

THE BEST OF AFGHAN COOKING

A culinary journey with more than 225 traditional recipes

Zarghuna Stanizai Adel

Hippocrene Books, Inc.
New York

All photographs by Zarghuna Stanizai Adel.
Map of Afghanistan, page 2: "20-Afghanistan-Vintage color dark stock illustration"
          © istockphoto.com/pop_jop

Book design by Acme Klong Design and K & P Publishing.

For information, address:
Hippocrene Books, Inc.
171 Madison Avenue
New York, NY 10016
www.hippocrenebooks.com

Cataloging-in-Publication data available from the Library of Congress.

ISBN: 978-0-7818-1443-0

Printed in the United States of America.

CONTENTS

ACKNOWLEDGMENTS

I would like to thank all my fans, followers, friends, and group members on social media from around the world, who not only supported me with endless likes and constructive comments on the older Afghan recipes that I rediscovered, but took the time to test them and truly made this cookbook come to reality.

Special thanks go to my brother, Dr. Khushal Stanizai, who laid the foundation for my work by constantly encouraging me throughout the entire project.

I thank my children, Omar and Eva, and my husband Fawad who patiently bore with my experimental cooking throughout the long years, and who constantly encouraged me.

If it hadn't been for my late mother, I wouldn't have the very rare recipes, such as *Halwa-e Safidak, Kulché Chaharmaghzi,* and *Tandoori,* among others, in this book.

I would like to thank Priti Gress my editor and the entire team of Hippocrene Books, Inc. for their wonderful job of editing, sales, and advertisement for this project.

Final and special thanks go to Rita Rosenkranz, my agent, for her support, guidance, and initial editing, and for finding a home for *The Best of Afghan Cooking.*

INTRODUCTION

Growing up in Kabul, I vividly recall the modest kitchen in my family home that featured a large fire-burning stove called a *chari*. As a curious seven-year-old, I remember wishing I could stir the giant pot of aged *lawangi* rice, enough to not only feed our large family of twelve but our family's cooks and housekeepers as well. The delectable aroma of spices wafting from an adjacent pot of meat and vegetable stew (*qurma*) was so enticing it made my mouth water. Unfortunately, I had to wait to taste it at the table with everyone else. My mother insisted that I could not stir any pot until I was tall enough to be able to see the inside of it.

When the day finally came and I *was* able to see the inside of the pot, my passion for cooking was ignited, inspiring me to learn the nuts and bolts of traditional Afghan cuisine through apprenticeships, where eyeballing measurements to evaluate a food's consistency was the gold standard. Simply put, I was cooking out of pure joy. I would volunteer to help my mother prepare delicacies like *ashak* dumplings. Throughout this time, there was not a single published Afghan cookbook that I could reference. Thus, mastering basic Afghan culinary skills required countless years of trial and error on my part, to successfully learn and memorize these extraordinary recipes that have been handed down through generations. Only then did Afghan cooking become second nature to me.

Then, of course, came the turmoil of war, which forced me to pack my culinary passion, along with the rest of my belongings, and leave Afghanistan forever. It would be twenty-five long years before I would revisit my homeland.

During this crucial visit in 2004, the Afghan culinary legacy that I had grown up with had all but vanished. Past generations of skillful cooks had either passed away or had been forced to flee the country, as I had. This left Afghanistan open to cultural influences from neighboring countries, as Afghan youths, returning home, brought with them the cooking cultures of the countries they had been living in. Except for some individuals in each surviving household who could still skillfully prepare authentic dishes, the food in every household now incorporated unfamiliar aromas, colors, and textures,

and even different names. Commercial cooking was likewise dominated by unskilled individuals, desperate to make a quick profit in a post-war capital city. It was no longer the food of the good old days.

This trip was a turning point in my life. It was heartbreaking to see my beloved home country go through such a bitter, backward transformation. I decided I had to give back to the place where I took my first steps, uttered my first words, and built the foundation of my character. I knew it would be a minuscule contribution, but still a first step. With renewed determination, I set out to restore and compile as many recipes as I could. I started from scratch, and through tireless experimentation, successfully recorded the timing, measurements, and procedures of every single recipe I knew by heart but had never seen in written form. I then proceeded to photograph them after each last try. During this process, it dawned on me that not only is every dish delicious and unique but also that Afghan food is very healthy, being prepared predominantly with whole foods and natural ingredients.

I completed most of this project, consisting of 225 recipes, in 2014. Positive feedback from friends and acquaintances who had tested my recipes filtered in from all over the world via phone, email, and social media and gave me great confidence that my project would be successful. I then introduced some of my finished recipes in Dari via social media. I founded a group that now reaches more than 120, 000 members and still growing, from all Dari-speaking countries like Iran, Tajikistan Kurds of Iraq, Afghanistan, and the Dari-speaking cooking enthusiasts around the world. Being bilingual, the Pashto-speaking population of Afghanistan has also contributed greatly to the completion of this project. I also posted select recipes to over 200,000 fans, friends, and followers on Facebook. My strong social media presence has resulted from my cooking posts. Fans and followers constantly support and welcome any new recipes I post. This enthusiasm and encouragement inspired me to create *The Best of Afghan Cooking*, a first-of-its-kind Afghan cookbook in the English language.

I believe that an entire generation of Afghan immigrants who are not familiar with their native language, and whose numbers reach the millions, will be delighted to see such an important aspect of their national heritage in print. Food lovers around the world will also be able to try recipes from a country that is constantly in the headlines, but that they know very little about. *The Best of Afghan Cooking* takes a modern approach to authentic recipes that have been modified for today's kitchens without sacrificing authentic flavor.

The history of Afghan cookery dates back thousands of years. Excavation of prehistoric sites suggests that farming communities in Afghanistan were among the earliest in the world. Afghans are known to have had domesticated livestock for thousands of years. It is believed that the tradition of grinding freshly harvested wheat into the finest flour originated in Afghanistan and that throughout the centuries fresh milk and its various by-products were used to make desserts.

Since ancient times, Afghan cuisine has also utilized unique ingredients common to neighboring regions. Located in the heart of central Asia, Afghanistan once served as the crossroads for diverse and exotic cultures. The ancient city of Kabul was the meeting point for European, Chinese, and Indian merchants as well as intellectuals and spiritual leaders. Thus, its multi-faceted culinary identity evolved, fusing various blends of recipes.

To this day Afghans have retained the tradition of preparing food with freshly harvested ingredients. In most villages located on the outskirts of Kabul, flour is still ground in local mills. Cows are also milked daily, and the milk is then processed into fresh butter. Dough prepared with fresh ingredients is shaped into bread, cookies, and cakes, before being baked in a pre-heated clay ground oven called a *tandoor*. The rich aroma of spices and the crispiness of roasted nuts combined with fresh milk and wheat create unique desserts that are simple to prepare but deliver impressive results.

It is my sincere hope that *The Best of Afghan Cooking* will serve as a valuable resource about a rich and unique, but tragically forgotten, culinary culture that is little known to the world.

Eggplant and Tomato Borani / *Badenjan Borani*

INDULGENCES
& APPETIZERS
Hawasana

Hospitality is a vital part of the Afghan code of honor. In Afghanistan, the best display of hospitality is to provide guests with special treats called *hawasana*. *Hawasana* have been around since ancient times. They are prepared mostly by females, for their best friends and favorite guests; with tender care by wives for their beloved husbands; and by grandmas for their precious grandchildren and other members of the family. For the most part, *hawasana* are about compassion and devotion to loved ones. If you are invited to share a platter of *ashak* (leek dumplings), you immediately know it is from a loved one. A variety of *bolani* and *sambosa* is prepared for engagement parties to please the daughter and impress the groom's side of the family.

Bolani (vegetable pastries) are one type of *hawasana*. *Bolani* are made with dough spread to a round sheet 10 inches in diameter, then filled with various vegetables or lentils and folded in half. They are then baked in a clay ground oven called a *tandoor* or fried on a griddle called a *taba*. *Bolani* take their name from *bolan*, a vegetable similar in taste and texture to the Chinese chive. This vegetable is abundant in spring when it turns the foothills of the Sher Darwaza and Asa Maee Mountains lush green. *Bolan* has been harvested throughout centuries by enthusiastic local women in colorful dresses strolling on the green to rejoice the arrival of the spring equinox while enjoying their free treat. Other varieties of *bolani* are prepared with a combination of potatoes and green onions, mung beans, pumpkins, and edible shamrocks.

Fried or baked *bolani* are served with a spicy yogurt dip or Afghan chutney on the side, and they last for days. During the Soviet occupation of Afghanistan, *bolani* served as a quick meal for the weary fighters. They were fetched by the younger boys and girls, even women, barefoot and hungry themselves, and carried through the hard terrain to the inaccessible mountains where the Mujahidin fighters had nested ready to fight the enemy. *Bolani* are widely sold at stalls in the cities as a quick snack but homemade *bolani* are tastier and customized with various spices and fried onions.

Hawasana, however, have also evolved alongside the fusion of various blends of ethnicities and cultures. Being at the crossroads of the earliest civilizations, Afghanistan has endured numerous invasions and served as a strategic location where the European, Chinese, and Indian merchants, intellectuals, and spiritual leaders met. It was the diversity of the visitors' cultures that left the legacy of diversity on the Afghan recipes. Most *hawasana* dishes have their roots in a specific region of the country. Detailed explanations with each recipe in this chapter shed light on the ingredients, origins, and brief histories of each *hawasana*.

Hawasana or specialty treats are served both as a main course or appetizer, depending on the ingredients. When meat is utilized in preparing the *hawasana*, it is considered a complete meal, like *ashak, mantu,* and *dolma*. However, other lighter *hawasana* recipes are mostly prepared with vegetables and are served as appetizers.

Ashak (leek dumplings) are considered the finest delicacy of all *hawasana* and are popular all over the country. In cities *ashak* are prepared with white flour dough. The dough is spread into paper-thin sheets that are then cut into rounds. However, in villages *ashak* are prepared in a super simple and fun communal way. One person shapes the dough into tiny balls and then each ball is passed on to the next person who will quickly shape it by hand into a pattie. The pattie is then transferred to the next person to be filled with *gandana* and then passed on to the person in charge of sealing the dumpling before it goes to the pot of boiling water for cooking. When it comes to the teamwork of extended families, *ashak* are magically prepared within minutes. Commercial wraps have also made *ashak*-making easy and fun. But whether using wraps or making your own, up to ten people can participate in this enjoyable assembly line to prepare *ashak*.

Afghans also use *ashak* for games and entertainment. At family parties, one single *ashak* is filled with hot pepper as a trap to make the receiver the next party thrower. The receiver of the super-hot *ashak* can, of course, refuse to eat it, but cannot refuse to invite everyone for an *ashak* party.

Other appetizers are prepared with vegetables, meat, and spices. Yogurt and garlic are traditional accompaniments for most of these dishes.

SAVORY YOGURT WITH PITA

Quruti

*Quruti is a quick, convenient and healthful meal prepared in Afghan villages from organic ingredients. A tangy by-product of milk (*qurut*) is heated and poured over bread chunks and then decorated with caramelized onion rings, walnuts, and spices. It is finished with a drizzle of garlic-flavored oil. Afghans love this simple and fun dish and often consider it a delicacy.*

2 cups qurut (page 319) or chaka (drained yogurt; page 318)
1 tablespoon garlic paste
1 teaspoon salt for chaka
1 small onion (¼ pound), sliced into rings
¼ cup ghee or melted butter
4 pita bread
Pinch ground turmeric
¼ teaspoon ground red or black pepper
½ teaspoon dried crushed mint
¼ cup chopped walnuts

In a small bowl whisk together the *qurut* or *chaka*, garlic paste, and 1 cup of water (if using chaka add 1 teaspoon of salt).

Fry the onion slices in the ghee on medium heat till golden brown. Turn the heat off. Using a slotted spoon, transfer the onions onto a plate and reserve. Also reserve the ghee in the pan.

Cut the pita bread into bite-size pieces and use them to cover the bottom and sides of a medium bowl.

Place the *qurut* mixture in a pot on medium heat and wait until it becomes hot, but not boiling. Remove from the heat and pour gently around the top of the pita bread.

Heat the reserved ghee in the pan and add turmeric. Mix and drizzle on top of the *quruti*. Sprinkle with pepper and mint. Decorate with the fried onions and walnuts. Serve warm.

STUFFED PASTA FLOWERS

Aikhanum

Makes 6 servings

Steamed or baked pasta flowers are stuffed with meat and vegetables, and served with split pea sauce, spices, and yogurt. This hawasana *dish comes from the northern provinces of the country, mainly Turkman and Uzbek populated areas. A three-tier steamer called a* mantu *steamer is used for steaming this treat. If you don't have a steamer, I've also given instructions for baking these in an oven. The pasta flowers in this recipe are four inches in diameter and each one is a serving.*

For the dough:
2 cups all-purpose flour
1 teaspoon salt
1 tablespoon oil
¾ cup water, room temperature

Mix the flour and salt. Add the oil and massage into the flour. Add the water and combine well. Transfer onto a board and knead the dough to homogenize. Cover and let rest for 30 minutes.

For the filling:
2 cups chopped onions
¼ cup oil
1 pound ground lamb or beef
1½ cups chopped green cabbage
1 teaspoon salt
1 teaspoon ground black pepper
2 teaspoons ground coriander seeds

In a mixing bowl, place the onions, oil, ground meat, cabbage, salt, pepper, and ground coriander seeds. Blend well with your hands for 5 minutes. Transfer into a pan and cook, covered, for about 20 minutes on a gentle heat, stirring occasionally, and breaking up any meat lumps until the mixture is dry. Set aside to cool.

For the sauce:
1 onion, finely chopped
¼ cup oil
2 tablespoons tomato paste
2 teaspoons garlic paste
½ teaspoon salt
½ teaspoon ground turmeric
¼ cup yellow split peas, soaked for
  1 hour

Fry the onions in oil to a golden color. Add the tomato paste and fry briefly. Add the garlic paste and fry for a minute. Add the salt, turmeric, and split peas. Add 2 cups of water and cook until split peas are tender and a thick gravy has formed. Keep warm.

For garnish:
1 cup chaka (drained yogurt; page
  318)
Pinch salt
1 teaspoon garlic paste
Dried mint
Cilantro leaves

Mix *chaka* with the salt and garlic paste and set aside.

To assemble the *aikhanum*:
Divide the dough into three equal balls. Cover the balls and rest for 15 minutes. Using a rolling pin stretch each ball into an 8- by 16-inch rectangle. Then divide each rectangle into two sections lengthwise so you have 6 strips. Divide the filling mixture into 6 equal portions. Spread each filling portion onto the dough lengthwise to cover half of the dough. Fold the uncovered portion over the filling and press to seal and brush lightly with oil. Roll the dough strips starting at the short end to make a flower. Pinch the ends so they don't come loose.

Cooking Method 1: Steaming
Arrange dough flowers on a greased *mantu* steamer and steam for about 45 minutes rotating the steamer pots until the pasta is soft and translucent. Spread half the seasoned *chaka* on a serving plate and spread half of the sauce on top. Place the pastry flowers on top of the chaka and sauce and drizzle the remaining sauce on top. Sprinkle with mint and cilantro leaves.

Cooking Method 2: Oven-baked
Mix half of the sauce with ½ cup water and pour in a casserole dish. Arrange the pastry flowers on top of the sauce. Pour the remaining sauce around and on top of the flowers and bake covered for 30 minutes in 375 degrees F oven. Serve as above.

LEEK DUMPLINGS WITH GROUND BEEF SAUCE
Ashak

Makes 8 servings

This delicacy, tender leek dumplings with a touch of yogurt served with a ground beef sauce, is prepared in all regions of the country. However, the finest ashak *is prepared in Kabul homes. In villages, the dough is shaped into tiny balls and flattened into thin patties for individual* ashak. *The ground beef and yogurt are fresh and organic. Afghans love to prepare* ashak *using the teamwork of family members (see chapter introduction, page 6).*

For the wraps:
4 cups all-purpose flour
1 teaspoon salt

Mix the flour and salt with 1½ cups water and knead well to form a firm dough. Let the dough rest for 15 minutes. Divide the dough into three balls and cover. Working with one ball, form the ball into a patty and then, using a rolling pin, spread into a thin sheet the thickness of a dumpling wrap. With a cookie cutter cut into 2½-inch rounds and sprinkle with flour. Do the same with the other balls of dough. Set aside four dough circles for the center flower (see below).

For the filling:
1½ pounds gandana, finely chopped and rinsed (leeks, scallions, or Chinese chives can be substituted)
2 teaspoons salt

Sprinkle the gandana/leeks with the salt and leave for about 15 minutes. Mix well then squeeze out the extra juices. Set aside.

Prepare the dumplings:
Dip your finger in water and run around the edge of a dough circle. Then place 1 tablespoon of the prepared filling in the center and fold over the dough to make a half-circle. Seal by pressing the edges together. Sprinkle with flour. Repeat with remaining dough circles.

Prepare the decorative center flower:
Overlap four dough circles in a straight line, moistening between the overlap areas generously so they can stick together by pressing them down. Place three tablespoons of the filling along the top of the circles. Fold the dough circles in half and then starting at one end roll loosely into a flower, leaving the top open. Pinch the end of the roll to seal. Adjust the flower petals by opening them more to a desired shape.

(continued on page 12)

Preparing the decorative center flower

Leek Dumplings with Ground Beef Sauce / *Ashak*

LEEK DUMPLINGS WITH GROUND BEEF SAUCE

(continued from page 10)

For the beef sauce:
4 cups chopped onions
¼ cup olive oil
¼ cup butter
1 teaspoon ground turmeric
1½ teaspoons salt
2 teaspoons cayenne pepper powder (optional)
1 tablespoon ground coriander seeds
1 tablespoon tomato paste
1½ pounds lean ground beef

Stir-fry onions in the oil and butter until golden. Add turmeric, salt, cayenne pepper powder, coriander seeds, and tomato paste. Stir-fry on medium heat for about 1 minute. Add the ground beef and stir to mix with the sauce on low heat, breaking up meat lumps. Stir in 1½ cups water. Cover and cook gently for about 20 minutes or until the water has evaporated. Spoon off most of the oil and discard. Keep warm.

For the topping:
2 cups chaka (drained yogurt; page 318)
2 teaspoons garlic paste
Pinch of salt
½ teaspoon dry crushed mint

Mix the *chaka* with the garlic paste and salt and set aside.

Cooking Method 1: Boiling
Mix 3 quarts of water with 1 teaspoon salt and bring to a rolling boil. Slide in the dumplings and boil gently for about 10 minutes, pushing the dimplings down into the water with a spatula for even cooking, until translucent and cooked through. Using a large slotted spoon catch a few dumplings at a time, letting the water drip back into the pot. Steam the flower separately using a steamer.

Method 2: Steaming
After filling the dumplings, arrange them, including the flower, on a well-greased steamer (*mantu*) and cook for about 40 minutes or until soft and transparent.

To serve:
Place the flower in the center of a serving plate. Spread half the *chaka* mixture onto the serving plate. Transfer the dumplings onto the *chaka* around the flower. Spoon the remaining *chaka* over the dumplings. Then pour the beef sauce evenly over the top of the dumplings and sprinkle with the mint.

STEAMED BEEF DUMPLINGS WITH SPLIT-PEA SAUCE

Mantu

Mantu is a popular dish from the northern provinces of the country, home to Uzbek and Turkman Afghans. Mantu consists of dumplings stuffed with beef, onion, and spices, and then steamed on the racks of a special steamer called a dayg mantu. Mantu *is served on a bed of drained yogurt (*chaka*) with split-pea sauce drizzled around the top. The dumplings are prepared from fresh dough spread into thin sheets and cut into squares. The use of commercial dumpling squares (Gayoza skins) is a time-saving and convenient way of preparing this elaborate dish.*

*For the dough:
4 cups all-purpose flour
1 teaspoon salt

*You can substitute square Gayoza skins for the dough squares.

Mix the flour with salt and 1½ cups water and knead well into a firm dough. Divide into 4 portions. Using a rolling pin, spread each portion into a rectangle, ⅛-inch thick. Cut each rectangle into equally divided squares, 3 to 4 inches each.

For the filling:
1 pound 85% ground beef
6 cups finely chopped onions
1½ teaspoons salt
1 teaspoon ground black pepper
1 tablespoon ground coriander seeds

Mix the ground beef, onions, salt, pepper, and coriander. Cook for about 20 minutes, stirring constantly on gentle heat. Then cook on a raised heat until juices evaporate. Let cool.

For the sauce:
1 cup yellow split peas
1 onion, finely chopped
¼ cup melted butter or oil
¼ teaspoon salt
Pinch ground turmeric
1 tomato blanched, skin removed and chopped

In a small saucepan boil the split peas in 1½ cups water for about 20 minutes. Drain and reserve, covered. Sauté the onions in oil to a light brown color. Add the salt, turmeric, and tomato. Stir-fry on low heat until tomatoes are dissolved. Add the split peas and stir to mix. Add 1 tablespoon water and simmer until oil starts to separate. Keep warm.

(continued next page)

STEAMED BEEF DUMPLINGS WITH SPLIT-PEA SAUCE

(continued from previous page)

For the topping:
2 cups chaka (drained yogurt; page 318)
2 teaspoons fresh garlic paste
Crushed dried mint
Crushed red pepper

Mix *chaka* and garlic paste together and set aside.

Assemble the dumplings:

On a smooth surface place 3 to 6 dough squares at a time. Then place 1 tablespoon of the prepared filling in the center of each square. Have two small bowls ready: one filled with water and the other with oil. Dip your finger in the water and run around the edges of each square. Bring two opposite corners together and pinch. Bring the remaining two opposite corners together and pinch with the first two. Seal the attaching edges thoroughly. Seal together the corners closest to each other on opposite sides.

Steam the dumplings:

Brush the surface of the steamers with oil and transfer the dumplings onto the steamers. Do not overcrowd them since it will block the holes and eventually block the steam. When the steamer's tiers are all filled, fill half of the lower boiler with boiling water and place on medium heat. Place the steamers on top of the boiler and steam the dumplings covered for about 20 minutes or until cooked through. Rotate steamer trays occasionally for even cooking.

To serve:

Spread half the seasoned *chaka* on a decorative platter and transfer the dumplings onto the *chaka* and top with the remaining *chaka*. Then spoon the split-pea sauce evenly over the top of the dumplings. Sprinkle with mint and red pepper. Serve warm.

Steamed Beef Dumplings with Split-Pea Sauce / *Mantu*

SQUASH BOLANI

Bolani Kadu

Makes 8 bolani

Thin dough rounds are stuffed with sweet and spicy butternut squash, shallow-fried or baked, and served with sauces and chutneys on the side. Butternut quash (kadu) is cultivated throughout the country, and when in season it is sold at stalls for cheaper. Squash is also utilized for preparing condiments such as squash pickles, turshi kadu (an appetizer), kadu borani, and soup. Seeds are saved either for next year's cultivation or for winter when they are roasted and salted for snacking.

For the dough:
1½ cups all-purpose flour
½ cup whole wheat flour
1 teaspoon active dry yeast
½ teaspoon salt
2 tablespoons oil, warmed
1 cup warm water

Place the flours, yeast, and salt in a mixing bowl and stir. Add the oil and rub into the flour. Add the warm water gradually and mix with hands into a soft, sticky dough. Transfer the dough onto a flour-dusted surface. With clean, flour-dusted hands knead the dough for about 5 minutes or until homogenized. Cover and set aside at room temperature to rise for 1 hour. Divide the dough into 8 equal portions and then form each portion into a ball. Cover and set aside, leaving spaces between balls for expansion.

For the filling:
1 pound butternut squash
1½ tablespoons olive oil
½ large onion, shredded
½ teaspoon salt
1½ teaspoons dried crushed
  red peppers
½ teaspoon garlic paste
1½ tablespoons sugar
¼ cup chopped cilantro
Oil for frying

Peel the squash and split. Remove the seeds and fiber from the bottom and then shred the squash. In a non-stick skillet, sauté the onions and squash together in the oil for about 7 minutes. Transfer to a mixing bowl. Add salt, crushed red peppers, garlic paste, sugar, and cilantro. Mix well and divide into 8 equal portions.

Make the bolani:

With the help of a rolling pin, spread one dough ball into a 7-inch circle. Then spread one portion of filling over half of the dough circle. Fold over the other half to make the *bolani*. Gently stretch out the *bolani* by pressing with palm till it has a 10-inch-long straight edge and then pinch the curved edges to seal. Work with the rest of the filling and dough to finish assembling the *bolani*.

Add ¼-inch of oil to a non-stick pan and heat. Fry the *bolani* in batches on both sides until golden and crisp. Drain on paper towels. Serve with chutney on the side.

MUNG BEAN BOLANI

Bolani Mash

Makes 10 servings

For these bolani, *cooked split mung beans (mash) are mixed with sautéed onions and spices and then stuffed in thin dough rounds. This* bolani *can be baked or shallow-fried and is served with sauces or chutney on the side. Bolani Mash is often served as a filling meal, taking into account its nutritious properties such as being a rich source of protein and fiber.*

For the dough:
1½ cups all-purpose flour
½ cup whole wheat flour
½ teaspoon salt
2 tablespoons oil, warmed
1 cup warm water

Mix the flours and salt in a bowl. Add the oil and rub into the flour. Add the warm water gradually and mix with hands into a soft, sticky dough. Transfer the dough onto a flour-dusted surface. With clean, flour-dusted hands knead the dough for about 5 minutes or until homogenized. Divide the dough into 10 portions and form each into a ball. Cover and set aside at room temperature to rest for an hour.

For the filling:
2 cups dried split mung beans
2 large onions
¼ cup oil
2 tablespoons minced garlic
½ teaspoon ground black pepper
2 teaspoons ground coriander
  seeds
1½ teaspoons salt
1 teaspoon dried crushed red
  peppers
Oil for frying

Soak the mung beans for 1 hour in water three inches above the beans. Place the bean pot over heat, bring to a boil, and cook for 30 minutes or until tender. Drain and reserve.

Peel and quarter the onions, top to bottom, and then slice each quarter across the grain. Sauté the onions in the oil until they start to change color. Remove from heat and add the garlic, black pepper, ground coriander seeds, salt, and crushed red peppers. Add the onion mixture to the mung beans and mix well. Divide mixture into 10 equal portions.

Make the bolani:
Spread out one dough ball into a 7-inch patty. Spread one portion of the filling to cover half of the dough. Fold over the other half and press gently on the filled dough to get rid of any bubbles, then pinch edges to seal. Repeat with the remaining dough and filling.

Cover a griddle with a film of oil and fry the *bolani* in batches until golden and crispy on both sides. Add oil for frying new batches as necessary. Drain on paper towels. Serve with chutney on the side.

LEEK AND POTATO BOLANI

Bolani Makhlut

Makes 8 bolani

Leavened, thin dough rounds are stuffed with a combination of leeks, potatoes, and spices. The stuffed dough is then shallow-fried on a griddle or non-stick pan, or baked in the oven, and then brushed with melted butter. Bolani are served with dips such as yogurt mixed with salt and powdered mint, or any chutney on the side. Bolani are popular in all regions of Afghanistan. Villagers prepare bolani with the vegetable of the season and bake them in the hot tandoor.

For the filling:
3 cups finely chopped gandana, washed and rinsed (a variety of leeks; scallions, Chinese chives, or leeks can be substituted)
4 cups shredded cooked potatoes
1 cup finely chopped cilantro
1 teaspoon salt
3 teaspoons dried crushed red pepper
½ cup fried sliced onions
1 tablespoon oil

Place the gandana/leeks in a mixing bowl and crush between hands to soften it. Add the potatoes, cilantro, salt, crushed red pepper, fried onions, and oil. Mix well with a fork until well blended and pasty. Divide into eight portions.

For the dough:
1½ cups all-purpose flour
½ cup whole wheat flour
½ teaspoon salt
1½ tablespoons oil, heated
1 teaspoon active dry yeast
1 cup warm water
Oil for frying

Place the flours and salt in a mixing bowl and whisk to combine. Add the heated oil and rub into mix. Dissolve the yeast in the warm water and add to the flour. Mix well and transfer to a flour-dusted board. With clean and flour-dusted hands knead the dough for about 5 minutes or until homogenized. Divide the dough into 8 equal portions, and then form each portion into a smooth ball. Cover and let stand in a warm place to rise for about 1 hour, depending on the surrounding temperature.

Spread one dough ball into a 7-inch circle. Spread one portion of the filling on half of the circle and fold over the other half to make a half-circle. Stretch the stuffed *bolani* with the palm of your hand, working from center and spreading it on both sides into a 10-inch long *bolani*. Fill the remaining dough balls. Pour a ½-inch oil into a frying pan and heat. Working in batches, fry the stuffed *bolani* on both sides and drain on paper towels. Add more oil as needed and adjust heat if the dough gets brown too quickly. When reheating leftover *bolani*, use a toaster oven.

LEEK BOLANI

Bolani Tandoori

Makes 6 bolani

These leek-filled Bolani Tandoori *are very popular in the villages. They are traditionally prepared in a triangular shape and baked in a clay ground oven, the* tandoor, *but domestic ovens serve well to prepare them. This* hawasana *is considered more healthful than their fried counterparts and they are usually served with chutney or yogurt on the side.*

For the dough:
2 cups all-purpose flour
½ teaspoon salt
2 tablespoons oil
1 teaspoon active dry yeast,
   dissolved in 1 cup lukewarm water
1 egg white, beaten

Mix the flour and salt in a mixing bowl. Add the oil and rub in by hand. Add the yeast solution to the flour and mix with hands until a soft dough is obtained. Transfer the dough to a clean surface. Wash hands and dry thoroughly. Then dust hands and the dough with flour and knead well until elastic and homogenized. Divide the dough into 6 equal portions and form each portion into smooth balls. Cover and set aside at room temperature to rise for 1 hour.

For the filling:
2 pounds gandana (a variety of
   leeks), finely chopped and washed
   and rinsed (scallions, Chinese
   chives, or leeks can be substituted)
2 teaspoons salt
Cayenne pepper powder to taste

Sprinkle salt on the gandana/leeks and mix. Set aside for about 20 minutes. Then crush the gandana/leeks with the palm of your hand. Drain the extra water and discard. Mix in the cayenne pepper powder and divide the leeks into 6 portions.

Prepare the bolani:
Heat the oven to 400 degrees F. Spread each dough portion into a circle 7 inches in diameter and arrange the leek portions in a triangle shape in the middle of each circle. Fold the edges over into a triangle. After sealing the *bolani*, transfer onto a greased baking tray, seam side down, and brush the tops with the beaten egg white. Bake for about 30 minutes or until golden. Serve warm with any chutney.

SPINACH BOLANI

Bolani Sabzi

Makes 14 bolani

These spinach-stuffed bolani *are prepared with fresh spinach, onions, and spices. This shallow-fried appetizer is best served with chutney on the side.*

For the dough:
3½ cups all-purpose flour
1½ teaspoons salt

In a mixing bowl mix the flour and salt. Add 1½ cups water gradually while rubbing the flour into a soft, sticky dough. Using dry hands knead the dough until homogenized. Transfer the dough onto a smooth surface and knead for 5 minutes. Divide the dough into two equal portions and shape the portions into cylinders. Using a sharp knife divide the cylinders into 7 equal portions, 14 in total. Shape each portion into a smooth ball, brush with oil, and cover with plastic wrap. Leave to rest for 20 minutes.

For the filling:
1 pound chopped fresh spinach
1 cup chopped cilantro
2 cups finely chopped onions
2 teaspoons garlic paste
1 teaspoon ground black pepper
2 teaspoons ground coriander seeds
1 teaspoon dried crushed red peppers
1½ teaspoons salt
4 tablespoons oil plus oil for cooking

Place all the filling ingredients in a mixing bowl, except the oil for cooking. Mix the ingredients well and divide the filling into 14 equal portions. Set aside.

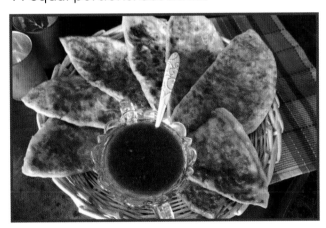

Prepare the bolani:
Working with one dough ball at a time sprinkle with flour and press gently into a patty 3 inches in diameter. Repeat with the rest of the balls and stack patties on top of each other. Leave to rest for 15 minutes. Using a rolling pin, spread each patty into a 7-inch circle.

Spread one portion of the filling on half of a dough circle and fold over the other half to cover. Pinch the open side to seal. Repeat with the rest of the dough and filling to finish all the *bolani*.

Heat 1 tablespoon of oil on a griddle on moderate heat and fry two *bolani* at a time for about 2 minutes on each side until golden and crisp. Adjust the heat if the *bolani* turns color too quickly. Repeat until all *bolani* are cooked, adding a little more oil when the griddle surface needs oil. Drain on paper towels. Serve with some chutney on the side.

EGGPLANT DIP

Badenjan Bharta

Makes 6 servings

This eggplant (badenjan) appetizer is prepared with spices and fried onions and served with nan. Young, good-quality eggplants (see Glossary, page 318) are carefully selected for this dish so the outcome is not bitter and seedy. This recipe is adapted from the Hindu-Afghan version of Afghan laghatak. Badenjan Bharta is a snack between meals and is a great dip for any Afghan nan or potato chips.

3 pounds eggplants
1 small onion, thinly sliced
3 tablespoons oil
1 tomato, finely chopped
2 teaspoons minced garlic
1 teaspoon salt, or as
  needed
1 tablespoon minced chilis
1 tablespoon olive oil
Pinch turmeric
Red chili flakes

With the help of a bamboo skewer make holes through the eggplants and then place in a casserole dish and bake for about 50 minutes at 375 degrees F, or until a knife can easily slice through the eggplants. Place the eggplants in a paper bag and close tight and leave to cool. Once they are cool, place the eggplants on a cutting board and peel. Cut each eggplant through the middle lengthwise and scoop out any seeds and discard. Then cut into small pieces and puree in the food processor. Set aside.

Brown half of the onion slices in the oil to a light golden color. Add the tomatoes and cook down for about 5 minutes on moderate heat. Add the garlic, salt, and chilies. Stir-fry for about 1 minute. Mix in the reserved eggplant puree and stir-fry for 1 minute. Transfer to a decorative dish.

Fry the remaining onion slices in the olive oil to a light brown color. Mix in the turmeric and fry for 15 seconds. Drizzle the onions and oil around the top of the dip and sprinkle with chili flakes. Serve warm or cool as a dip with Afghan nan (page 188).

EGGPLANT YOGURT DIP

Badenjan Laghatak   Makes 6 servings

*Badenjan Laghatak is a healthful appetizer that requires no frying. It is prepared with eggplants (*badenjan*), organic yogurt, and spices. It can be served as a dip with Afghan* Nan Tabaee *(page 196), potato chips, French fries, or vegetables such as cucumbers, celery, and carrots.*

1 large, seedless eggplant
   (about 1½ pounds)
¼ pound chaka (drained
   yogurt; page 318)
1 teaspoon salt
1 tablespoon minced onion
2 teaspoons minced garlic
1 tablespoon lemon juice
Tomato, cilantro leaves, sesame
   seeds, and extra virgin olive oil
   for garnish

With the help of a bamboo skewer make holes through the eggplant and then place in a casserole dish and bake for about 50 minutes at 375 degrees F or until a knife can easily slice through the eggplant. Place the eggplant in a paper bag, close tight and leave to cool. Once cool, transfer the eggplant onto a cutting board and peel. Cut the eggplant through the middle lengthwise and scoop out any seeds and discard. Then cut into small pieces and puree in the food processor.

Place eggplant puree in a bowl and add the *chaka*, salt, onion, garlic, and lemon juice. Mix well. Transfer to a decorative dish. Drizzle the oil around the top of the eggplant. Decorate with the tomato and cilantro leaves. Sprinkle with the sesame seeds. Serve as a dip.

EGGPLANT BORANI

Badenjan Borani

Makes 4 servings

This eggplant appetizer goes through three stages—dehydrating, frying, and steaming with layers of tomatoes. It is served on a bed of drained yogurt, mixed with salt and garlic. Afghan Nan Taba-ee (page 196) tastes great with this appetizer. Badenjan Borani makes a light snack or starter with other main dishes. This dish is loved by all Afghans and does not belong to any specific region.

1 pound seedless eggplant (see Glossary, page 318), sliced
Salt
Oil for frying
1 large tomato, sliced
½ teaspoon tomato paste
¼ teaspoon ground turmeric
1 cup chaka (drained yogurt; page 318)
Red flaked pepper and dried mint for garnish

Sprinkle the eggplant slices on both sides lightly with salt and place in a colander, arranging tightly. Leave for 20 minutes or so to sweat. Gently pat each eggplant piece with a paper towel. Pour 3 inches of oil into a small pan and heat. Fry a few eggplant pieces at a time to a golden color and drain on paper towels.

In a cooking pot arrange half of the tomato slices. Then arrange the fried eggplant on top of the tomatoes and place the remaining tomato slices on the top. Dissolve the tomato paste and turmeric in ¾ cup water and pour it around the top of the tomatoes. Cover and cook for about 15 to 20 minutes on moderate heat until the oil separates. Uncover and continue to cook to rid of any juices.

Spread half of the *chaka* on a serving plate. Arrange the eggplant-tomato mixture on the plate. Decorate with the remaining *chaka*, red pepper flakes, and mint. Serve warm.

EGGPLANT, ONION AND TOMATO BORANI

Borani Lowabdar

Makes 6 servings

Eggplant (badenjan) *is a popular vegetable in Afghanistan and is cultivated throughout the country. This eggplant appetizer is considered a delicacy for most households. The eggplant is fried before steaming in a sauce of fried onions and tomatoes.* Badenjan Lowabdar *is served with Afghan nan (page 188) or plain rice (chalow, page 147) on the side.*

3 pounds seedless eggplants (see page 318),
   peeled and chopped into bite-size pieces
1 cup finely chopped onions
½ cup olive oil
½ teaspoon ground turmeric
2 teaspoons tomato paste
½ cup chopped tomatoes
2 teaspoons ground coriander seeds
Salt and pepper to taste
1 cup chaka (drained yogurt; page 318)
1 teaspoon minced garlic
1 teaspoon dried mint flakes

Sprinkle the eggplant pieces with salt and leave for 20 minutes to sweat.

Stir-fry the onions in the olive oil over medium heat until they start to change color. Pat the eggplant pieces dry, and stir-fry with the onions until the vegetable starts to brown. Add the turmeric, tomato paste, tomatoes, ground coriander, and salt and pepper. Stir-fry on low heat until the tomatoes are dissolved. Add 1 cup of water. Stir well, and then cover and cook on low heat until the eggplants are soft, and all the liquid has been absorbed, about 10 to 15 minutes. Spoon off the extra oil and discard.

Mix the *chaka* with the garlic. Spread half the *chaka* on a serving plate and top with the eggplant mixture. Top with the remaining *chaka*. Sprinkle with the mint flakes and serve warm.

POTATO BORANI

Borani Kachalu

Borani Kachalu is a popular Afghan dish prepared with Afghan potatoes, widely cultivated in Afghanistan, particularly in Bamiyan province. Fried wedges of potato are steamed in tomato and onion sauce to make this appetizer. A drizzle of fried onions, yogurt, and spices complete it and it is then served with nan.

1 cup chaka (drained yogurt; page 318)
2 teaspoons minced garlic
1¼ teaspoons salt
½ cup thinly sliced onions
¼ cup oil
1 pound potatoes, peeled and each cut into
  4 wedges
¼ teaspoon ground turmeric
1 teaspoon tomato paste
1 green chili, sliced
Dried mint, crushed chilies, and cilantro for
  garnish

Whisk together the *chaka*, garlic, and ¼ teaspoon of the salt. Set aside.

Stir-fry the onion slices in the oil until a light brown color is achieved. Remove onions with a slotted spoon and reserve.

Lower the potato wedges into the same oil and stir-fry on moderate heat for about 5 minutes. Add the turmeric, tomato paste, and remaining salt. Stir-fry for another minute. Add ¾ cup of water and stir. Cover and simmer for about 15 minutes or until the potatoes are tender and the liquid has evaporated.

Spread half of the *chaka* on a serving plate. Transfer the potatoes to the bed of *chaka*. Drizzle the remaining *chaka* and any remaining sauce around the top of the potatoes. Sprinkle with the fried onions, green chili slices, dried mint, crushed chilies, and cilantro. Serve immediately with nan.

BANANA SQUASH BORANI

Borani Kadu

Makes 4 servings

Banana squash (kadu) is fried and served in sauce on a bed of yogurt with a drizzle of caramelized onions and spices. Toasted Afghan nan tastes great with this appetizer. This borani *is mostly prepared in autumn when the squash is in season and plentiful. Squash, which grows in most regions of the country, is also utilized for preparing other foods such as soup,* sambosa, *and* bolani. *When squash is used in condiments, sugar is added with vinegar for that sweet and sour taste (see* Turshi Kadu, *page 206).*

1 pound banana or butternut squash
½ onion, sliced
1 cup oil for frying
½ teaspoon salt
1 tablespoon sugar
½ teaspoon cayenne pepper powder
1 teaspoon tomato paste
1 cup chaka (drained yogurt, page 318)
1 teaspoon garlic paste
1 teaspoon dried mint

Peel the squash and chop it into 1½-inch rectangular pieces with ¼-inch thickness.

Stir-fry the onion slices in the oil over medium-high heat until golden. Remove with a slotted spoon. Let cool.

Fry a few pieces of squash at a time for 2 minutes on each side in the same oil, and then drain on paper towels. Transfer fried squash to a medium-sized saucepan. Whisk together ¾ cup water, the salt, sugar, cayenne pepper powder, and tomato paste. Sprinkle evenly around the top of the squash. Cover and cook on low heat for about 10 minutes or until squash is oily and transparent.

Mix the *chaka* with the garlic paste and a pinch of salt. Spread half of the *chaka* onto a large plate. Mound half of the prepared squash on top of the *chaka*. Sprinkle with the fried onions. Spoon the remaining squash on top of the onions. Pour over the remaining *chaka* evenly and sprinkle with dried mint. Serve warm with nan.

YELLOW MUNG BEANS

Dahl

Afghan dahl *is prepared with yellow mung beans and sour plums, and is flavored with orange peel, garlic, and ginger, and then finished with a drizzle of garlic-flavored oil and spices. It is served with nan.* Dahl *has been served in Afghanistan for as long as the Hindu and Sikh Afghans in many regions of the country have called Afghanistan their home. Variations in* dahl *cooking are the result of recipe modification by Muslim Afghans eager to learn the tasty and spicy recipes from their fellow Hindu and Sikh Afghans.*

2 cups dried yellow mung beans
½ cup oil
1 large onion, finely chopped
½ teaspoon ground turmeric
2 teaspoons ground cumin seeds
½ tablespoon ground coriander
  seeds
½ teaspoon ground fresh ginger
1½ teaspoons salt
1 tomato, chopped
3 green chilis, finely chopped
  (optional)
12 dried sour plums (alu bukhara)
½ tablespoon grated orange peel

For the garnish:
1 tablespoon oil
½ tablespoon minced garlic
½ tablespoon dried chili
  flakes

Cook the mung beans in 5 cups of water for about 45 minutes on moderate heat, until the grains disintegrate and a thick soup is obtained.

Meanwhile, to prepare the sauce, heat the oil in a skillet and add the onions and stir-fry to a golden color. Add turmeric, ground cumin seeds, ground coriander seeds, and ginger. Stir on low heat for 1 minute. Add the salt, tomatoes, and green chilis and stir for another minute until the tomatoes are cooked down. Add the prepared mung beans to the sauce and stir to mix. Add the dried sour plums and orange peel and simmer until the fruit is tender. Transfer to a serving bowl.

To garnish, heat the 1 tablespoon oil and fry the garlic and chili flakes in it for 30 seconds. Pour over the top of the *dahl* and serve with nan.

Yellow Mung Beans / *Dahl*

STUFFED BELL PEPPERS

Dolma e Morch

Makes 7 servings

Oven-baked bell peppers (morch) are stuffed with ground beef, basmati rice, herbs, and spices. Dolma e Morch is a complete meal when served with toasted Afghan nan. When prepared in villages, the stuffed peppers are tightly arranged in a clay or stone pot and drizzled with the sauce. Then the pot is lowered onto the glowing wood particles of a pre-heated ground oven (tandoor) for slow cooking. The outcome is aromatic and delectable.

For the sauce:
2 large tomatoes
2 large onions, finely chopped
¼ cup oil
3 tablespoons tomato paste
1 teaspoon salt
1 teaspoon ground turmeric
1 tablespoon minced garlic
½ teaspoon dried chili flakes
1 teaspoon ground coriander seeds
1 cup chopped cilantro

Submerge the tomatoes in boiling water for 1 minute. Remove and dip in cold water. Remove skin and chopped them finely. Stir-fry the onions in the oil over medium heat until golden. Add the tomatoes and stir-fry until the tomatoes are dissolved and the sauce gets oily. Add the tomato paste and stir-fry for about 30 seconds on low heat. Add the salt, turmeric, garlic, chili flakes, and ground coriander seeds. Stir for another 30 seconds. Add 1 cup water and stir. Simmer until the sauce is thick and oily. Sprinkle with chopped cilantro. Keep warm.

For the stuffing and peppers:
7 medium bell peppers (the color of your choice)
1 pound lean ground beef
1 cup finely chopped onions
1 cup finely chopped tomatoes
1½ teaspoons salt
1 teaspoon ground black pepper
2 teaspoons garlic paste
½ tablespoon ground coriander seeds
1½ teaspoons ground turmeric
½ cup Baghlan or Basmati rice, soaked in a small saucepan in 1 cup water for 2 hours
1 cup chopped fresh dill

Slice the tops off the bell peppers and reserve. Remove the membranes and seeds from the peppers and discard them. Preheat oven to 400 degrees F.

Place the ground beef and onions in a skillet. Add the chopped tomatoes, salt, pepper, garlic paste, ground coriander seeds, and turmeric. Stir on medium heat for about 7 minutes until tomatoes are wilted. Cover and cook on low heat for an additional 5 minutes (cook on a high heat uncovered if there is water). Boil the rice for about 3 minutes. Drain and add to the meat. Add the dill. Mix well.

Stuff and bake the peppers:

Divide the beef mixture into 7 portions and spoon into each pepper. Pour 1½ cups boiling water into a two-quart oven-proof casserole that will hold all the peppers in one layer and arrange the stuffed peppers tightly in it. Place the tops beside the peppers and cover the dish with aluminum foil. Bake for about 1 hour.

Remove the cover and broil the peppers on high for about 4 minutes or until peppers start to turn brown. Cover peppers with tops. Spread the reserved sauce on a large serving plate. Transfer the peppers one by one with the help of a tong and large spoon for bottom support onto the bed of sauce. Serve warm with toasted Afghan nan.

STUFFED INDIAN EGGPLANTS

Badenjan Shekampur

Makes 6 servings

Indian eggplants (badenjan), the size of small apples, make a favorite standing vegetable for this dish. Oblong eggplants of the same size can work as well. "Shekampur" means "stuffed belly." The shell of the eggplant is stuffed with eggplant flesh, meat, and vegetables, sprinkled with spices and baked. This appetizer is considered a fancy dish and is prepared for festive gatherings. Other times Badenjan Shekampur *is enjoyed as a main course when served with nan and* doogh *(Tangy Yogurt and Cucumber Drink, page 314).*

6 Indian eggplants, the size of small
  apples
Oil as needed for coating plus
  4 tablespoons
1 cup finely chopped onions
1 cup ground beef
½ teaspoon ground turmeric
1 cup finely chopped bell pepper
1 cup finely chopped tomatoes
1 teaspoon salt
1 teaspoon pepper (optional)
1 tablespoon garlic paste
2 tablespoons ground coriander
  seeds

Cut around the stems of the eggplants and save for tops. Scoop out the flesh, leaving ⅛-inch thickness on the skin. Chop the flesh finely and reserve. Grease inside and outside of the eggplants and their tops liberally with oil, and arrange them on a baking tray, placing the tops beside the eggplants. Broil on high for about 10 minutes and set aside.

To prepare the filling, fry the onions in the 4 tablespoons oil to a golden color. Add the ground beef and turmeric and stir to cook for 5 minutes. Add the chopped eggplant flesh, bell peppers, tomatoes, salt, pepper, garlic paste, and ground coriander. Mix well and cook covered on moderate heat for 10 minutes until the meat and eggplant flesh are cooked and the liquids have evaporated, leaving an oily sauce. Spoon the oil out and discard.

Heat the oven to 400 degrees F. Divide the filling among the 6 eggplant shells. Place them on a baking tray and cover with aluminum foil. Do not bake the eggplant tops. Bake for 40 minutes or until fork-tender. Cover with the tops of the eggplants and serve.

STUFFED GREEN CABBAGE

Boqcha Karam

Makes 4 servings

"Boqcha" means "bundle." Meat, vegetables, and spices are used to stuff green cabbage (karam) leaves in a bundle. The baked boqcha are then served on a bed of tomato sauce with nan on the side. Green cabbage is more popular in Afghanistan than red cabbage and is utilized widely for culinary purposes.

1 head green cabbage
¼ cup butter
¼ cup oil
2 cups finely chopped onions
2 tomatoes, blanched and chopped
1 teaspoon salt
¾ cup tomato sauce
½ cup finely chopped bell pepper
1 tablespoon ground coriander
  seeds
6 ounces ground turkey or beef
1 cup cooked rice
2 cloves garlic, crushed
2 green chilies, finely chopped
Chopped cilantro to garnish

Submerge the cabbage in a large pot of simmering water for 5 minutes. Then peel off the outer four leaves and reserve. Preheat the oven to 375 degrees F.

Heat the butter and oil in a saucepan and fry the onions until golden brown. Add the tomatoes and fry until wilted and dissolved. Add the salt, tomato sauce, bell peppers, and ground coriander seeds. Add ¾ cup water. Stir and transfer half of the sauce to a second saucepan. Add the ground turkey or beef to the first pan and stir. Cover and cook on low heat for about 30 minutes. Remove from heat and mix in rice and allow to cool.

Add the garlic and chilies to the second pan of sauce. Cover and simmer for about 5 minutes. Set aside.

Lay out the four reserved cabbage leaves and divide up the meat mixture placing some in the center of each leaf. Fold over the bottoms, tops, and sides. Then place in an ovenproof dish seam side down. Bake covered for 45 minutes.

Reheat the reserved sauce and pour into a large serving platter or bowl. Transfer the stuffed cabbages onto the sauce, and garnish with cilantro.

GREEN CABBAGE ROLLS

Dolma e Karam

Makes 20 rolls

For this recipe green cabbage (karam) leaves are stuffed with meat, rice, vegetables, and spices, and baked with a tomato and onion sauce. In Afghanistan, cabbage rolls are mostly prepared in larger cities in domestic ovens when cabbage is in season. In this version of stuffed cabbage, the sauce is drizzled on top of the rolls. Dolme e Karam is usually prepared for large feasts and it is used as both an appetizer and a main course.

For the cabbage:
1 large head of cabbage, center core removed

Place the cabbage, cored side down, in a large pot of boiling water. Cover and simmer for 12 minutes. Remove cabbage to a large bowl reserving the boiling water. Separate the soft leaves away from the core leaving any that are still hard. Return the cabbage head to the simmering water and continue to simmer until softened. Remove the head and take off remaining leaves until you have a total of 20 leaves. Scrape off the thick part of the spine of each leaf for easier rolling.

For the filling:
1 cup finely chopped onions
1½ tablespoons oil
½ tablespoon minced garlic
1 cup tomato sauce
1½ teaspoons salt
1 teaspoon ground black pepper
1 pound ground beef or turkey
1 cup basmati rice, soaked for
  4 hours
½ bunch chopped cilantro
½ teaspoon Palow Spice Blend
  (page 319)

Stir-fry the onions in the oil to a golden color. Add the garlic and stir until it is fragrant. Add the tomato sauce, salt, and pepper and simmer for about 5 minutes. Set aside to cool.

Add the meat, rice, cilantro, and spice blend to the cooled onion mixture. Combine well.

Place about 3 tablespoons of the filling in the center of a cabbage leaf, shaping the filling into an oblong across the spine near you. Fold the two sides of the leaf over the filling. Then fold over the edge near you and roll the leaf away from you. Stuff the remaining cabbage leaves in the same way.

For the sauce:
1 cup finely chopped onions
2 tablespoons olive oil
½ cup tomato sauce
½ teaspoon salt
6 mini sweet peppers, sliced

Stir-fry onions in 1 tablespoon olive oil to a golden color. Add the tomato sauce and fry for 1 minute. Add 1½ cups water and the salt and simmer for 5 minutes.

Preheat oven to 350 degrees F. Pour half of the prepared sauce in a 13-by-9-inch baking dish or use two smaller pans. Arrange the cabbage rolls over the sauce seam side down. Pour the remaining sauce evenly over the top of the rolls. Place the sweet pepper slices on top of the rolls. Cover the pan tightly with foil and bake for 75 minutes. Remove from oven and brush with the remaining 1 tablespoon olive oil. Cook uncovered for 15 minutes.

POTATO FRITTERS 1

Pakowré Kachalu 1   Makes 4 servings

This affordable snack is prepared with breaded potatoes that are deep-fried and served with hot sauces, chutneys, and dips on the side. Pakowra is also prepared as street food in the populated areas and commercial zones of Afghanistan. Due to the growing population of the larger cities such as Kabul, the demand for potatoes has resulted in the cultivation of this vegetable in many provinces, particularly in Bamiyan.

1½ cups chickpea flour
1 teaspoon cayenne pepper
  powder
1½ teaspoons salt
1 teaspoon baking powder
Oil for frying
1½ pounds potatoes, peeled
  and thinly sliced

In a mixing bowl, mix the chickpea flour, cayenne pepper powder, salt, and baking powder. Add water gradually as needed while mixing until a thick mixture with pea soup consistency is obtained.

In a deep saucepan, heat 4 inches of oil on medium heat. Place a small drop of batter in the oil—if it sizzles and rises quickly to the top, the oil is ready. Lower 4 to 5 potato slices in the batter, coating them thoroughly. Then lift the coated potato slices one at a time with a slotted spoon, letting the access batter drain back to the bowl and lower into the hot oil. Fry for 5 minutes or until golden and crisp on both sides. Drain on paper towels. Continue until all slices are fried, removing any fried batter lumps as they form on the oil surface as you go. Serve the fritters hot with the chutney of your choice or yogurt dip on the side.

POTATO FRITTERS 2

Pakowré Kachalu 2

Makes 6 servings

This potato cutlet is prepared with shredded potatoes (kachalu) mixed with spices, and shallow-fried after being dipped in flour and breadcrumbs. Pakowré Kachalu is prepared more in the cities during the month of Ramadan. A platterful of pakowré kachalu with a little bowl of dips such as chutney or seasoned yogurt is passed around among the fasting family members to break their fast before the prayers. Ramadan dinner starts with a mild soup and is served after the prayers.

6 cups shredded cooked potatoes
2 eggs, whites and yolks
   separated
1½ teaspoons salt
4 green chilies, seeded and finely
   chopped
1 teaspoon ground coriander
   seeds
1 teaspoon ground cumin
1 teaspoon garlic powder
½ teaspoon cayenne pepper
   powder (optional)
1 cup all-purpose flour
1 cup dried breadcrumbs
Oil for frying

Place the potatoes in a mixing bowl. Add the egg yolks, salt, green chilies, ground coriander seeds, cumin, garlic powder, and cayenne pepper powder. Mash the potatoes with a fork as you mix them with the added ingredients. Divide the potato mixture into 12 portions.

In a small bowl beat the egg whites slightly. Place the flour on a plate and the breadcrumbs on another plate. Heat 3 inches of oil in a skillet. Rub some additional oil in palms of hands lightly to avoid stickiness. Then form one portion of the potato mixture into a patty ¼-inch thick. Coat the patty lightly with flour, rub the egg white liberally all over the patty, and then dip on both sides into the breadcrumbs. Lower the patty into the pre-heated oil. Fry on both sides on medium-high heat until golden and crisp. Then drain on paper towels. Repeat the procedure with the rest of the patties, frying 3 to 4 patties at a time. Serve warm with any chutney.

BEEF OR LAMB SAMBOSA

Sambosa Khanagi

Makes 25 sambosa

To make traditional sambosa*, homemade (*khanagi*) dough squares are stuffed with organic meat, vegetables, and spices. This recipe calls for the pastry to be baked in a domestic oven but* sambosa *are traditionally baked in ground ovens called* tandoors *in Afghan villages. This snack can be preserved for a week, and for this reason they were often packed for long trips in the old days. Large quantities of various* sambosa *are prepared for the fasting month of Ramadan as a starter before prayers and the main course.*

For the dough:
2½ cups all-purpose flour
1½ teaspoons active dry yeast
½ tablespoon sugar
½ teaspoon salt
1 cup warm milk
⅓ cup oil

In a bowl mix together the dry ingredients. Add the milk and oil. Knead well to homogenize and form into a soft dough and then cover and set aside to rise for about 1½ hours.

For the filling:
½ pound ground beef or lamb
1½ cups finely chopped onions
1 teaspoon salt
1 tablespoon oil or butter
2 medium potatoes, finely
  chopped
1 carrot, finely chopped
2 minced green chilies, or to taste
¼ teaspoon ground black pepper
2 teaspoons minced garlic
2 teaspoons ground coriander
  seeds
White of one egg, beaten

Place the meat, onions and ½ teaspoon of the salt in a skillet and sauté for about 10 minutes breaking up the meat as it cooks.

Heat the oil or butter in a separate skillet and stir-fry the potatoes, carrots, and chilies with the remaining salt until fork tender. Add the meat mixture to the fried vegetables. Sprinkle the black pepper, garlic, and ground coriander seeds over the meat and vegetables and mix well.

Assemble and bake the *sambosa*:
Preheat the oven to 375 degrees F. Using a rolling pin spread the dough into a rectangle ⅛-inch thick and cut into four-inch squares. Place 1 tablespoon of the filling on half of each square diagonally and fold over the other half to make triangles. Seal the edges and brush with egg white. Place in a single layer on a baking sheet and bake for about 25 minutes. Serve with chutney on the side.

PUFF PASTRY BEEF SAMBOSA

Sambosa Goshti

Makes 30 sambosa

For these sambosa, puff pastry is filled with ground beef, onion, and spices and baked. They are then sprinkled with powdered sugar and served along with sweet pastries and tea. Sambosa Goshti are traditionally prepared for celebratory occasions such as weddings, Eid, and engagement parties. The most popular beverage served with this pastry is Qaimaq Chai (page 311).

1 pound ground beef
4 cups finely chopped onions
1 teaspoon salt
2 teaspoons ground black
  pepper
2 teaspoons ground coriander
  seeds
15 sheets of 5x5 puff pastry
1 egg yolk beaten with
  1 tablespoon milk
½ cup powdered sugar

Sauté the ground beef in a non-stick pan for about 10 minutes on moderate heat, breaking up any lumps until the meat dries out. In a food processor, grind the cooked beef to breadcrumb consistency and return to the pan. Add in the onions. Stir-fry the beef and onion mixture for about 10 minutes until onions are dry and cooked through. Add the salt, pepper, and ground coriander seeds. Mix and simmer for about 5 minutes. Remove from heat and allow to cool completely. Preheat the oven to 375 degrees F.

Thaw the puff pastry sheets until bendable but not too soft. Working with one sheet, keep the rest refrigerated. Cut the sheet in half diagonally to make two triangles. Place 1 tablespoon of the filling on half of each triangle and fold to make smaller triangles. Pinch the edges by hand and then seal completely with the tines of a fork. Place the filled pastry on a cookie sheet lined with parchment paper. Prepare the remaining *sambosa* in the same way.

Brush the *sambosa* with the egg yolk mixture. Bake for about 30 minutes or until golden and crisp. Remove from oven and let cool for about 10 minutes. Sprinkle with the powdered sugar.

Ghiyas-ud-Din Shah Sambosa / *Sambosa Ghiyas Shahi*

The Best of Afghan Cooking

GHIYAS-UD-DIN SHAH SAMBOSA

Sambosa Ghiyas Shahi

Makes 25 sambosa

The recipe for this ancient fried pastry, which is filled with ground meat and spices, dates back 500 years to the Khilji dynasty of Afghan rulers in India and is included in the ancient cookbook, Nemmatnama. *The pastry is named after the Khilji king, Ghiyas-ud-Din Shah. "Sambosa" is spelled "sanbosa" in the ancient cookbook, which is the current spelling used in Afghanistan.*

For the dough:
2½ cups all-purpose flour
1½ teaspoons active dry yeast
½ tablespoon sugar
½ teaspoon salt
⅓ cup oil
1 cup warm milk

In a bowl mix the flour, yeast, sugar, and salt. Massage the oil into the flour. Add the milk gradually and knead for about 5 minutes to homogenize and form into a soft dough. Cover and place at room temperature for about 1½ hours to rise.

For the filling:
1 pound ground beef
1 pound onions, finely chopped
1 teaspoon salt
½ teaspoon ground black pepper
2 teaspoons minced garlic
2 teaspoons ground coriander seeds
Pinch saffron dissolved in
  1 teaspoon rose water
1 tomato, finely chopped and
  sautéed
Oil for frying

Sauté the ground beef and onions for about 10 minutes, breaking up any lumps. Raise the heat if there is liquid and boil off. Add the salt, pepper, garlic, coriander, rose water mixture, and tomatoes and combine them. Set aside to cool.

Assemble and fry the sambosa:
Divide the dough into 4 portions and shape them into balls. Working with one ball cover the rest. Shape the ball into a patty, and then roll out into a thin sheet and cut into 3-inch circles. Fill each circle with one tablespoon of the beef filling and fold them to make half circles. Pinch the edges to seal. Work with the rest of the dough and filling until all *sambosa* are prepared. Cover and let rest for 30 minutes.

Reseal the edges of each *sambosa* using the tines of a fork. Heat 3 inches of oil in a skillet and fry as many *sambosa* as the skillet can hold. Drain on paper towels.

POTATO AND GARBANZO SNACK

Shournakhod

Makes 6 servings

This deliciously filling and appetizing snack is prepared with slow-cooked, tender garbanzo beans and thin potato slices, soaked in the juices of the beans and chutney and sprinkled with salt and pepper. This street food has been around for years to serve students, employees, shoppers, and movie-goers.

1 cup uncooked garbanzo beans
2 teaspoons baking soda
1 pound small potatoes
Chutney Gashniz (page 212) or Chutney Morch Sorkh (page 213) to taste
Salt and black pepper to taste

Soak the garbanzo beans in water 4 inches above the bean level for 4 to 6 hours in a small cooking pot.

Add the baking soda to the bean pot and stir to dissolve. Bring to a boil. Reduce heat to low. Cover and cook until the beans are creamy and can be easily smashed between fingers. The juices should barely cover the top of the beans. If beans float in juices boil further uncovered. Leave to cool.

Meanwhile, boil the potatoes until a knife can slice through but not too soft. Let cool by placing in cold water for easy peeling. Then peel and slice into thin slices. Divide the potatoes among 6 serving plates. Then divide the beans by mounding on top of the potatoes. Saturate with bean juices and sprinkle with the chutneys and salt and pepper to taste. Serve as a snack.

HOT AND SPICY FRIED NOODLES

Simian

Makes 4 servings

These hot and spicy fried flour noodles are served with sweets to balance the flavors, particularly on Eid feasts where tables are loaded with a variety of Afghan sweets such as sugar-coated almonds candies, and sweet pastry. This snack is widely prepared commercially and is adopted from the Hindus and Sikh Afghans. Note that you will need a pasta maker for this recipe.

1 cup all-purpose flour
½ cup chickpea flour
1½ teaspoons cayenne pepper powder
2½ teaspoons ground cumin
2 teaspoons salt
1 teaspoon ginger powder
2 tablespoons oil
Yellow food coloring to your taste
Oil for frying

Place the flours in a mixing bowl. Add the cayenne pepper powder, cumin, salt, ginger powder, 2 tablespoons of oil, food coloring, and ½ cup water. Knead to form a firm dough. Divide the dough into two portions. Shape each portion into an oblong patty. Working with one patty at a time feed the dough into a pasta maker, adjusting the machine to the smallest noodle setting (5).

Meanwhile, heat 3 inches of oil in a saucepan. Oil is ready when a small portion of noodles dropped in it sizzles and rises to the top quickly. Fry a handful of noodles at a time until crisp. Drain on paper towels and let cool. Serve as a snack.

Turnip and Pasta Soup / *Omaché Shalgam*

SOUPS

Shourba

Afghan soups are served both as a light appetizer before a meal or as hearty meals on their own, especially when bread is cut into pieces and soaked in the soup. Rich and tasty, Afghan soups may serve different purposes; while *Omaché Shalgham* (Turnip and Pasta Soup) relieves coughs and sore throat, *Mashaba* (Beef and Bean Soup) makes a filling meal. *Yakhni Morgh* (Chicken and Split Pea Soup) is mild and soothing after surgeries or for a high fever.

Many shapes of pasta are used in Afghan soups but if you don't have the time to make homemade pasta there are easy substitutes. The noodles for *Aush* (Hearty Flour Noodle and Meatball Soup) are usually prepared at home from freshly harvested wheat flour after it is sieved for white flour. Outside of Afghanistan fresh noodles are a good substitute for *aush* noodles. For the tiny homemade pasta that resembles rice grains used in *Omaché Shalgham*, pastina or orzo can be substituted. *Lakhshak* (Vegetable Soup with Egg Noodles) requires larger squares of pasta prepared with eggs. Italian *quadrucci* pasta is a perfect replacement for its Afghan counterpart.

In the grapevine countryside, specifically north of Kabul, soups are prepared very hot and spicy to balance the intense sweetness of the grapes that are consumed any time of the day in summer and the mulberry dessert, *chukida*, enjoyed in the wintertime.

When bread is soaked in soups, the soup is called *shourba* and is considered a meal. It is usually prepared with meat, vegetables, beans, potatoes, and bread, and slow-cooked with spices. This carbohydrate-, vitamin-, and protein-rich meal is not only tasty, but it is nutritious and healthy as well. *Shourba* is traditionally believed to be the meal of the people, and is considered the national dish of Afghanistan.

A simpler form of *shourba* is *piawa*, where the bread is soaked in soup. The only meat incorporated into *piawa* is ground beef in the form of meatballs. Other variations are egg and dried fruit *piawa*. Simple and tasty, *piawa* is considered the poor man's delight.

HEARTY FLOUR NOODLE AND MEATBALL SOUP

Aush

For this winter soup, flour noodles are cooked with spicy meatballs in an onion and yogurt sauce. Fresh baby spinach leaves and a sprinkle of pepper and mint add to its beauty and flavor. From the high-altitude provinces along the Hindu-kush Mountains such as Badakhshan to the deserts of the southwest regions such as Kandahar and Farah, Afghans prepare this complete meal in their homes.

For the meatballs:
½ **pound lean ground beef**
¼ **teaspoon salt**
¼ **teaspoon ground black pepper**
½ **cup minced onions**
½ **teaspoon garlic paste**
½ **teaspoon ground coriander seeds**

In a small bowl, massage all the ingredients for the meatballs until well-blended and sticky. Shape into 1-inch balls and set aside.

For the soup:
2 **cups finely chopped onions**
¼ **cup oil**
½ **cup chopped tomatoes**
2 **teaspoons salt**
½ **teaspoon ground turmeric**
2 **quarts boiling water**
5 **ounces fresh flour noodles or vermicelli**
½ **cup chopped cilantro**
2 **cups baby spinach leaves**
2 **cups qurut (page 319) or chaka (drained yogurt; page 318), room temperature**
1 **teaspoon ground black pepper**
1 **teaspoon dried mint leaves**

Fry the onions in the oil to a golden color. Add the tomatoes, salt, and turmeric. Stir for 1 minute. Lower the meatballs into the sauce. Cover and simmer for 20 minutes.

Add the boiling water, noodles, cilantro, and spinach. Cover and cook on moderate heat until noodles are tender. Turn the heat off and let stand for 5 minutes. Gently fold in the *qurut* or *chaka*. Sprinkle with pepper and mint. Serve immediately.

TEAPOT SOUP

Chainaki

Called the teapot soup, Chainaki is a commercial meal served in the teahouses of Afghanistan ("chainak" means "china or clay teapot"). The meat of a freshly slaughtered lamb is carefully selected from the neck or shoulder of the animal, with the bone and fat attached. The meat, cut into pieces, is placed in china teapots, together with vegetables and spices, and then slow-cooked in a clay oven underground (tandoor) or on special grills, until the meat is falling off the bone. It is served with Afghan flat nan. Travelers' demand for something filling gradually converted the old-time teahouses to restaurants, but the serving dishes remain teapots to this day. Electric slow-cookers achieve similar results at home.

2 pounds lamb on the bone, cut into 6 portions
1 onion, sliced
1 teaspoon ground turmeric
3 green chilies
2½ teaspoons salt
½ large tomato, sliced
2 cloves garlic, crushed
½ cup dried split yellow peas
6 cups boiling water
1 teaspoon ground black pepper

Place the lamb and onion slices in a slow cooker. Add turmeric, chilies, salt, tomato slices, garlic, and split yellow peas. Stir well. Add the boiling water. Cook the soup on low for 6 hours.

Serve the soup with Afghan bread and salad or vegetables on the side. Or cut the bread into bite-size pieces and divide among four bowls, then saturate with the soup and top with the meat. Sprinkle with black pepper. Serve the salad on the side.

Vegetable Soup with Egg Noodles / *Lakhshak*

VEGETABLE SOUP WITH EGG NOODLES

Lakhshak

For this soup, pasta is prepared with organic eggs, shaped into thin sheets and cut into small squares noodles. The noodles and mung beans are then cooked in a sauce of onions, tomatoes, and spices. Qurut *is folded in before serving. Chaka (drained yogurt) can be used as a substitute for* qurut. *This soup serves as a full meal and is considered a winter soup.*

*For the pasta:
½ cup all-purpose flour
Pinch salt
1 egg
2 tablespoons water

*Italian quadrucci pasta can be used as a substitute for the homemade pasta

Mix the flour with the salt. Break the egg into a separate bowl and beat with a fork. Add ½ of the egg to the flour. Massage the egg into the flour. Gradually add the water and mix with a fork. Transfer onto a dusted surface and knead for about 5 minutes to homogenize. Shape into a ball and set aside for 15 minutes to rest. Flatten the ball into a rectangle ⅛-inch thick. Cut the rectangle into 1-inch squares.

For the soup:
½ onion, sliced; and 1 onion, finely chopped
¼ cup oil
1 large tomato, chopped
½ teaspoon ground turmeric
1 teaspoon tomato paste
2 teaspoons salt
1 teaspoon ground black pepper
1 cup mung beans, washed and presoaked for 4 hours and drained
1½ pounds spinach leaves
4 chopped sweet chilies
½ cup qurut (page 319) or chaka (drained yogurt; page 318)
1 teaspoon garlic paste

Brown the onion slices in the oil. Remove from oil and reserve.

Stir-fry the chopped onions in the same oil until the onions start to change color. Add the chopped tomato to the onions and cook down for about 3 minutes. Add the turmeric, tomato paste, salt, pepper, mung beans, and 8 cups water. Add the pasta squares and cook for about 30 minutes.

Add the spinach and sweet chilies and cook for about 10 to 15 minutes. Transfer to a serving dish. Mix the *qurut* or *chaka* with the garlic paste and then fold gently into the soup. Sprinkle with the fried onions.

BEEF AND BEAN SOUP

Mashaba

This rich, filling soup is prepared with beef, various beans, and barley cooked in onion juices and spices. Qurut is folded in gently when the soup is ready to be served. Badakhshan is the home of authentic Mashaba *which takes its name from mung beans* (mash) *and juices* (aba). *Mung beans have many culinary uses in Afghan kitchens and at least half of the many varieties of rice dishes are prepared with them.*

1 onion, finely chopped
¼ cup oil
1 small tomato, chopped
1½ cups ground beef
1 teaspoon ground turmeric
1 tablespoon ground coriander seeds
2 teaspoons salt
1 cup chopped fresh dill
1 cup mung beans
¼ cup dried white beans, soaked for
  6 hours and drained
¼ cup pearl barley
1 cup qurut (page 319) or chaka (drained
  yogurt; page 318)*
1 tablespoon garlic paste
Pinch ground black pepper
Pinch crushed red peppers

Fry onions in oil to a light golden color. Add the tomatoes and fry until the tomatoes are dissolved and oily. Add the beef and turmeric and stir-fry for 2 to 3 minutes. Add the ground coriander seeds and salt. Add 8 cups water, dill, mung beans, white beans, and barley. Simmer for about 30 minutes or until the beans and barley are tender. For a thicker and creamier consistency boil the soup further on higher heat.

Turn the heat off. Mix the *qurut* or *chaka* with garlic paste and ½ cup of water and fold into the soup. Sprinkle the soup with the peppers. Serve immediately.

*Chaka (drained yogurt) can replace the qurut *but the flavor will not be quite the same.*

Beef and Bean Soup / *Mashaba*

TURNIP AND PASTA SOUP

Omaché Shalgham

Makes 4 servings

This turnip (shalgham) and pasta soup is prepared with turnip slices slow-cooked in a thick onion sauce. It is flavored with multiple spices and vegetables and served with nan on the side. The pasta is prepared with the right consistency so it can be broken into tiny pieces. This soup is more desirable in winter and turnips are said to have soothing effects on coughs and respiratory problems.

*For the pasta:
½ cup whole wheat flour
Pinch salt
2 tablespoons water

*Pastina or orzo can be used as a substitute for the homemade pasta

In a small bowl mix the flour and salt. Add the water and massage in to break the dough into tiny pieces the size of wheat grain. Set aside.

For the soup:
1 onion, finely chopped
3 tablespoons oil
1 tomato, finely chopped
2 teaspoons tomato paste
2 teaspoons chopped garlic
1 teaspoon salt
¼ teaspoon ground turmeric
2 medium turnips, peeled, quartered, thinly sliced
1 cup sliced sweet peppers
½ bunch cilantro
1 tablespoon lemon juice
1 teaspoon crushed dried mint
¼ teaspoon ground black pepper

Stir-fry the onions in oil over low heat until lightly golden. Add the tomato, tomato paste, garlic, salt, and turmeric. Stir-fry until the tomatoes cook down and dissolve. Add the turnips and stir-fry for another 5 minutes. Add 7 cups of water and bring to a boil. Stir and cover to cook on low heat for about 30 minutes.

Add the pasta, sweet peppers, and cilantro. Cook for 10 minutes. Drizzle with lemon juice and sprinkle with mint and black pepper. Serve warm.

BREAD AND EGG SOUP

Piawé Tokhm

Piawa Tokhm *is a simple but nutritious meal of bread soaked in onion soup and topped with eggs, apricots, and sour plums. Less commonly,* Piawa *is sometimes prepared with meatballs. A sprinkle of black pepper is what distinguishes this soup from others. Another name for* Piawa, *which is considered the meal of the poor, is* Eshkana.

2 cups thinly sliced onions
¼ cup olive oil
½ teaspoon ground turmeric
1 tablespoon lemon juice
2 tablespoons sugar
1 teaspoon salt
8 dried sour plums
8 dried apricot halves
5 cups boiling water
4 large eggs
6 small pita bread
Ground black pepper to taste

In a large saucepan stir-fry the onion slices in the oil over medium heat till golden. Add turmeric, lemon juice, sugar, salt, plums, apricots, and boiling water. Cover and cook on low heat for about 10 minutes or until the apricot halves and plums are tender. Lower the heat to simmer.

Break the eggs one at a time into a separate bowl and then slide gently into the simmering soup. Cover and cook until the eggs are set.

Cut the pita bread into bite-size pieces and then divide them among four serving bowls. Saturate the bread with the soup broth and top each with an egg making sure each bowl has an equal amount of the fruits. Sprinkle with pepper. Serve immediately.

SPICY SOURDOUGH SOUP

Qulur Trush

Makes 4 servings

This unique soup from the western region of Herat is prepared by cooking mung beans and dried meat (landi) in an onion sauce. A spicy sourdough powder (fermented dough is dried and ground into a powder in large quantities and saved for winter uses) is incorporated into the soup in the last 10 minutes. The spicy Qulur Trush is a complete meal served with Afghan nan.

*For the *Qulur Trush* Powder:
3 cups flour (your choice of type)
1 tablespoon ground turmeric
1 tablespoon ground coriander
  seeds
2 teaspoons active dry yeast
2 teaspoons ground cumin
3 teaspoons ground pepper of your
  choice
6 teaspoons salt
1 cup tomato sauce
½ cup yogurt
2 tablespoons minced garlic

* *Makes 3 cups; you need 1 cup for this soup; store the remaining powder in a jar in the refrigerator for later use*

In a mixing bowl whisk together the flour, turmeric, coriander, yeast, cumin, pepper and salt. Add the tomato sauce, yogurt, and garlic. Mix well. Transfer to a flour-dusted board and knead for 5 minutes into a smooth, firm dough. Cover the dough and leave it at room temperature for about 2 days or until the dough is fermented and smells sour.

Preheat the oven to 375 degrees F. Punch down the dough and shape it into a 2-inch-thick disc. Place on a cookie sheet and bake in the oven for about 30 minutes. Remove from oven and cover with kitchen towels. Leave to cool completely. Break the disc into smaller pieces and grind into a powder with breadcrumb consistency (if the bread is too soft for grinding, leave uncovered for another day and then grind).

For the soup:
1 pound dried meat chunks (you
  can substitute with fresh beef or
  lamb)
1 onion, finely chopped
¼ cup oil
¼ cup mung beans
1 cup Qulur Trush Powder (above)

Soak the dried meat in water overnight to rid of extra salt in it. Drain and rinse with cool water. (Skip this step for regular meat.)

Stir-fry the onions in the oil to a golden color. Add the meat and stir-fry for 2 minutes. Add 8 cups of water and cook the meat for about 1 hour or until the

meat is barely tender. Add the mung beans and cook for about 30 minutes or until the meat and beans are tender. Remove from heat and let the soup cool.

Add the Qulur Trush Powder gradually while mixing rapidly with a spoon so it doesn't get lumpy. Cook the soup further for about 10 minutes on low heat, stirring. Serve.

MEAT, BEAN, AND VEGETABLE SOUP

Shourba

Makes 4 servings

Shourba *is perhaps the most traditional food in Afghanistan. Lamb, vegetables, and legumes are slow-cooked in onion. Like most Afghan soups, shourba is quite substantial and is often prepared as a meal. This soup is served with bread pieces soaked in the broth and topped with the meat, beans, and vegetables and sprinkled with black pepper and cilantro. A salad, Salatè Maida (page 73), is usually served on the side.*

4 cups finely chopped onions
¼ cup olive oil
1½ pounds beef chuck, neck bones, or lamb shoulder, cut into chunks
3 teaspoons salt
½ teaspoon ground turmeric
1 tablespoon garlic paste
½ cup chopped tomatoes
1 tablespoon tomato paste
1 large potato, quartered
4 whole chilies
1 large carrot, cut into 4 pieces
¾ cup cooked garbanzo beans
¾ cup cooked pinto beans
1 cup chopped cilantro
8 pita bread, cut into pieces
Ground black pepper

In a six-quart pot, stir-fry onions in oil on medium heat to a golden color. Add the meat, salt, turmeric, garlic paste, tomatoes, and tomato paste. Fry until the meat is golden and tomatoes are dissolved. Add 3 cups of water. Cover and cook on low heat until the meat is tender, about 1½ hours for beef and 2 to 2½ hours for lamb. Add the potatoes, chilies, and carrots 30 minutes before the finish time for meat.

Add both beans, the cilantro, and 4 cups of water. Cover and boil gently for a further 10 minutes. Fill four bowls with the bread pieces and saturate evenly with the soup broth. Top with meat, beans, and vegetables. Sprinkle with pepper. Serve warm.

CHICKEN AND RICE SOUP

Shourba Berenj

Makes 6 servings

This soup (shourba) is prepared with rice (berenj), chicken, and turnips cooked in onion juices. Dill and garlic give this shourba a unique aroma and flavor. If you use leftover meat and rice, this tasty shourba can be prepared in minutes. When served with Afghan flatbread, it is often considered a main course; other times it is served as a starter. Shourba Berenj can also be prepared with ground meat sauce or tiny meatballs.

1 cup finely chopped onions
1½ tablespoons olive oil
2 chicken legs, meat pulled off the bones and cut into bite-size pieces
1 tablespoon minced garlic
1 teaspoon ground turmeric
¾ cup chopped tomatoes
1 tablespoon tomato sauce
2 teaspoons salt
1 large turnip, shredded
6 cups boiling water
¾ cup short-grain rice, washed and drained
1 cup chopped red sweet peppers
1 tablespoon lemon juice
¼ cup chopped fresh dill
Pinch ground black pepper

In a four-quart pot, stir-fry the onions in the oil over medium heat until light golden. Add the chicken leg meat and stir-fry on low heat for about 5 minutes. Add the garlic and turmeric and stir for 1 minute. Add the tomatoes, tomato sauce, and salt. Stir until the tomatoes are melted down. Add the turnips, boiling water, and rice. Cover and cook on low heat for about 45 minutes.

Add the sweet peppers, lemon juice, and half of the dill. Cook covered on low heat for about 10 minutes. Sprinkle with pepper and the remaining dill. Serve immediately.

Red Lentil Soup / *Soupè Adas Surkh*

RED LENTIL SOUP

Soupé Adas Surkh

Makes 4 to 6 servings

For this soup red split lentils are cooked in water first and then a thick sauce of onions and tomatoes flavored with ginger, cumin, and garlic is prepared separately and folded into the lentil soup. The use of bay leaves in the lentil boiling process is adopted from Hindu and Sikh Afghans who serve this soup on their daily menus. This soup is delectable and nutritious.

For the soup:
1 cup dried red split lentils
2 bay leaves
1-inch piece fresh ginger
½ teaspoon ground turmeric
2 teaspoons salt or to taste
1½ quarts boiling water
1 cup chopped cilantro
Cilantro leaves and dried red
   pepper flakes for garnish

Wash the lentils and soak for about 1 hour. Drain the lentils and place them in a large saucepan. Add the bay leaves, ginger, turmeric, salt, and boiling water. Cover and cook for about 30 minutes on moderate heat; or pressure cook for about 10 minutes. Set aside.

For the sauce:
2 tablespoons olive oil
Pinch whole cumin seeds
1½ cups chopped onions
2 teaspoons minced garlic
1 cup chopped tomatoes
1 chili, finely diced

In a separate pan heat the oil on medium heat and stir-fry the cumin seeds for 1 minute. Add the onions and stir-fry until the onions change color. Add the garlic and stir-fry for 1 minute. Add the tomatoes and chili and cook down until the tomatoes are dissolved and the oil separates.

Add the sauce to the lentil soup. Add the 1 cup cilantro, mix well, and simmer for 5 minutes. Transfer to a bowl and garnish with cilantro leaves and dried red pepper flakes. Serve with Afghan nan on the side.

MEATBALL AND BARLEY SOUP

Soupé Jow

Makes 4 servings

Tender pearl barley and meatball soup is prepared with onions and vegetables, and flavored with spices. This soup serves as a starter. When served as a main course, Afghan nan on the side completes the meal. A variation of this soup is prepared with pelted wheat or other meat, mostly leftover.

For the meatballs:
½ **pound lean ground beef**
½ **teaspoon salt**
½ **teaspoon ground black pepper**
½ **cup finely chopped onions**

For the soup:
1½ **cups finely chopped onions**
¼ **cup olive oil**
1 **cup finely chopped tomatoes**
1 **teaspoon ground turmeric**
½ **tablespoon minced garlic**
2 **teaspoons ground coriander seeds**
1½ **teaspoons salt**
¾ **cup uncooked pearl barley**
½ **each red and green bell peppers,
    sliced**
½ **teaspoon ground black pepper**
**Dried mint and cilantro leaves for
    garnish**

Place the ground beef in a mixing bowl. Add the salt, black pepper, and onions. Massage in until well combined. Form the beef into balls the size of gumballs. Set aside.

In a pot, stir-fry the onions in the oil into a golden color. Add the tomatoes and stir until wilted. Add the turmeric, garlic, ground coriander seeds, and salt. Fry for 1 minute. Add the meatballs and simmer covered for about 5 minutes. Shake the pot to stir the meatballs. Add the barley and 5 cups of water. Cook on low heat for about 30 minutes, stirring occasionally. Add the bell pepper slices. Stir to mix and cook on gentle heat for 15 minutes.

Sprinkle the black pepper and dried mint around the top of the soup and garnish with cilantro leaves. Serve warm.

CHICKEN AND SPLIT PEA SOUP

Yakhni Morgh

Makes 4 servings

This chicken (morgh) and split pea soup is prepared with the meat of cage-free, organic chickens. Broth soup (yakhni) is perhaps the most simple and easy to prepare of all Afghan soups. The chicken is mixed with all the ingredients in a cooking pot and the soup will be ready to serve in 30 minutes. This soup serves as a nice starter as well as a good soup for the ill.

8 chicken thighs & drumsticks
2 cups chopped onions
1 teaspoon salt
¼ teaspoon ground turmeric
Pinch ground black pepper
8 cups boiling water
⅓ cup yellow split peas
½ cup cilantro leaves

Skin the chicken and trim any visible fat. Wash thoroughly and place in a six-quart stockpot. Add the onions. Sprinkle with salt, turmeric, and pepper. Pour in the boiling water and the split peas. Bring to a rolling boil on high heat. Lower the heat, cover, and continue to cook on low heat for about 30 minutes. Add the cilantro and simmer for a further 5 minutes.

Sheep Feet Soup / *Soupé Pacha*

SHEEP FEET SOUP

Soupé Pacha

Makes 4 servings

Sheep feet (pacha) are slow-cooked with garbanzo beans and pelted wheat for this soup and flavored with fried onions, garlic, and black pepper. A drizzle of lemon completes the dish. This soup is a delicacy. After Eid Al-Adha when sheep are sacrificed, the meat is distributed to the neighbors and the needy. The sheep legs, head, and tripe are set aside for special dishes like tripe soup (shourba shekamba), head and leg soup (shourba kala pacha), and tongue palow (palow zoban). Note that there is pre-soaking of the wheat and garbanzo beans before this soup can be put together.

4 sheep feet (see Glossary, page 320)
Boiling water to clean the feet
2 large onions, finely chopped
¼ cup cooking oil
1 cup pelted wheat, soaked for
  4 hours
1 cup dried garbanzo beans, soaked
  for 4 hours
2 tablespoons minced garlic
1½ teaspoons ground turmeric
8 cups boiling water
2 teaspoons salt or as needed
1 tablespoon lemon juice
Freshly ground black pepper for
  garnish
Cilantro leaves for garnish

Place the sheep feet in a pot and pour in enough boiling water to cover the feet. Boil for about 10 minutes. Drain and rinse with cool water.

In a separate pot, fry the onions in the oil to a light golden color. Turn the heat off. Arrange the sheep feet on top of the fried onions. Add the wheat, beans, garlic, and turmeric. Stir well and add the boiling water. Cover the pot and simmer the sheep feet for 6 hours or until the beans and wheat are tender and the meat is falling off the bone.

Discard the bones. Add the salt and lemon juice and stir the soup. Simmer for an additional 10 minutes. Transfer to soup bowls. Garnish with black pepper and cilantro.

SPINACH BEAN SOUP

Soupé Sabzi   Makes 6 servings

This spinach soup is prepared with beans, lentils, pasta, and vegetables, garnished with yogurt and fried onion rings, and spiced up by dill, garlic, parsley, and cilantro. Lentils and beans make this soup filling, particularly when served with toasted Afghan nan on the side. Spinach is cultivated in Afghanistan and is always fresh. The yogurt is usually made at home from organic milk.

For the soup:

3 tablespoons oil
2 cups finely chopped onions
1 tablespoon minced garlic
2 teaspoons salt
2 teaspoons ground turmeric
½ cup yellow lentils
8 cups boiling water
½ cup cooked red kidney beans
½ cup cooked white beans
½ cup cooked garbanzo beans
3 ounces fresh noodles
1 tablespoon dry dill
7 ounces frozen chopped spinach,
   water removed
1 cup chopped parsley
1 cup chopped cilantro

Heat the oil in a soup pot and sauté the onions on moderate heat. Add the garlic and stir for 1 minute. Add the salt and turmeric. Add the lentils and 4 cups of boiling water. Cook for about 30 minutes until lentils are tender. Add the three beans, noodles, dill, spinach, parsley, cilantro, and the remaining 4 cups of boiling water. Simmer until the noodles are tender.

For garnish:

1 onion, sliced into rings
Oil for frying
1 cup chaka (drained yogurt; page 318), mixed with salt to taste
1 tablespoon dried mint

Fry the onion rings in the oil until golden and crisp. Drain and reserve. Divide the soup into bowls. Drizzle with *chaka* and decorate with fried onion rings. Sprinkle with dried mint.

Spinach Bean Soup / *Soupé Sabzi*

Tomato and Onion Salad / *Salaté Watani*

SALADS

Salata

Salads in Afghanistan are prepared with fresh organic vegetables. These days even war-stricken rural Afghans have a small garden in their backyards.

Salads comprise two categories, one of which is the traditional vegetables on a plate. Vegetables such as radishes, cucumbers, red onions, and tomatoes are sliced and arranged nicely on a platter, sprinkled with salt, and drizzled with the juice of a lemon. Leafy vegetables like lettuce are used as a bed for the sliced vegetables, and mint sprigs and cilantro are arranged nicely as a garnish for the salad plate. Sliced salads are served widely with any main course such as *shourba* or rice dishes. This type of salad is not considered formal, except when served with meat dishes when the vegetable slices are arranged with the meat on one platter.

In the second category, salads are the chopped and mixed variety flavored with salad dressing that are recommended for festive events and guests.

Traditionally, a salad was a meal complement during late spring through early autumn when vegetables were abundant in the old days. Before the arrival of harsh winters, families would hastily stock up their supplies of many varieties of vegetables and make them into colorful, mouthwatering pickles. During wintertime, when vegetables disappeared from the markets, pickles came to the rescue. Today vegetables from the eastern, tropical regions of Afghanistan are sold by vendors throughout the year.

Vegetables are also consumed before they get to the kitchen. In villages, women, men, and children can be seen strolling through the weeping willows by the gurgling creeks to their gardens. They don't leave their patch without munching on young cucumbers sprinkled with salt, or dipping the crisp leaves of edible shamrocks in salt.

Certain salads are prepared when fruits and vegetables of the season are abundant. Cucumbers are in season in the Spring, while pomegranates are harvested in the Fall. Daikon radishes are available throughout the year and are sliced and served with a variety of dishes. The most popular vegetables and herbs for salad preparation are tomatoes, onions, cucumbers, radishes, mint, and cilantro.

POMEGRANATE SALAD

Salaté Anar   Makes 6 servings

The best quality pomegranate (anar) grows abundantly in Afghanistan, particularly in Kandahar and Tagab. When pomegranates are in season, Salatè Anar is prepared in households and served with rice dishes. The salad is tangy and sweet and pomegranate seeds add crunchiness. Pomegranate juices are also used in savory cooking for rice coloring and flavor.

For the salad:
½ large cucumber
2 cups chopped daikon radishes
½ cup sliced white onions
½ cup chopped red bell pepper
⅓ cup finely chopped cilantro
1 small pomegranate
1 head green lettuce

Peel the cucumber, split lengthwise, and then scoop out the seeds if any. Dice and place in a mixing bowl. Add the radishes, onions, bell peppers, and cilantro. Seed the pomegranate and add the seeds to the salad.

For the dressing:
1 small pomegranate
1 tablespoon lemon juice
1 teaspoon sugar
½ teaspoon dried crushed mint
¼ teaspoon ground black
  pepper
¼ teaspoon salt

Place the pomegranate on a hard surface and press with thumbs on all sides until the fruit is soft and squishy. Poke a hole on one side and squeeze the juice out into a bowl. Measure juice to ¼ cup and place in a small bowl. Add the lemon juice, sugar, dried mint, pepper, and salt. Mix well.

Add the dressing to the salad and toss to mix and then transfer to a bed of green lettuce leaves. Serve immediately.

CUCUMBER AND YOGURT SALAD

Salaté Maust

This refreshing versatile salata is perfect for warm summer days and is served as a starter or as a dip with most vegetable fritters or kabobs. It is prepared with organic cucumbers and homemade yogurt (maust) with the addition of onion, garlic, salt, and pepper. A quick yogurt drink (doogh) is often prepared from this salad by adding cool water or club soda before serving.

2 cups plain yogurt
½ teaspoon salt
2 teaspoons crushed dried mint
1 teaspoon garlic paste
1 cup peeled and finely chopped cucumbers
½ cup finely chopped onions
Mint powder and cucumber slice for garnish

Place the yogurt in a mixing bowl. Add the salt, mint, and garlic paste. Whisk the yogurt until smooth. Add the cucumbers and onions. Fold in gently. Chill for an hour before serving. Transfer the yogurt into a serving bowl. Decorate with the powdered mint and cucumber slice.

Vegetable Salad with Pine Nuts / *Salaté Jalghoza*

The Best of Afghan Cooking

VEGETABLE SALAD WITH PINE NUTS

Salaté Jalghoza

This mixed vegetable salad is prepared with roasted garlic and pine nuts (jal-ghoza). Olive oil, lime juice, crushed dried mint, salt, and pepper are added for flavor. Pine nuts are the edible kernels of pine trees grown in the forests of eastern Afghanistan. Due to time-consuming and costly harvesting, pine nuts are pricey, but this expensive nut is versatile in cooking due to its mild, nutty flavor. This salata *is prepared when pine nuts are in season and tastes great with most kabobs.*

For the dressing:
1 head garlic
2 tablespoons olive oil
1 tablespoon lime juice
½ teaspoon crushed dried mint
Pinch each salt and ground black
　pepper

Preheat the oven to 400 degrees F. Cut off the tail of the garlic head then cut through the middle crosswise and place on a cookie sheet with the cut sides up. Drizzle 1 teaspoon oil on the garlic cloves and bake for about 25 minutes or until roasted.

Squeeze the garlic cloves out of the skins. Then mash when cool. Mix the garlic, lime juice, mint, salt, pepper, and the remaining oil to make the dressing.

For the salad:
1 large tomato, chopped
4 scallions, chopped
¼ head romaine lettuce, chopped
1 cup chopped cucumbers
1 cup parsley or cilantro leaves
1 tablespoon roasted pine nuts

In a mixing bowl, place the tomatoes, scallions, lettuce, cucumbers, and parsley.

Drizzle the prepared dressing around the top of the salad and toss to mix. Sprinkle in the pine nuts and serve immediately.

BEETROOT SALAD

Salaté Lablabu

Cooked beetroots (lablabu) are mixed with shallots and fresh mint sprigs for this delicious salad. Olive oil, lemon juice, salt, pepper, and garlic make up the dressing and walnuts are added for crunchiness. Beetroots are cultivated in the north of Kabul. Tons of sugar is produced in the sugar factory of Baghlan using the beetroot harvest. When in season, cooked beetroot converts to a street snack sold at stalls in Afghan cities.

For the salad:
1 pound beetroots
1 small shallot, peeled
   and sliced into rings
¼ cup fresh mint leaves
¼ cup coarsely chopped
   walnuts

For the dressing:
2 tablespoons extra virgin
   olive oil
Juice of 1 lemon
½ teaspoon salt
½ teaspoon ground black
   pepper
2 teaspoons garlic paste

Chop off the tops and tails of beetroots. Place the beetroots in a pot with enough water to cover. Cook for about 60 minutes or until tender. Set aside until cool enough to handle. Wearing rubber gloves (to protect your hands from turning beet red) peel the warm beetroots and cut into strips and transfer to a salad bowl. Add the shallot rings and mint leaves.

In a separate small bowl mix oil, lemon juice, salt, pepper, and garlic paste.

Drizzle the dressing around the top of the salad. Sprinkle the salad with the walnuts and serve immediately.

MIXED VEGETABLE SALAD WITH LIME DRESSING

Salaté Maida

Makes 4 servings

*This mixed vegetable salad with lime dressing is popular and versatile. It tastes great with any rice dish as well as stews (*qurma*) and soups that require the soaking of bread pieces in them. The aroma of lime, garlic, and mint adds to the uniqueness and taste of the finely chopped vegetables (*maida*).*

For the dressing:
½ cup lime juice
¼ teaspoon ground black pepper
½ teaspoon dry powdered mint
1 teaspoon minced garlic
Pinch of salt
3 tablespoons olive oil, optional

In a small mixing bowl, mix the lime juice, pepper, powdered mint, garlic, and salt. Drizzle in the olive oil and mix.

For the salad:
1 cup finely chopped tomatoes
1 cup finely chopped cucumbers
1 cup finely chopped radishes
1 cup finely chopped onions
½ cup finely chopped cilantro
½ cup finely chopped fresh mint

Toss together all the vegetables for the salad. Pour the dressing on top of the salad and mix well. Transfer to a salad bowl and serve.

DAIKON RADISH SALAD

Salaté Muli

Makes 4 servings

Daikon radishes (muli) are cultivated in Afghanistan. This vegetable is in season at the same time as sour oranges are harvested in the citrus-growing regions of the east. So, the fruit and vegetable marry well and are often served together on a traditional destarkhwan *(food laid out on the floor on a large piece of cloth). This recipe is the modern presentation of* Salaté Muli *and is great with hot and spicy food or grilled meat.*

1 pound daikon radishes
½ cup chopped cilantro

For the dressing:
¼ cup lime juice
¼ teaspoon salt
Crushed chilies to taste
1 tablespoon olive oil
1 tablespoon grated orange peel;
  or juice of 1 orange

Scrape the radishes and split into halves crosswise. Slice half of the pieces into rounds. Using a kitchen peeler peel the rest into thin ribbons. Add the cilantro to the ribbons and mix. Arrange the sliced radish slices around a serving plate.

In a mixing bowl mix the ingredients for the dressing and pour on top of the radish ribbons. Toss to mix and transfer onto the middle of the serving plate.

TOMATO AND SHALLOT SALAD

Salaté Watani

Makes 4 servings

This tomato and shallot salad is mostly served with soup. However, when served with meat stew (qurma) and Afghan nan, this salata creates a full meal. It also tastes great with rice dishes and most grilled meats. When sliced, organic Afghan vegetables waft a rich and appetizing aroma.

2 shallots
1½ large firm tomatoes
½ cup cilantro leaves, chopped
4 scallions, chopped
1 teaspoon dried mint flakes

For the dressing:
Juice of ½ lemon
1 tablespoon olive oil
Pinch of ground black pepper
¼ teaspoon salt

Cut off the top and tail of the shallots and then halve lengthwise. Remove the outer skin. With the flat side down, slice shallot halves thinly across the stripes, one at a time. Slice the tomatoes in the same way. Place the tomatoes and shallots, in a mixing bowl. Add the chopped cilantro and scallions.

Mix the lemon juice, olive oil, pepper, and salt for the dressing in a small bowl and then add to the salad. Toss well and sprinkle with mint flakes.

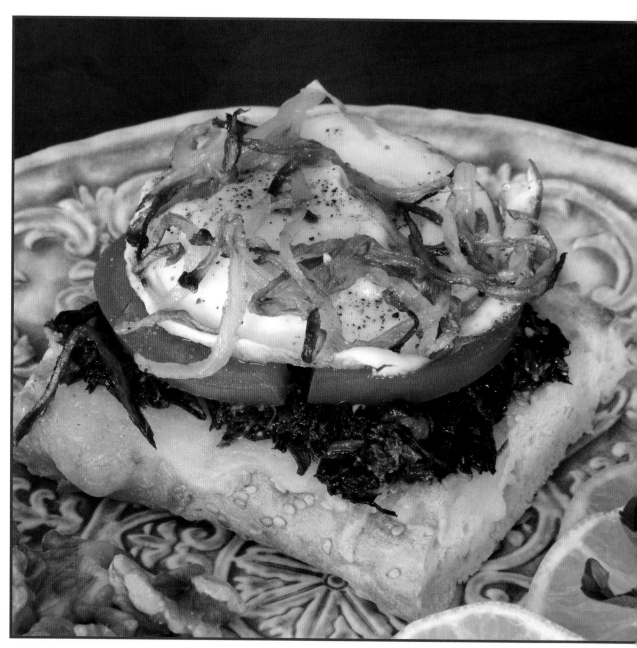

Egg and Spinach Open-faced Sandwich / *Tokhm ba Sabzi*

EGG DISHES

Tokhm

In Afghanistan, eggs are mostly consumed at breakfast. Most eggs are 100 percent organic, and the yolks are a deep yellow color. Leftover chicken or beef are sometimes added to the eggs to prepare *karaee* for a quick and convenient breakfast. When eggs are prepared with vegetables like onions and tomatoes, they serve as a quick meal. Hard-boiled eggs are used as a garnish for salads and kabobs.

A simple and easy soup prepared with eggs is *Piawé Tokhm* (page 53), a nutritious meal prepared by poaching eggs in onion juices and spices, pouring them over bread pieces in a bowl, and sprinkling the dish with crushed walnuts. In the old days, *piawa* was said to be the food of the poor.

Eggs are also used to prepare some desserts. One exceptionally unique yet delicious dessert that is prepared with eggs is *Abreshum Kabob* (page 86). It is an egg thread dessert fried in oil. The ancient dessert is said to take its name from the silk threads, *abreshum*. Sprinkled with ground cardamom and pistachios, this crispy dessert is bathed in sugar syrup to perfection.

Hard-boiled eggs are used for consumption and entertainment on the festive days of Nawruz and Eid. Hard-boiled eggs are traditionally dyed using natural, organic dye extracted from red onion skin, walnut shells, pomegranate shells, beet juice, and even grass. The rich-colored eggs are then used in contests during Eid celebrations by children and teens. The contest involves knocking two eggs together—the person with the cracked egg is the loser and the holder of the intact egg then wins the cracked egg. The harder the shell of the hard-boiled egg, the better the chance of winning when they are knocked together. Some eggshells are said to be so hard that they could win against dozens of eggs in a single egg fight. The egg fight usually is played by the children and teens in brand new clothes they wear for the first time for Eid. At the end of the day, victorious children are seen strolling proudly with a full wicker basket of colorful cracked eggs to share with their families. The colors and designs on the eggs are then copied by the family's women who would be the masters of decorating eggs for the coming Eid.

DEEP-FRIED BEEF-COATED EGGS

Kabob Nargisi

For this recipe hard-boiled eggs are coated with ground meat, breaded, and fried. This light meal is served with chutney and nan on the side. Whether fried like shami kabob *and* abreshum kabob, *steamed such as* kabob daygi, *or grilled like* kabob seekhi, *Afghans call them "kabob." Having yellow and white colors in the center, this treat is also called* Nargisi Kabob *(Narcissus Kabob).*

1 pound lean ground beef
½ cup cooked or canned garbanzo
  beans
1 pound cooked potatoes
½ cup minced onions
1 teaspoon salt
1 tablespoon ground coriander
  seeds
½ teaspoon ground black pepper
2 teaspoons minced garlic
1 egg, plus 1 egg mixed with
  1 tablespoon water
8 hard-boiled eggs, shells removed
1 cup flour
1 cup dried bread crumbs
Oil for frying

Place the ground beef in a mixing bowl. Mash the beans and potatoes and add to the meat. Add the onions, salt, ground coriander seeds, black pepper, garlic, and 1 egg. Knead the meat until well blended and sticky. Divide the meat into 8 portions.

Working with one portion, shape into a patty. Lightly dust 1 hard-boiled egg with flour and place it in the center of the patty. Coat the egg evenly with the patty. Smooth any bumps or cracks on the meat. Repeat with remaining hard-boiled eggs.

Coat the meat-covered eggs lightly with flour, then brush with the egg wash and coat with the bread crumbs. Heat oil in a large pot and deep-fry the kabobs to a golden color. Drain them on paper towels. Split lengthwise to serve with chutney and bread.

STEAMED EGGS IN FRIED MEAT SAUCE

Karaee Tokhm

Sunny-side-up eggs (tokhm) served on a bed of cooked meat that's been sautéed with vegetables and spices, this dish is best served with Afghan nan on the side. Using leftover grilled meat or ground meat qurma saves time when making this and adds to the flavor of this filling breakfast. Karaee Tokhm is traditionally prepared on Friday mornings (Jumma) which is the start of a Muslim weekend. In fact, in much of the Muslim world, the modern weekend is adapted to allow Friday as a day off from work to accommodate the congregational prayer.

2 tablespoons olive oil
½ cup finely chopped onions
¼ cup finely chopped bell pepper
½ cup finely chopped tomatoes
½ pound barbecued meat or any
  leftover meat, cut into ½-inch
  pieces
Salt and pepper to taste
4 eggs
¼ cup chopped cilantro

In a medium-size fryer, heat oil for 1 minute. Stir-fry onions, bell peppers, and tomatoes for 1 minute on high heat. Add the meat. Sprinkle with salt and pepper, then cover and cook on low heat for about 5 to 7 minutes until the vegetables are tender, and the meat has been heated through.

Make four openings in the prepared meat mixture the size of large eggs. Break the eggs one at a time into a small bowl, and then gently slide into pan to fill the openings. Sprinkle eggs with salt and pepper, then cover and cook to the desired consistency.

Transfer to a plate and garnish with the chopped cilantro. Serve warm with hot sauce and nan for breakfast.

EGG PANCAKES WITH MEAT AND ONIONS

Shesh Taranga

Makes 8 to 10 servings

Egg pancakes serve as a bed for sautéed meat, onions, walnuts, and spices drizzled with lemon. This is a modern version of the Shesh Taranga *of the old days when onions and eggs were cooked in layers and then cut into squares.* Shesh Taranga *is tasty and filling. Leftover meats facilitate the preparation and determine the main flavor of the dish.*

¼ cup olive oil
½ onion, sliced
Salt and pepper
½ cup ground cooked meat
½ cup crushed walnuts
½ teaspoon crushed dried
  mint
6 large eggs
½ teaspoon baking soda
  dissolved in 2 teaspoons
  milk
1 teaspoon flour
1 clove garlic, crushed
2 tablespoons lemon juice

Prepare 2 pans for cooking, each 6 inches in diameter. Divide the oil between the pans. In the first pan, stir-fry the onion slices until they start to turn color. Turn the heat off. With a spatula spread the onions evenly on the oil bed and sprinkle with a pinch each of salt and pepper. Cover with a layer of the meat and then the crushed walnuts. Sprinkle with mint. Keep warm.

Meanwhile, break the eggs into a separate bowl. Add the baking soda mixture, flour, garlic, and a pinch each of salt and pepper. Mix until well blended and pour into the second pan. Cover and cook on moderate heat until eggs are set, about 10 minutes. Flip the eggs and place them on a plate. Slide the prepared onion mixture from the first pan on top of the cooked eggs. Drizzle with the lemon juice. Serve warm for breakfast.

EGGS IN TOMATO SAUCE

Tokhm wa Badenjan Rumi

Makes 4 servings

Sunny-side up fried eggs (tokhm) on a bed of sautéed vegetables, mainly tomatoes (badenjan rumi), is the most versatile dish in the country. In both the countryside and the cities fresh tomatoes, chili peppers, and onions are harvested and cooked together with organic eggs from cage-free chickens. This dish, served with homemade nan for breakfast, is a popular breakfast treat throughout the country.

1½ tablespoons cooking oil
1½ cups finely chopped onion
1 green chili, finely chopped
2½ cups finely chopped tomatoes
½ cup fresh cilantro
4 large eggs
Salt and pepper to taste

Place a large skillet over medium heat. Add oil and heat for 1 minute. Add the onions and the chili and stir-fry until the onions turn transparent. Add the tomatoes and cook for about 4 to 5 minutes until the tomatoes are tender. Sprinkle the cilantro around the top of the cooked vegetables.

With a spatula make 4 openings in the sauce the size of the eggs. Break eggs one by one in a separate small bowl and then gently slide into the openings. Sprinkle with salt and pepper and continue to cook on low heat until the eggs are the desired consistency. Serve warm with nan for breakfast.

Two-Onion Eggs / *Tokhm e Dopyaza*

TWO-ONION EGGS

Tokhm e Dopyaza

Makes 4 to 6 servings

To the Afghans a meal without onions is like a pretty woman without charisma (Nan e bay pyaz, zan e bay naz.) "Dopyaza" means "containing two types of onions." For this recipe green onions are chopped and mixed with eggs and steamed over white onion rings and tomatoes. In Afghanistan this breakfast dish is prepared with all organic ingredients—eggs from the backyard coops and vegetables from the backyard gardens. The aroma and sweetness of caramelized onions make this dish special. Tokhm e Dopyaza can also serve as a quick lunch or dinner.

6 large eggs
½ cup chopped green onions
¼ cup chopped cilantro
½ teaspoon salt
½ teaspoon ground black pepper
¼ teaspoon ground turmeric
¼ cup melted butter or oil
1 yellow onion
1 small tomato

Break the eggs into a mixing bowl. Add the green onions and cilantro. Sprinkle in half the salt and pepper. Add the turmeric. Using a fork mix well until well combined.

Place the butter or oil in a medium-sized pan. Peel the onion and cut it in half. Slice the half onion across into ¼-inch thick slices and arrange around the edge of the pan. Slice the tomato into rings ¼-inch thick, and arrange inside the onion circle. Cook on medium heat for about 2 minutes or until the bottom of the vegetables start to brown.

Pour the prepared beaten egg mixture around the top of the onions and tomatoes. Cover tightly and cook on low heat for about 10 minutes or until set. Place a plate on top of the pan facing the eggs and flip the pan. Serve with tea and any Afghan nan for breakfast.

GANDANA OMELET

Tokhm wa Gandana

Makes 4 servings

Organic gandana with eggs, bell pepper, cilantro, and spices complete this breakfast cake served with toasted Afghan nan on the side. Gandana, used widely in Afghan cookery, is a cultivar of a wild variety of leeks. Leeks or Chinese chives are good substitutes.

1 cup finely chopped onions
½ cup finely chopped red bell
  pepper
2 tablespoons melted butter
¼ pound chopped gandana or
  leeks or Chinese chives
4 eggs
½ cup chopped cilantro
½ teaspoon salt
½ teaspoon ground black pepper

In a saucepan, stir-fry the onions and bell peppers in half of the butter on medium heat until the peppers are wilted down and the onions transparent, about 5 minutes. Add the gandana/leeks, and stir-fry for another minute on high heat. Remove the pan from heat.

Break the eggs into a mixing bowl and whisk until smooth. Add the prepared gandana/leek mixture to the eggs. Then add the cilantro, salt, and black pepper and mix gently. Place the remaining butter in the same saucepan over low heat. Then gently slide in the egg mixture. Cover the pan and cook for about 10 minutes, until the bottom side is set. Flip over to the other side and cook for another 5 minutes. Serve warm with nan and fresh gandana, preferably for breakfast.

EGG AND SPINACH OPEN-FACED SANDWICH

Tokhm ba Sabzi

Makes 4 servings

Fried eggs (tokhm) on a bed of toasted Afghan flat nan with sautéed to-matoes and dill-flavored spinach (sabzi) makes for a delicious breakfast. Caramelized onions give this breakfast dish a unique flavor.

½ cup sliced onions
2 tablespoons oil
3 firm Roma tomatoes, sliced
6 cups spinach leaves, chopped
2 teaspoons dried or fresh dill, chopped
4 squares (3½-inch) Afghan flatbread
2 cups shredded or chopped Swiss cheese
4 eggs
Salt and black pepper to taste

In a frying pan, stir-fry the onion slices in oil over medium heat to a golden color. Remove the onions and reserve. In the same pan fry the tomato slices on both sides on high heat for about 30 seconds and remove with a slotted spoon and reserve. In the same oil add the spinach. Sprinkle with dill, salt, and pepper, and sauté for about 3 minutes or until wilted. Remove the spinach and reserve.

Lay the four nan squares out and top each with one-fourth of the cheese. Then top each with one-fourth of the spinach and tomatoes. Place in a toaster oven and toast until the cheese has melted. Remove to four plates.

Crack the eggs into the same pan. Cover with a tight-fitting lid and cook for 3 minutes, or until whites are set. Place one egg in the center of each sandwich and sprinkle with salt, pepper, and fried onions. Serve warm.

EGG THREAD DESSERT

Abreshum Kabob

Makes 15 rolls

Egg Thread Dessert is prepared with syrup and cardamom. "Abreshum" means "silk" and "kabob," when used as a verb, means "searing in hot oil" or "grilling over an open fire." The egg threads, called the silk threads in this recipe, are mostly prepared in Kabul and other larger cities. The outcome is sweet, crisp, and aromatic. Abreshum Kabob is served with plain green or black tea on the side.

3 eggs
¾ cup sugar
1 teaspoon lemon juice
½ teaspoon ground saffron
Oil for frying
1 teaspoon ground cardamom
2 teaspoons ground pistachio

Whisk the eggs in a small deep saucepan until smooth but not frothy and let stand at room temperature for 4 hours.

Place the sugar in a small saucepan and add ½ cup water and stir to dissolve. Bring the sugar solution to a boil on moderate heat. Stir in the lemon juice and saffron. Boil for about 7 minutes until bubbly syrup is obtained. Keep warm.

Heat one inch of oil in a 12-inch frying pan. Submerge your hand into the egg mixture until well coated. Then string the egg rapidly over the hot oil in a circular motion, palm down. Repeat 12 times, making a mesh of egg threads, like a fabric. Let the mesh fry until golden.

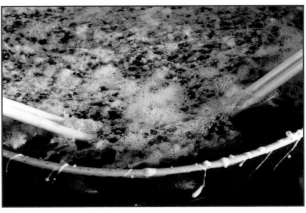

Then place one edge of the "omelets" near you and using skewers on both sides roll loosely away from you. Transfer the kabob onto a serving tray with the seam-side down.

Sprinkle with 1 tablespoon of warm sugar syrup. Cut the roll into three equal portions and sprinkle with cardamom and ground pistachios.

Repeat the above until all the egg mixture is used up. Serve cool.

Lamb and Quince Stew / *Qurme Behi*

AFGHAN STEWS
Qurma

Qurma is a dish made by frying solid ingredients and onions in oil and then cooking them in liquid and serving with the resulting gravy. *Qurma* ingredients are usually meat, fruits, lentils, and vegetables. When *qurma* is prepared without meat it is called *qurma bagari*. With delectable aromas and great taste, *qurma* is a healthy component of a satisfying meal. Most *qurma* are served with bread or plain white rice, *chalow*, on the side.

Lamb has always been the favored meat in Afghanistan, with chicken as a second choice in some instances. Beef is generally considered to be of mediocre quality, consumed if at all by the poorer classes. Certain spices are used for certain meats. The spices and vegetables used for beef are milder and refreshing, such as ground coriander seeds, tomatoes, and bell peppers. Chicken meat, on the other hand, is stir-fried with spices of intense flavor and aromas like garlic, curry powder, and cumin. Lamb is prepared with medium spices. The raw smell of chicken and fish is eliminated by incorporating ground turmeric. Turmeric also gives most qurma dishes a beautiful color and flavor. Turmeric is also said to have a therapeutic effect and healing role in wounds and inflammations.

Meat *qurma* can be combined with fruits and vegetables. Fruits and vegetables in *qurma* cookery are available year-round in Afghanistan thanks to the climatic extremities of the different regions. While it snows hard in Kabul, people still enjoy cauliflower for *qurma* from the eastern cities like Jalalabad. Cherry *qurma*, a product of high altitudes like Kabul, is enjoyed in the summer heat of Jalalabad.

The cooking process for Afghan stews is completed in three stages. It always starts with stir-frying onions in oil. Then meat or vegetables are seared in the onions on high heat. When spices and other ingredients like tomato paste and fresh tomatoes are added, the heat is reduced to medium, before the *qurma* is simmered in its sauce or water to a thorough tenderness. A typically finished *qurma* has no extra liquid in it. Afghan stews are thickened by onion gravy once the liquid evaporates.

Qurmas served with *chaka* (drained yogurt) are called *lawang*. Most *lawang* dishes are prepared with special spices like black pepper, ginger, and cardamom. The most popular *lawang* of the old days used to be prepared with game meats such as quail and partridge with cloves (*lawang*) as the main spice, thus the name of the stew.

CHICKEN AND SOUR CHERRY STEW

Qurmé Alubalu

Makes 4 to 6 servings

Sour cherry (alubalu) stew is prepared with chicken, sour cherries, onions, and spices. Sour cherries grow in higher altitudes like Kabul where it snows in winter. The Paghman district located in the west of Kabul is known for the best quality regular and sour cherries. Sour cherries are edible and taste good with a sprinkle of salt to balance the tanginess. However, in culinary uses, sugar is added for the sweet and sour taste. This qurma *is served with plain* chalow *rice on the side.*

1½ pounds cherries, preferably sour, pits removed
1 tablespoon sugar
2 teaspoons juice of fresh ginger
2 cups finely chopped onions
½ cup oil
1½ pounds chicken legs and thighs, fat and skin removed
¼ teaspoon ground turmeric
1 teaspoon salt
1 teaspoon ground coriander seeds
1 teaspoon cayenne pepper powder (optional)
1 teaspoon ground cardamom

In a saucepan mix together the cherries, sugar, ginger juice, and ½ cup water. Cook down covered on low heat until cherries are soft and the mixture is reduced to a thick sauce. Keep warm.

Meanwhile, in a six-quart pot, fry the onions in the oil over medium heat until the onions start to brown. Add the chicken pieces, turmeric, salt, ground coriander seeds, cayenne pepper powder, and cardamom. Stir-fry for about 3 to 5 minutes. Add 1½ cups water. Stir and then cover and cook on low heat until the chicken is tender in a thick sauce. Boil uncovered if there is extra liquid. Fold the prepared cherries into the *qurma*, and serve with plain *chalow* (page 147).

SWEET AND SOUR CHICKEN AND TOMATO STEW

Qurmé Badenjan Rumi

Makes 4 servings

This sweet and sour chicken and tomato stew is usually served with nan or plain rice on the side. This dish is prepared mostly in late summer when tomatoes (badenjan rumi) are ripe and plentiful. The acidic taste of the tomatoes is balanced by incorporating sugar into the stew. Ginger and cardamom distinguish this qurma *from other stews.*

3 cups finely chopped onions
⅓ cup oil, divided
2 pounds boneless, skinless chicken meat,
  cut into 2-inch pieces
1 tablespoon ground coriander seeds
1½ teaspoons salt
1 teaspoon ground turmeric
2 teaspoons minced garlic
2 cups skinned and chopped tomatoes
1 8-ounce can tomato sauce
1 tablespoon sugar
1 tablespoon juice of fresh ginger
6 cardamom pods, cracked
½ bell pepper, sliced
½ jalapeño pepper, sliced
1 tablespoon lemon juice
1 tablespoon chopped cilantro

On medium heat stir-fry onions in half of the oil until golden. Add the chicken and sear for about 2 minutes. Reduce the heat. Add the ground coriander seeds, salt, and turmeric. Fry for 1 minute. Pour in ½ cup of water. Stir, cover, and cook on low heat for about 5 minutes. Set aside.

In a separate pan, fry the garlic in the remaining oil for 1 minute. Add the chopped tomatoes and stir-fry until tomatoes are cooked down. Add the tomato sauce and fry for 1 minute. Add the sugar, ginger juice, cardamom pods, bell peppers, and jalapeño. Fry for 1 minute.

Add the tomato mixture to the chicken and fold gently. Simmer for 15 minutes until the peppers are tender and the meat is cooked through. Drizzle the lemon juice around the top of the *qurma* and decorate with cilantro. Serve with plain rice or nan on the side.

CHICKEN AND POMEGRANATE STEW

Qurmé Anar

This sweet and sour chicken stew is cooked in onion sauce with spices and pomegranates (anar). It is usually served with chalow rice (page 147). The best quality pomegranates are grown in many provinces of Afghanistan, particularly Kandahar and the Tagab district of Kapisa province.

1¼ pounds pomegranate seeds, plus
  additional for garnish
Sugar and lemon as needed
1 onion, finely chopped
3 tablespoons oil
1½ pounds chicken parts, skinned
½ teaspoon ground turmeric
1 teaspoon garlic paste
1 teaspoon ginger paste
1 teaspoon salt
½ tablespoon ground coriander seeds
5 cardamom pods, cracked

Puree the pomegranate seeds and squeeze through a sieve, discarding any solids. Boil for about 10 minutes until the juice is reduced to ½ cup. Depending on the pomegranate variety, for tarter fruit add sugar to taste, and for sweeter fruit add lemon to taste. Set aside.

Fry the onions in oil to a golden color on moderate heat. Add the chicken and turmeric. Stir-fry for 3 minutes. Add the garlic paste and ginger paste and fry for 1 minute. Add the salt, ground coriander seeds, cardamom pods, and 1 cup of water. Stir and cover. Simmer until chicken is tender and a thick sauce is formed.

Add the prepared pomegranate syrup to the meat sauce and fold gently. Sprinkle with additional pomegranate seeds. Serve warm.

Chicken and Pomegranate Stew / Qurmé Anar

SWEET AND SOUR CHICKEN STEW

Qurmé Chashnidar

Makes 4 to 6 servings

This sweet and sour chicken stew is cooked in onion gravy and spices with a touch of lemon and sugar and served with nan or plain white rice (chalow). Afghan chicken meat is packed with flavor. In post-war Afghanistan, with an overpopulated capital and larger cities, backyard farming is becoming popular, and in the suburbs, Afghans raise their chickens cage-free and organic.

3 cups finely chopped onions
⅓ cup oil
6 chicken drumsticks and
   thighs, skin removed
1½ teaspoons salt
1 tablespoon ground
   coriander seeds
1 tablespoon garlic paste
1 teaspoon ginger powder
½ teaspoon ground turmeric
2 tablespoons tomato paste
1 cup chopped tomatoes
Juice of one lemon
¼ cup brown sugar
½ red bell pepper, sliced
½ green bell pepper, sliced
½ cup chopped cilantro

Stir-fry onions in oil to a golden color on high heat. Add the chicken pieces, and sear for about 5 minutes. Reduce heat to medium-low and add the salt, ground coriander seeds, garlic paste, ginger powder, and turmeric. Stir-fry for 1 minute. Add the tomato paste and tomatoes, and fry until tomatoes are dissolved. Add 1¼ cups of water. Stir, cover, and cook on medium heat for about 30 minutes.

Raise the heat and boil uncovered if there is water in the stew. Once the water has evaporated, add the lemon juice, brown sugar, and bell peppers. Fold in gently. Cover and simmer for a further 5 to 10 minutes. Sprinkle with cilantro. Serve warm with *chalow* (page 147) or nan.

CHICKEN AND MUSHROOM STEW

Qurmé Lawangé Samaruq

Chicken breast meat and mushrooms (samaruq) are sauteed with spices and folded into garlic-flavored yogurt. Qurut, a tangy counterpart of yogurt, is replaced by chaka in this recipe. In the old days, nonpoisonous mushrooms were harvested from the wild and used for delicacies such as this recipe. In today's Afghanistan, mushrooms are cultivated on private farms by women in the post-war cities. Homegrown mushrooms are safe and appear to have made a place on the Afghan food spread, the destarkhwan.

16 ounces white button mushrooms, sliced
¾ cup olive oil
2 cups sliced onions
2 pounds chicken breasts, cut into
  bite-size pieces
3 tablespoons finely chopped green chilis
1 teaspoon salt
2 teaspoons ground turmeric
1 teaspoon ground black pepper
½ teaspoon ground cumin
2 cups chaka (drained yogurt; page 318),
  room temperature
1 teaspoon garlic paste
1 cup chopped cilantro

In a saucepan sauté the mushrooms in the oil for about 1 minute. Remove the mushrooms with a slotted spoon and reserve. Stir-fry the onion slices in the same oil until the onions start to change color. Add the chicken breast pieces to the onions and sauté for about 5 minutes on moderate heat. Add the chilis and sauté an additional 2 minutes. Add the salt, turmeric, black pepper, and cumin. Return the mushrooms to the pan. Sauté for 1 minute on low heat.

In a small bowl, whisk the *chaka* with the garlic paste and a pinch of salt to a honey consistency (add a little water if necessary). Add the prepared *chaka* and cilantro to the chicken and mushroom mixture and fold in gently. Remove from heat and let the *qurma* set for about 5 minutes until the sauce has thickened and oil separates. Serve with Afghan nan or plain *chalow* (page 147).

LAMB AND MANGO STEW

Qurmé Am

Makes 6 servings

For this qurma, *after lamb stew is prepared with onions, tomato paste, and spices, fresh slices of mango (am) are added and simmered. Mangos grow only in the citrus-growing eastern districts of Afghanistan and are sold at the stalls in Kabul and other larger cities. Mangos are pricy and considered for special condiments or* qurma. *This* qurma *is usually served with plain rice.*

1½ cups finely chopped onions
⅓ cup olive oil
1½ pounds lamb, cut into bite-size
   pieces
1½ teaspoons salt
½ teaspoon ground turmeric
2 teaspoons ground coriander
   seeds
2 teaspoons tomato paste
2 teaspoons garlic paste
3 green mangos, peeled and sliced
5 mini sweet peppers
3 green chilies, sliced
Cilantro leaves to garnish

Fry the onions in the oil until onions start to brown. Add the lamb, salt, and turmeric. Stir-fry on medium heat until golden, about 5 to 7 minutes. Add the ground coriander seeds, tomato paste, and garlic paste. Stir-fry on low heat for about 1 to 2 minutes. Add 1 cup of water. Cover and cook on low heat until the meat is tender, about 1½ to 2 hours.

Add the mangos and sweet peppers. Cover and cook for about 10 minutes. The *qurma* is done when the juices are reduced to a thick gravy and oil forms on top 5 minutes after the dish is removed from heat. Sprinkle with the cilantro and serve with Afghan nan or *chalow* (page 147).

LAMB AND EGGPLANT STEW

Qurmé Badenjan

*Good quality eggplants (*badenjan*) are peeled, fried, and then folded into a lamb stew. Chalow rice is recommended as a complement with this dish, although Afghan flat nan can be utilized as a scoop.*

1 pound seedless eggplants, peeled and chopped
4 cups finely chopped onions
¼ cup oil
2 pounds lamb, cut into 2-inch chunks
1½ teaspoons salt
¼ teaspoons ground turmeric
½ teaspoon cayenne pepper powder
½ tablespoon ground coriander seeds
1 tablespoon tomato paste
1 tablespoon garlic paste
2 cups blanched, peeled, and chopped tomatoes
Oil for frying

Sprinkle the eggplant pieces with salt and set them aside to sweat for about 20 to 30 minutes.

Fry the onions in the oil to a golden color. Add the lamb and brown. Reduce heat to medium. Add the salt, turmeric, cayenne pepper powder, ground coriander seeds, tomato paste, and garlic paste and fry for 1 minute. Slide in the tomatoes gently and cook down to dissolve. Add 1½ cups of water and stir. Cover and cook on low heat for about 1½ hour or until meat is tender. Then if needed, boil the stew uncovered on a higher heat for any excess water to evaporate. Keep warm.

Meanwhile, in a small saucepan heat the oil for frying. Pat-dry the eggplant pieces using paper towels and lower a handful at a time into the hot oil and fry until golden. Drain on paper towels. Lower the fried eggplant into the prepared meat stew and fold in gently. Simmer for 10 minutes until the oil separates. Remove oil and discard. Serve the *qurma* with Afghan nan or preferably with short-grain rice (*bata*) or *chalow* (page 147).

LAMB AND QUINCE STEW

Qurmé Behi

Makes 4 servings

Slices of fresh quince (behi) are simmered with spicy lamb stew and served with chalow rice or flat nan. Quinces ripen in the fall in the cooler climates of Afghanistan. When incorporated in meat stews, the grainy pulp and the sweet aroma of quince make the dish delectable and special.

2 cups finely chopped onion
⅓ cup olive oil
1 pound lamb, cut into bite-size
  pieces
1 teaspoon salt
½ teaspoon ground turmeric
1 tablespoon ground coriander
  seeds
2 teaspoons tomato paste
2 teaspoons garlic paste
1 teaspoon ginger paste
1 large quince, seeds removed and
  sliced
3 green chilies, sliced

Fry the onions in the oil until onions start to brown. Add the lamb, salt, and turmeric. Stir-fry on medium heat until golden, about 5 to 7 minutes. Add the ground coriander seeds, tomato paste, garlic paste, and ginger paste. Stir-fry on low heat for about 1 to 2 minutes. Add 1 cup of water. Cover and cook on low heat until the meat is half-cooked, about 30 minutes or so.

Add the quince and chilies. Cover and simmer for another 60 minutes. The *qurma* is done when the juices are reduced to a thick gravy and the oil forms on top 5 minutes after the dish is removed from heat. Serve with Afghan nan or *chalow* (page 147).

LAMB AND POTATO STEW

Qurmé Kachalu

Makes 6 servings

Lamb is stewed in onion gravy and spices and then simmered with pota-toes (kachalu) and served with nan or plain rice for this version of qurma. *Ex-cept when prepared as French fries to compliment certain fried kabobs or as snacks such as* bolani *and* pakowra, *potato dishes are prepared for everyday meals—never for guests since they are considered cheap and mostly avail-able to needy Afghans. Potatoes are cultivated all over the country, particu-larly in the Bamiyan province.*

4 cups finely chopped onions
⅓ cup olive oil
1½ pounds lamb on the bone, cut
   into 3-inch chunks
½ teaspoon ground turmeric
2 teaspoons salt
2 tablespoons ground coriander
   seeds
1 tablespoon garlic paste
2 tablespoons tomato paste
1 cup blanched, peeled and
   chopped tomatoes
3 cups boiling water
2 chilies, finely chopped (optional)
1½ pounds potatoes, peeled and cut
   into thirds
½ bunch cilantro, chopped

Stir-fry the onions in the oil to a light golden color on high heat. Add the lamb and sear on high heat for about 4 minutes, stirring constantly. Add the turmeric, salt, and ground coriander seeds and stir-fry on medium heat for about 1 minute. Add the garlic paste and tomato paste and stir-fry for about 1 minute. Add tomatoes and stir-fry until wilted and dissolved. Stir in the boiling water. Cover and cook on low heat for about 2 hours.

Add the chilis and potatoes. Stir. The sauce should cover the potatoes—add more water and stir if necessary. Simmer covered for 30 minutes or until the potatoes are fork-tender.

Raise the heat and boil uncovered to rid of any extra water. Remove from heat. Spoon off and discard any fat that forms on top after the qurma sits for 5 minutes. Sprinkle with cilantro. Serve warm with nan or *chalow* (page 147).

Lamb and Split Pea Stew / *Qurmé Dalnakhud*

LAMB AND SPLIT PEA STEW

Qurmé Dalnakhud

For this qurma, *lamb is cooked in onion gravy and spices, folded in with split peas* (dalnakhud) *and sour plums, simmered, and served with nan or plain rice. This lamb stew is the most versatile* qurma *prepared in almost every Afghan home and is served in many variations. When served with plain rice it is called* Qurma Chalow; *when layered with plain rice and steamed it is called* Chalow Ladam; *and when used as the topping for short-grain rice* (shoula) *it is called* Shoulé Ghorbandi. *But the most basic method of serving this dish is using a flat nan to scoop up the* qurma.

3 cups finely chopped onions
⅓ cup olive oil
1½ pounds lamb with bone, cut into
   small chunks
2½ teaspoons salt
1 teaspoon cayenne pepper powder
1 tablespoon ground coriander seeds
½ teaspoon ground turmeric
2 tablespoons minced garlic
½ cup chopped tomatoes
Pinch ground saffron
½ cup dried yellow split peas, washed
10 dried sour plums
6 sweet peppers

Stir-fry the onions in the oil to a golden color on high heat. Add the lamb and sear for about 5 minutes. Reduce the heat to medium. Add the salt, cayenne pepper powder, ground coriander seeds, and turmeric. Stir-fry for about 1 minute. Add the garlic and stir-fry for 1 minute. Add the tomatoes and fry until dissolved. Add 2 cups of water and saffron. Mix well, and then cover and simmer over low heat for about 1½ hours or until the lamb is just tender and a thick sauce is formed. If too watery, boil on high for a few minutes to evaporate extra water.

Add the yellow split peas to the *qurma* and cook on low heat for 20 minutes. Fold in the dried sour plums and sweet peppers. Cover and simmer for 7 minutes. Spoon off any fat and discard. Add a little olive oil if desired. Serve warm with *chalow* (page 147) or nan.

LAMB AND TURNIP STEW

Qurmé Shalgham

Makes 6 servings

This sweet and spicy lamb qurma *is cooked in onion sauce and simmered with ginger, turnip* (shalgham) *slices, and peppers. Afghan turnips are crisp, juicy, and mild. They are favored in cold seasons and when cooked in Om-ache Shalgham* (Turnip and Pasta Soup), *the soup makes a good home remedy for cold and respiratory problems.*

3 cups finely chopped onions
½ cup oil
1 pound boneless lamb, cut into
   2-inch chunks
1½ teaspoons salt
½ teaspoon turmeric
½ tablespoon ground coriander
   seeds
2 teaspoons tomato paste
2 teaspoons minced garlic
1 teaspoon minced ginger
½ cup chopped tomatoes
2 medium turnips, peeled and
   cut into bite-size pieces
2 tablespoons brown sugar
2 green chilies, chopped
1 red bell pepper, cut into 6
   pieces
Few leaves of cilantro

Stir-fry the onions in the oil to a golden color on moderate heat. Add the lamb and sear until golden. Add the salt, turmeric, and ground coriander seeds and stir for 1 minute. Add the tomato paste, garlic, and ginger and stir on low heat until the garlic becomes aromatic. Stir in the tomatoes until dissolved. Stir in 2 cups of water, cover and cook on low heat until the meat is just tender, about 1 to 1½ hours.

Stir the stew and add the turnips. Cover and cook on low heat for about 30 more minutes or until the turnips are tender and transparent.

Gently fold in the brown sugar, chilies, and bell pepper and simmer for 7 to 10 minutes. Garnish with cilantro. Serve with *chalow* (page 147) or nan.

BEEF AND RHUBARB STEW

Qurmé Rawash

Makes 4 servings

Here beef stew is cooked in onion gravy and spices, steamed with rhubarb (rawash), and served with nan or chalow. This dish is more popular in the spring season when the red and green of the rhubarb stalks and leaves attract visitors to the foothills of mountains and creek sides for the harvest. The leaves are not edible. However, the stalks are peeled and often eaten raw with just a sprinkle of salt.

½ pound rhubarb
2 cups finely chopped onions
¼ cup olive oil
1½ pounds beef shanks, cut
  into 3-inch chunks
¼ teaspoon ground turmeric
1½ teaspoons salt
1 tablespoon ground coriander
  seeds
1 tablespoon garlic paste
1 tablespoon tomato paste
1 cup sliced bell peppers
1 tablespoon brown sugar

Peel rhubarbs, chop off leaves and discard, and then cut stalks into 3-inch pieces.

Stir-fry the onions in the oil on high heat to a golden color. Add the beef shanks and sear to a golden color. Reduce the heat to medium-low. Add turmeric, salt, ground coriander seeds, garlic paste, and tomato paste. Stir-fry for another minute. Add 2 cups water. Cover and cook on low heat for 1½ to 2 hours or until meat is tender and a thick sauce has formed.

Add the bell peppers and brown sugar. Mix well, and then arrange rhubarb pieces on top of the stew. Cover and simmer for 10 to 15 minutes or until rhubarbs are tender and creamy. Serve warm with nan or preferably with *chalow* (page 147).

MEATBALL STEW

Qurmé Koufta

For this stew, ground meat is rubbed with minced onions, tomatoes, chopped cilantro, salt, and black pepper into a smooth paste. The paste is then shaped into balls and the spicy meatballs are simmered in onion sauce and spices. This versatile dish can be served with pasta, nan, plain rice (chalow; page 147), shoulas (short-grain rice dishes), or Piawa (Bread and Egg Soup, page 53). Beef is most commonly used for this qurma. Ground turkey and chicken are healthier choices and ground lamb can be substituted as well.

For the meatballs:
1½ pounds lean ground meat (beef, lamb, turkey or chicken)
1 cup minced onions
½ cup minced tomatoes
1 cup chopped cilantro
1 tablespoon garlic paste
1 teaspoon ground black pepper
1½ teaspoons salt
1 egg

Place the meat in a mixing bowl. Add onions, tomatoes, cilantro, garlic paste, pepper, salt, and egg, and then mix in and massage until sticky. Set aside.

For the sauce:
2½ cups finely chopped onions
⅓ cup olive oil
2 tablespoons tomato paste
½ teaspoon ground turmeric
1 teaspoon salt
Shredded bell peppers to garnish

Stir-fry the onions in the oil to golden color. Add the tomato paste, turmeric, and salt. Stir-fry for another 2 minutes on medium heat. Add ½ cup water and stir. Lower the heat to simmer.

Shape the meat mixture into egg-sized balls with wet hands and then lower into the sauce one at a time in a single layer. Arrange any remaining balls over the spaces between the balls of the first layer. Cover and cook for about 30 minutes on a gentle heat.

Stir and let stand for 5 minutes for the oil to form on the surface of the *qurma*. Spoon the oil off and discard. Garnish with peppers and serve with any pasta, bread, or rice.

FRIED FISH STEW

Qurmé Lawangé Mahi

*Fried fish (*mahi*) fillets are simmered in onion sauce and spices, folded with creamy yogurt, and served with nan for this delicious* qurma *variation. The use of cloves (*lawang*) and cardamom with the incorporation of* chaka *(drained yogurt) is what makes this dish unique. Afghans have stopped using cloves in this type of* qurma *recipe but the* qurma *continues to be called* lawang.

1 cup finely chopped onions
¼ cup olive oil
½ teaspoon salt
½ teaspoon ground turmeric
3 cloves garlic, crushed
1 teaspoon ginger powder
4 green chilies, finely chopped
1 large tomato, blanched, peeled, and
  chopped
1 teaspoon tomato paste
Oil for frying
1½ pounds wild tilapia fillets, cut into
  2-inch pieces
½ cup chaka (drained yogurt; page 318)

Stir-fry the onions in the oil to a golden color. Add salt, turmeric, garlic, and ginger powder. Stir-fry on low heat for about 1 minute. Add the chilies, tomatoes, and tomato paste. Stir-fry until the tomatoes are dissolved. Turn the heat off and set aside.

Pour a thin layer of oil into a separate frying pan and heat. Sear the tilapia in the hot oil for about 2 minutes on each side or until golden on both sides.

Gently fold the fried fish into the prepared sauce. Simmer for 3 minutes. Spread half the *chaka* on a serving dish and top with the fish stew. Then top with the remaining *chaka*. Serve warm with nan.

GAME HEN STEW WITH SPICES

Qurmé Lawang

Makes 4 servings

This ancient dish was originally prepared with game birds such as quails with the main spice distinguishing it from other qurma *being the clove (la-wang). The game bird was marinated with spices and stewed in onion gravy and folded into a byproduct of milk* (qurut). *However, Afghans now often use other meats such as chicken or lamb for this stew and have eliminated the use of* lawang *and other spices over the long years. The* qurut *has been replaced by drained yogurt* (chaka).

For the hen:
½ tablespoon garlic paste
½ tablespoon ginger paste
2 teaspoons ground turmeric
1 teaspoon ground coriander seeds
1½ teaspoons salt
1 tablespoon olive oil
1½-pound game hen or wild bird,
  cut into pieces

Mix the garlic paste, ginger paste, turmeric, ground coriander seeds, salt, and oil in a large bowl. Transfer the game hen pieces to the spice bowl and massage with the spices. Cover and let marinate in the refrigerator for about 6 hours.

For the spices:
2 whole cloves
5 whole cardamom pods, cracked
¼-inch piece cinnamon stick

Tie all the spices into a small cheesecloth.

For the stew:
1 cup sliced onions
⅓ cup oil
¼ cup finely chopped chilies
  (optional)
½ cup chopped cilantro
1 cup chaka (drained yogurt; page
  318), room temperature
Pinch of salt
1 teaspoon garlic paste, room
  temperature
Ground black pepper and crushed
  red chilies to garnish

In a 6-quart pot stir-fry the onions in the oil on moderate heat until they begin to change color. Add the marinated game hen pieces to the onions and stir-fry on moderate heat until the meat is golden, trying not to burn the onions. Add the chilies and 1 cup of water. Toss in the tied spices and stir. Cover and simmer until the meat is tender and juices are reduced to a thick gravy, about 45 minutes (game birds cook a little longer than game hens.)

Remove the tied spices and discard. Sprinkle the *qurma* with the chopped cilantro. In a small bowl stir together the *chaka*, pinch of salt, and garlic paste. then fold the *chaka* gently into the *qurma*. Transfer to a serving dish and sprinkle with black pepper and chilies. Serve with *chalow* (page 147) on the side.

OKRA STEW

Qurmé Bamia

For best results, Afghans stir-fry the okra (bamia) first to rid it of sliminess before simmering it in the prepared sauces. A variety of hot peppers and a drizzle of lemon make this qurma delectable. Okra is also served with meat qurma by incorporating it into the qurma halfway through the meat cooking, after being stir-fried. Qurmé Bamia can be served with nan or plain rice .

2 pounds fresh okra
1½ cups finely chopped onions
⅓ cup olive oil
2 cups finely chopped tomatoes
1 teaspoon salt
2 teaspoons ground coriander
  seeds
¼ teaspoon ground turmeric
2 teaspoons tomato paste
2 teaspoons garlic paste
½ teaspoon cayenne pepper
  powder
½ tablespoon lemon juice

Cut the stems off the okras, wash, and pat dry with a kitchen towel.

Fry the onions in the oil over high heat until golden. Reduce the heat to medium. Add the okras and stir-fry for about 3 minutes. Add the tomatoes, salt, ground coriander seeds, turmeric, tomato paste, garlic paste, and cayenne pepper powder. Stir on low heat until the tomatoes are dissolved. Add 1 cup of water, stir well and bring to a fast boil. Reduce heat to low and simmer covered for about 20 minutes or until okra is tender.

Transfer to a serving bowl. Drizzle with the lemon juice. Serve hot with nan or *chalow* (page 147).

SWEET AND SOUR CARROT STEW

Qurmé Zardak

Makes 6 servings

Stir-fried sweet and sour carrots are steamed in onion juices and spices and served with nan on the side. Carrots (zardak) are a popular vegetable in Afghanistan. They are used in preparing a sweet called Halwa Zardak *(page 259) and add flavor and color to* shourba *soups. Afghans also consume this healthy vegetable just by munching on it or making juices. Carrots are also cut in thin strings and fried with raisins for the famous* palow *topping.*

3 cups finely chopped onions
½ cup cooking oil
2 pounds carrots, chopped
2 tablespoons salt
1 teaspoon cayenne pepper powder, or finely chopped green chilies
1 tablespoon tomato paste
2 teaspoons minced garlic
1 cup chopped tomatoes
1 tablespoon lemon juice
2 tablespoons sugar

In a skillet, stir-fry the onions in the oil over high heat until the onions turn golden. Add the carrots and stir-fry for about 10 minutes on medium-low heat or until carrots turn dryer and softer to the bite. Add the salt, cayenne pepper powder, tomato paste, and garlic. Stir-fry for 1 minute on medium heat. Add the tomatoes and fry until dissolved. Add 2 cups water and the lemon juice. Stir and cover to cook on low heat for about 45 minutes or until carrots are tender and all liquid is absorbed. Add sugar in the last 10 minutes of the cooking time. Serve warm with Afghan nan.

CAULIFLOWER STEW

Qurmé Gulpi

This vegetable qurma is prepared with cauliflower (gulpi) cooked in a sauce of onion gravy, spices, and vegetables, and served with nan on the side. Cauliflower is cultivated in the citrus-growing districts in the east of Afghanistan like Jalalabad. Cauliflower is harvested in winter and sold at the stalls in Kabul and other cold cities, together with sour oranges and other citrus fruits. Fritters prepared with cauliflower are often served as a starter in the month of Ramadan before a meal.

1 teaspoon salt
1 tablespoon tomato paste
½ teaspoon cayenne pepper
  powder
¼ teaspoon ground turmeric
1 teaspoon garlic paste
2 cups finely chopped onions
¼ cup olive oil
1 pound cauliflower florets
Juice of ½ sour orange or lemon
¼ cup red and green bell pepper
  slices

Dissolve the salt, tomato paste, cayenne pepper powder, turmeric, and garlic paste in 1 cup of water. Set aside.

In a 6-quart pot stir-fry the onions in the oil to a light golden color on high heat. Add the prepared sauce and the cauliflower florets. Mix well to coat florets. Add 2 cups of water in a thin stream, not touching the sauce-coated florets. Cover and cook on medium heat for 20 minutes or until the cauliflower is barely tender.

Drizzle with the orange or lemon juice and gently mix in the bell peppers. Cook uncovered on medium-high heat for about 10 minutes or until most of the liquid has been absorbed and the cauliflower is fork-tender when pierced in the stem. Serve with nan.

FRIED CAULIFLOWER STEW

Qurmé Gulpi Beryan   Makes 4 to 6 servings

In this version of cauliflower stew, the cauliflower is fried first and then simmered in a sauce of onions, tomatoes, and spices. Afghans consider cauliflower (gulpi) an inferior vegetable unless it is cooked with certain spices in a certain way so the outcome is not mushy and sloppy. Frying saves this vegetable from being categorized as unenticing and bland.

1½ pounds cauliflower florets
Oil for frying
1 cup chopped onions
¼ cup olive oil
1 teaspoon garlic paste
1 cup blanched, peeled, and
   chopped tomatoes
½ cup tomato sauce
1 teaspoon salt
3 chilies, chopped
2 teaspoons ground coriander seeds

Split the florets lengthwise. Heat 3 inches of oil in a small saucepan. Then fry the cauliflower florets, a few at a time, with the flat side down until golden. Turn on the other side and fry. Drain on paper towels.

Meanwhile in another pan, fry the onions in ¼ cup olive oil on high heat until golden. Add the garlic paste and fry for 1 minute. Add the tomatoes and stir-fry on medium heat until the tomatoes are dissolved. Add ½ cup of water, the tomato sauce, salt, chilies, and ground coriander seeds. Stir well.

Place the fried cauliflower florets in a medium saucepan and pour the prepared sauce over the top of the florets. Cook covered on low heat until fork-tender. Serve warm.

CABBAGE AND BELL PEPPER STEW

Qurmé Karam

Makes 6 servings

Cabbage (karam) and bell peppers are sautéed with onions and spices for this vegetable stew. This cabbage dish is not a filling meal on its own but it tastes great with any fried or grilled kabob. Since Afghanistan has a diverse geographical nature, cabbage cultivation alternates between tropical zones and higher altitudes. Thus, it is available throughout all four seasons.

2-pound head of cabbage
3 cups finely chopped onions
½ cup oil
¼ teaspoon ground turmeric
2 tablespoons tomato paste
1 tablespoon garlic paste
2 teaspoons salt
2 teaspoons lemon juice
2 each red, yellow, and green
   mini sweet peppers
1 tablespoon chopped parsley

Remove the hard stock of the cabbage at the bottom and discard. Chop the rest into 1-inch pieces.

In a large non-stick saucepan stir-fry the onions in the oil to a light golden color on high heat. Reduce the heat to medium. Add the turmeric, tomato paste, garlic paste, and salt. Stir-fry for 1 minute. Add the cabbage and stir-fry on medium heat for about 5 minutes, or until the cabbage is wilted. Stir in the lemon juice. Cover and continue to cook on low heat for 45 minutes, stirring occasionally and adjusting heat to a lower degree if the vegetable starts to stick to the bottom of the pot.

Add the sweet peppers in the last 10 minutes. Raise the heat and cook uncovered to rid of any extra water. Garnish with parsley and serve warm with nan.

PURSLANE AND MUNG BEAN STEW

Qurmé Khurfa

Makes 4 servings

Purslane (khurfa) and mung beans are cooked together and steamed with onion and tomato sauce. Purslane grows in the wild in Afghanistan and by the creeks in the villages. This succulent, packed with omega 3, can be eaten raw in salads. Mung beans as the protein source in this qurma *makes it a good candidate for being served as a meal.*

¼ cup whole mung beans
2 cups boiling water
2 pounds fresh purslane
½ large yellow onion, finely
  chopped
¼ cup oil
2 teaspoons minced garlic
½ teaspoon ground turmeric
2 teaspoons ground coriander
  seeds
1 teaspoon ground black pepper
1 teaspoon tomato paste
½ teaspoon salt
1 small tomato, sliced

Place the mung beans and 2 cups of boiling water in a pot. Cook covered for about 15 minutes on low heat. Add the purslane. Stir well and cook covered for 15 minutes until there is no more visible liquid at the bottom of the pot. Set aside.

Meanwhile, prepare the sauce: In a small saucepan fry the onions in the oil over medium heat until the onions start to change color. Add the garlic, turmeric, ground coriander seeds, and pepper. Stir-fry briefly until they are aromatic. Add the tomato paste and salt and stir-fry for 1 minute. Add the tomato slices and cook down on low heat until the oil has separated.

Add the prepared sauce to the purslane mixture. Stir well. Cover and steam on low heat for about 10 minutes. Serve with Afghan nan on the side.

BEAN STEW

Qurmé Lobia

Makes 4 servings

Beans (lobia) cooked in a sauce of fried onions, tomatoes, and spices, and served with nan or rice on the side is a rich source of protein so usually served as a main course. Basket-loads of various lobia have been found at the busy Mandawi Bazaar for centuries. The most popular lobia cultivated in the country, particularly in the northeast districts, are kidney beans, navy beans, and blackeye peas, all called "lobia," but referred to by their colors.

2 (16-ounce each) cans red
   kidney beans or pinto beans*
3 cups finely chopped onions
¼ cup olive oil
2 teaspoons tomato paste
4 green chilies, chopped
2 teaspoons ground coriander
   seeds
1 teaspoon ground cumin
½ teaspoon salt
1 teaspoon garlic paste
1 tomato, blanched, peeled and
   chopped
½ tablespoon lemon juice

Drain the red kidney or pinto beans and rinse thoroughly.

Stir-fry the onions in the olive oil over high heat to a golden color. Add the tomato paste, chilis, coriander, cumin, salt, and garlic paste. Stir-fry on medium heat for 1 minute. Add the tomatoes and stir-fry until dissolved. Add the beans and enough water to cover the beans. Cover and cook on low heat for about 20 minutes.

If the sauce has not thickened, boil uncovered on medium heat to allow the liquid to thicken. Stir in the lemon juice. Simmer for 5 minutes. When the sauce thickens and the oil separates the *qurma* is ready.

You can also use dried beans for this stew. Soak them for 4 hours and then drain. After you make the sauce add the beans with 1 extra cup of water and simmer for 45 minutes or until the beans are tender.

SPINACH AND DILL STEW

Qurmé Sabzi

This dill-flavored spinach (sabzi) dish is prepared with gandana (a type of leek) and spices, and usually served with a meat stew topping and nan on the side. This spinach dish is particularly prepared for the Afghan new year, Nawruz, which falls on the spring equinox. Spinach symbolizes a fertile and productive year ahead.

2 pounds fresh spinach
2 cups finely chopped gandana, leeks, or green onions
⅓ cup olive oil
½ teaspoon salt
1 teaspoon cayenne pepper powder (optional)
½ tablespoon garlic paste
¼ cup chopped fresh dill
2 tablespoons of any meat qurma per serving

Boil the spinach briefly. Drain and submerge in chilled water. Drain.

In a medium-size skillet sauté the leeks in the oil until wilted. Add the spinach. Turn the heat to medium and add the salt, cayenne pepper powder, garlic paste, and dill. Mix well, cover, and cook until the spinach is reduced to one-quarter of its volume, about 20 minutes.

If spinach is still watery, cook further on a higher heat, uncovered, until all the liquid has evaporated. Transfer to a serving bowl. Top with any meat stew. Serve warm with nan or plain rice (*chalow*, page 147).

VEGETABLE DOUGH BALLS

Kololè Khamiri

Makes 5 servings

Vegetable dough balls are cooked in tomato sauce and served with a drizzle of dried and fresh mint and Afghan nan. "Kolola" means "round" and "khami-ri" means "made of dough." This healthy meal is called "dough balls" because the dough is used during the preparation as a binding agent to make the vegetables stick together. Depending on the season, various leafy and solid vegetables can be chopped and used in these balls. Cooking times for most substitute vegetables will remain the same.

For the sauce:
2 tablespoons tomato paste
⅓ cup oil
1½ cups chopped tomatoes
1 teaspoon salt
½ teaspoon turmeric
1 tablespoon ground coriander
   seeds

Stir-fry the tomato paste in the oil over a moderate heat for about 2 minutes. Add the tomatoes and stir-fry for another 2 minutes on low heat until the tomatoes are dissolved. Add the salt, turmeric, and ground coriander seeds. Stir for 1 minute and set aside.

For the dough balls:
1½ cups peeled and finely
   chopped eggplants
1 cup finely chopped potatoes
½ cup finely chopped onions
½ cup finely chopped tomatoes
3 green chilis, finely chopped, or
   to taste
½ cup finely chopped cilantro
1 tablespoon garlic paste
1 teaspoon ground black pepper
1 tablespoon ground coriander
   seeds
½ teaspoon salt
1 teaspoon oil
½ cup all-purpose flour
Red pepper flakes, mint powder,
   and fresh mint sprigs for
   garnish

In a mixing bowl, place the eggplants, potatoes, onions, tomatoes, chiles, and cilantro. Add the garlic paste, black pepper, ground coriander seeds, salt, and oil. Rub the mixture together gently so that the vegetables are coated evenly with the spices and oil. Sprinkle the flour gradually around the top of the mixture. Using a fork combine the flour with the mixture until a soft, sticky, and shapeable mixture is achieved.

Divide the vegetable mixture into 10 equal portions and with wet hands form each portion into a ball.

Add 2 cups of water to the reserved sauce and bring to a gentle boil. Gently lower the dough balls into the simmering sauce. Cook the balls for about 15 to 20 minutes on a gentle heat, stirring gently every 5 minutes until most of the water evaporates leaving behind a thick sauce.

Transfer the balls onto a decorative dish and pour the sauce over the balls. Sprinkle with dry and fresh mint and chili flakes and serve with toasted Afghan nan.

Ground Chicken Kababs / *Kabob Naichee*

MEAT & FISH DISHES

Kabobs

In Afghan tradition "*kabob*" refers to all solid meat and fish dishes that are consumed with bread and condiments on the side. *Kabobs* can be fried, steamed, grilled, or baked. They have been part of the Afghan menu since the early days when deep in the valleys, shepherds grilled chunks of mutton on makeshift fires. The meats used for *kabobs* are chicken, beef, lamb, fish, and veal with lamb being the most favored. Fat is left on the meat for flavor and tenderness. When it comes to Afghan *kabobs*, there is nothing such as rare, medium, or well done. Each *kabob* has to be well done, yet tender and tasty.

Since Afghanistan is a landlocked country, fish caught from the local rivers is the only seafood known in Afghan cuisine. In this book, rainbow trout and tilapia fish are selected as a replacement for Afghan fish.

A lack of chicken farms in the rapidly growing population of Afghanistan had made chicken meat one of the most expensive poultries in the country. Chicken would have only been served at a celebration. However, Afghan chickens, raised in the backyards of small private farms, are organic, grazing on mineral-rich soil and picking on nutrient-rich vegetables. The meat flavor is strong and tasty, and the meat is more muscular with less visible fat on it.

Restaurant eating in Afghanistan is mostly for foreigners. Afghans, on the other hand, enjoy their time out by arranging picnics by the gurgling streams under huge trees or by the river banks. Charcoal is used in portable grills. Singing and dancing are widely popular in the atmosphere pervaded by the appetizing smells of the various *kabobs*. Whether steamed, fried, or roasted *kabobs* are mostly prepared at home for a picnic (*mayla*), dinner guests, or festive occasions.

Kabobs at the market stalls are made fresh on charcoal grills. These commercial *kabobs*, mostly lamb and fat cubes, are threaded on skewers alternately—one cube of fat and four cubes of meat per skewer. Flat skewers are used to thread the *kabob* meat, particularly the ground meat. The meat is marinated with onion puree, garlic, yogurt, and pepper overnight in large quantities. Salt is added just before grilling. These *kabobs* are consumed by people on long shopping sprees, employees on their lunch break, and moviegoers before or after a popular movie. The man grilling the *kabobs* (the *kababi*) sprinkles the *kabob* with sour, powdery *ghoray angur* or sumac and places a loaf of nan on top of the *kabob* before serving it to his customer. A variety of chutneys are served with these grilled meats.

BEEF PATTIES

Chapli Kabob

Makes 24 patties

These fried and spicy ground beef patties are prepared with chickpea flour, scallions, coarsely ground coriander seeds, and spices, topped with fried tomato slices, and served with Afghan nan. This street food is popular in the eastern districts of Afghanistan such as Jalalabad. Homemade Chapli Kabobs come out fancier and healthier as they avoid the repetitive use of burned oil in larger quantities as is true with the commercial version.

2 pounds 80%-lean ground beef
2 cups finely chopped green onions
2 onions, minced and patted dry
1 bunch chopped cilantro
1 tomato, finely chopped
1 tablespoon minced garlic
1 tablespoon minced ginger
1 egg
¼ cup all-purpose flour
¼ cup chickpea flour
2 tablespoons ground coriander seeds
2 teaspoons salt
1 tablespoon crushed dry chili
1 teaspoon ground black pepper
Oil for deep frying
24 tomato slices

Place all ingredients for the *kabob* except the oil and tomato slices in a mixing bowl. Working with your hands, mix the ingredients until well-blended and sticky. Divide the mixture into 24 portions. With clean, oiled hands form each portion into a patty ¼ inch in thickness.

Heat 2 inches of oil in a large fryer on medium-low heat. Fry 4 patties at a time for about 4 minutes on each side, or until golden. Drain on paper towels. Place on a baking tray and keep warm in the oven at 160 degrees F while frying the remaining patties.

Once all the patties are cooked, drain the oil from the pan, reserving a thin film, and return the pan to the heat. Arrange the tomato slices in a single layer in the pan (you might have to do in batches) and let them cook and caramelize slightly on medium heat. Transfer onto the center of each *kabob* and serve.

Beef Patties / *Chapli Kabob*

BEEF SHORT RIBS

Kabob Qaburgha   Makes 6 servings

Beef short ribs (qaburgha) are slow-cooked in water, drained, sprinkled with spices, and then broiled in the oven. Afghans consider beef to be a cold food that causes muscle spasms and joint pain in certain people. So ginger has wide culinary use in beef preparation to suppress muscle inflammation. Beef is available domestically. All over Afghanistan, even the smallest and poorest farmers keep at least one cow to provide their subsistence requirements for dairy products and in all regions cattle are very important to cultivate the land and for beef production.

6 pounds beef short ribs
1 large onion, sliced
3 tablespoons salt
1 teaspoon ground turmeric
Mint leaves and lemon slices to
  garnish

For seasoning mixture:
3 tablespoons garlic paste
1 tablespoon ginger paste
1 tablespoon ground black pepper
1 tablespoon salt
½ cup olive oil

Place the short ribs in a 12-quart stockpot. Add the onion slices, the 3 tablespoons salt, and turmeric. Add enough water to cover the short ribs. Place on high heat and bring to a rolling boil. Cover, reduce heat, and cook on a slow simmer for about 2½ hours or until meat is almost falling off the bone.

Make the seasoning mixture: In a small mixing bowl, mix the garlic paste, ginger paste, pepper, salt, and olive oil. Set aside.

Drain the short ribs and arrange the them in a large ovenproof tray with meat-side up. Then brush thoroughly with the prepared seasoning mixture. Broil on low for 5 minutes in a preheated oven. Garnish with mint leaves and lemon slices. Serve warm with nan.

BEEF, GARBANZO BEAN, AND POTATO KABOBS

Kabob Shami

Makes 4 servings

This kabob is prepared with a combination of ground beef, garbanzo beans, and potatoes. The addition of cilantro and mild spices makes this kabob unique. They are served with fresh tomatoes and Afghan nan on the side. Leftovers can be crumbled and cooked with eggs and tomatoes in the morning. Kabob Shami is served cold as well and makes a versatile meal for a picnic (mayla). (Sham is another name for the Syrian capital, Damascus, and the Syrian Shami, though with the same name, is prepared as patties and uses different ingredients.)

1½ pounds stew beef
1 large onion, chopped
4 cups boiling water
1 cup cooked garbanzo beans
½ pound cooked potatoes
2 chili peppers
2 large eggs
1½ teaspoons salt
1 teaspoon ground black pepper
1½ teaspoons ground coriander
  seeds
1 teaspoon ground cumin
1 tablespoon garlic paste
2 egg whites, beaten
Oil for frying
Tomatoes, cilantro, and chili
  pepper to garnish

In a stockpot, cook the meat and onions in the boiling water for about 15 minutes. Drain and let cool.

Using a meat grinder grind the meat, onions, garbanzo beans, potatoes, and chilies, one at a time, into a mixing bowl. Add the two eggs, salt, pepper, coriander, cumin, and garlic paste. Working with your hands mix together well. Divide the mixture into 2- or 3-tablespoon portions.

Heat 3 inches of oil in a smaller saucepan to 270 degrees F (medium-high). Shape each meat portion into an oblong sausage. Rub the sausages with egg white, and then fry 5 or 6 at a time, turning occasionally for even browning, until golden and crispy. Drain on paper towels. Garnish with tomatoes, cilantro and pepper to serve.

AFGHAN MEATLOAF

Kabob Qalebi

Makes 6 servings

"Qalib" means "mold." This kabob is prepared with lean ground beef, veg-etables, onions, and spices that are pressed in a mold and baked. The kabob is served sliced with fresh tomatoes, greens, and nan on the side. When pre-pared for special occasions and parties, this kabob makes 8 quarter-pound slices. Kabob Qalebi is served cool and can make a great snack when used in sandwiches or packed for a picnic (mayla).

2 pounds lean ground beef
½ cup finely chopped red bell
  pepper
1½ cups minced onions
2 teaspoons salt
1 teaspoon ground black pepper
1 tablespoon ground coriander
  seeds
½ cup tomato sauce
2 large eggs
1 cup minced carrots
1 cup chopped cilantro
1 egg white, beaten
Parsley and tomato to garnish

Preheat the oven to 400 degrees F.

In a mixing bowl, place the ground beef, bell peppers, onions, salt, black pepper, coriander, tomato sauce, eggs, carrots, and cilantro. Working with your hands, massage the meat until well combined. Then press the mixture into a 9-by-5-inch or 1.5-quart oven-proof rectangular dish. Cover with aluminum foil and bake for 75 minutes.

Drain the juices off the meatloaf if any. Un-mold the meatloaf onto a baking tray, upside down. Brush the loaf with the egg white and broil, uncovered, on low for 5 minutes or until golden brown on the top. Slice and serve.

GRILLED LAMB SKEWERS

Kabob Teka

"Tika" means "bits or pieces" in the Dari language. In cooking it is traditionally referring to small pieces of boneless lamb on skewers cooked on a charcoal grill. Kabob Teka is marinated in onion juices and mild spices before grilling. Kabob Seekhi is another name used for this street food, served in the commercial areas of towns to shoppers, moviegoers, students, and workers. In the homemade version, the lamb is threaded on the skewer (seekh) alternately with vegetables, while in the commercial version pieces of fat are threaded between the lamb pieces.

2½ pounds boneless lamb, cut into 2-inch cubes
1 cup onion puree
1½ teaspoons cayenne pepper powder
½ cup plain yogurt
1 tablespoon garlic paste
1 large onion
1 large tomato
½ green bell pepper
2 teaspoons salt
8 flat skewers
1 tablespoon sumac
4 Nan Taba-ee (page 196)

Place the lamb in a glass mixing bowl. Add the onion puree, cayenne pepper powder, yogurt, and garlic paste. Mix well. Cover with plastic wrap and let marinate in the refrigerator overnight.

Let the marinated lamb sit at room temperature for 2 hours before grilling. Meanwhile chop the onion and tomato into 1-inch square cubes. Blanch the bell pepper in simmering water until soft and flexible then cut into 1-inch squares. Add the salt to the marinated lamb and mix well. Thread the lamb and vegetables alternately onto flat skewers, until the skewers are full (about 8 skewers).

Preheat a grill on medium heat. Grill the kabobs for about 10 minutes, turning from time to time, until the kabobs are golden. Sprinkle with the sumac. Serve on a bed of *nan taba-ee.*

Slow-Cooked Steamed Lamb / *Kabob Daygi*

The Best of Afghan Cooking

SLOW-COOKED STEAMED LAMB

Kabob Daygi

Tender slow-cooked lamb on the bone is steamed with sautéed onions and peppers and served with Afghan nan. This slow-cooked and steamed kabob is prepared in pots (dayg) and therefore, it is called "daygi," meaning "food cooked in a pot." Kabob Daygi is convenient and easy to prepare at home for picnics (mayla) as it can be served cold.

2 pounds lamb on the bone, cut into
  2½-inch chunks
1½ teaspoons salt
Pinch turmeric
1 tablespoon ground coriander seeds
3 large onions, sliced
Juice of ½ lemon
2 chili peppers
½ cup oil
2 tomatoes, sliced
1 teaspoon ground black pepper

Place the lamb and 1 cup water in a pot and sprinkle with the salt, turmeric, and ground coriander seeds. Add the slices of 1 onion. Drizzle with the lemon juice. Cover and cook over moderate heat until the meat is tender and juices are reduced to a thick sauce. If needed, to rid of extra water boil on high heat uncovered.

In a separate pan, sauté the remaining onion slices and the chilis in the oil over medium heat until the onions start to change color. Add the tomatoes and fry for about 2 minutes until tomatoes are wilted and oily.

Transfer the onion mixture to the lamb and fold in gently. Cover the pot with a towel and secure it with the lid. Steam on low heat for about 30 minutes. Transfer to a serving plate. Sprinkle with black pepper. Serve with Afghan nan on the side.

GROUND LAMB AND BEEF SKEWERS

Kabob Qeema

Makes 8 skewers

"Qeema" (which means "ground meat") is mentioned in the Nemmatnama cookbook written during the reign of the Khilji dynasty of Afghan rulers five hundred years ago. The word keema is still used for ground meat in India. This kabob is a tender and juicy ground lamb and beef combination, marinated in ground onions and spices, grilled, and served with charred tomatoes on a bed of Afghan nan. For tender kabob the meat must contain at least 20% fat which gives flavor and color and then drips away in the heat, leaving behind tender and juicy kabob.

1 pound lamb (20% fat),
   ground twice
1 pound beef (20% fat),
   ground twice
1½ large onions, minced
1½ teaspoons salt
2 teaspoons ground black
   pepper
1½ teaspoons ground
   turmeric
6 medium tomatoes
Oil as needed
Sumac
Nan Taba-ee (page 196)
Flat skewers

Place the ground beef and lamb in a mixing bowl. Squeeze out the juices of the onions and reserve the juice. Add the onions, salt, black pepper, and turmeric to the ground meat. Mix well. Massage the meat mixture for about 10 minutes until well-blended and sticky. Cover the bowl with cling wrap and refrigerate for 4 hours until the meat gets firm.

Divide the meat into 8 equal portions. Working with one portion of meat, moistened your palm with the reserved onion juices and shape the meat into a 4-inch-long roll. Thread the roll onto a flat skewer, positioning the roll in the middle. Working quickly, stretch the meat to the top and bottom of the skewer by gently squeezing it in your palm so the kabob is about 9 by 1½ inches and covers the skewer. Pinch the start and end of the kabob to seal. Dip

your palm in onion juices again and make crosswise grooves on the kabob by pressing between fingers. Repeat with the remaining meat portions. Return kabobs to the refrigerator.

Split the tomatoes and brush well with oil. Clean the grill and preheat for about 10 to 15 minutes on medium heat. Brush the grill rack with oil thoroughly. Remove the kabobs from the refrigerator and place them on the grill. Place the tomatoes with the cut side up around them. Start turning the kabobs after 1 minute. Turn every few minutes for 7 to 10 minutes or until the kabobs start to turn golden. Sprinkle with sumac and serve warm with the grilled tomatoes and *nan taba-ee* on the side.

Braised Lamb and Onions / *Dopyaza*

BRAISED LAMB AND ONIONS

Dopyaza

The word "dopyaza" pertains to having two types of onions (pyaz) in a single dish. In this recipe, pungent yellow onions are used in the cooking process, while mellow red onions are served with the cooked meat separately. Tender lamb on the bone is slow-cooked in onion gravy and steamed with yellow onion slices. Dopyaza is usually served with marinated red onions, tender split peas, and a sprinkle of black pepper. Afghan flat nan is served on the side. This kabob is traditionally served without being warmed and thus makes a convenient food for a picnic (mayla).

½ cup dried yellow split peas
1 red onion, sliced into rings
1 cup lime juice
1½ pounds lamb shoulder (on the
   bone with fat), cut into 3-inch
   chunks
1 teaspoon salt
½ cup chopped yellow onions, plus 3
   large yellow onions, sliced into rings
3 tablespoons oil
Pinch salt
½ teaspoon ground black pepper

In a small pan boil the split peas in 1 cup of water for 20 minutes. Drain, rinse and reserve. Soak the red onions in the lime juice in a small bowl and set aside.

In a pot, mix the lamb chunks, salt, and the ½ cup chopped onions. Add 2 cups water. Cover and cook on low heat for about 2 hours or until lamb is tender and is easily falling off the bone and the juices are reduced to a thick onion sauce. For any extra water cook uncovered on high heat to reduce water.

In a separate pan, sauté the yellow onion rings in the oil and sprinkle with a pinch of salt. Fold the onions gently with the meat. Transfer to a small platter. Drain the split peas and red onions and arrange by the lamb. Sprinkle the lamb with black pepper. Serve warm or cool.

LAMB, NAN, AND YOGURT TREAT

Kabob Roi Nan

Makes 4 servings

"Kabob Roi Nan" means "kabob served on nan." Lamb is slow-cooked in onion and tomato gravy until tender and all the juices have evaporated. It is then served on a layer of toasted nan, chaka (drained yogurt), and chopped gandana (chopped scallions or leeks are a good substitute for gandana). This dish is a treat served to special guests.

For the lamb:
2 cups sliced onions
¼ cup olive oil
¼ cup butter
1 pound lamb shoulder chops, cut
  into 1½-inch pieces
1 teaspoon salt
½ teaspoon ground black pepper
  or cayenne pepper powder
¼ teaspoon ground turmeric
1 teaspoon tomato paste
Red pepper flakes, green chilies,
  and tomato rose for garnish

Stir-fry the onions in the oil and butter on medium heat to a golden-brown color. Add the lamb, salt, pepper, and turmeric. Brown the lamb on low heat. Add the tomato paste and 1 cup of water. Stir and then bring to a boil on high heat. Reduce heat, cover and simmer on a low heat until meat is tender. The sauce should be thick but juicy. If it is still watery boil on medium heat uncovered for a few minutes. Skim off any excess oil. Keep warm.

For the kabob bed:
3 Nan Taba-ee (page 195) or 3 store-
  bought pita bread, quartered
2 tablespoons butter
¾ pound chopped gandana, leeks,
  or scallions
1½ cups chaka (drained yogurt;
  page 318)
1 teaspoon minced garlic
Pinch of salt

Fry the nan/pita quarters in the butter on medium heat until they start to change color—not too crispy. Transfer the fried nan/pita onto a platter.

Wilt down the gandana/leeks in the same butter for a minute. Mix the *chaka* with the garlic and pinch of salt. Top the nan/pita with the seasoned *chaka* and gandana/leeks. Arrange the lamb on top. Sprinkle with red pepper flakes and garnish with green chilies and the tomato rose. Serve warm.

Lamb, Nan, and Yogurt Treat / *Kabob Roi Nan*

MARINATED CHICKEN DRUMSTICKS WITH POTATOES

Kabob Ran Morgh

Makes 4 to 6 servings

Chicken (morgh) marinated in spices, baked, and served with spicy roasted potatoes on a bed of green lettuce is a delicious family dinner. Backyard poultry production has always been a major contributor to family nutrition in Afghanistan. The Food and Agriculture Organization of the United Nations (FAO) aimed at introducing production systems for small-scale family-managed poultry production, specifically targeted to provide income for women. Women now have responsibility for more than 90 percent of the village production of eggs and poultry meat.

For the chicken:
3 pounds chicken drumsticks
1½ teaspoons salt
2 teaspoons garlic paste
½ teaspoon ground turmeric
¼ cup hot sauce (optional)
¼ cup olive oil
Lettuce and chopped cilantro to
   garnish

Wash and pat-dry the drumsticks, and then make cuts through to the bone. Place in a glass bowl. Add the salt, garlic paste, turmeric, hot sauce, and oil. Massage the chicken with the oil and spices thoroughly. Cover and place in the refrigerator for about 4 hours.

Preheat the oven to 400 degrees F. Transfer the chicken to an ovenproof dish. Cover with foil and cut small slits through the foil with a sharp knife. Roast the chicken for 40 minutes. Meanwhile, prepare the potatoes.

For the potatoes:
1½ pounds potatoes, peeled and
   cut into 1-inch pieces
2 tablespoons oil
½ teaspoon salt
½ teaspoon ground black
   pepper
1 teaspoon garlic paste
1 teaspoon ground turmeric

Place the potatoes in a mixing bowl. Add the oil, salt, pepper, garlic paste, and turmeric. Mix well.

When the chicken is done roasting for 40 minutes, baste it thoroughly with the pan juices and add the potatoes to the pan by arranging them in empty spots around the chicken. Roast for a further 40 minutes until the chicken and potatoes are cooked through.

Transfer the chicken and potatoes onto a bed of lettuce leaves. Sprinkle with cilantro. Serve warm.

GROUND CHICKEN SKEWERS

Kabob Naichaee

Makes 6 servings

Spicy ground chicken is threaded onto wooden skewers (naicha), baked in the oven, and served with grilled tomatoes, lemon slices, and Nan Taba-ee *(page 196). Arabic toasted pita bread or Spanish toasted flour tortilla can be used as a replacement for the nan. This* kabob *can be stored in the refrigerator for up to a week and leftovers are great in the morning when crumbled and sautéed with vegetables and used as a bed for eggs.*

2 pounds ground chicken (dark meat)
1 large onion, ground and juices
  drained
2 teaspoons salt
1 teaspoon ground cumin seeds
1 teaspoon ground coriander seeds
1 tablespoon garlic paste
½ teaspoon ginger paste
1 green chili, pureed
1 bunch cilantro, chopped
3 tablespoons oil
Tomatoes, lemon slices, and cilantro
  to garnish
6 wooden skewers, soaked in water
  for 30 minutes

Place the ground chicken in a mixing bowl. Add the ground onion, salt, cumin, coriander, garlic paste, ginger paste, pureed chili, and chopped cilantro. Using your hands massage the ingredients together until combined and sticky. Cover and let stand in the refrigerator for an hour to get firm.

Heat the oven to 375 degrees F.

Towel-dry the skewers. Divide the chicken mixture into 12 portions. Shape the portions into oblong shapes and put 2 on each skewer. Place across a cake pan with the skewers sitting on the rim so the pan catches the juices. Brush the *kabobs* with oil and place the cake pan in the middle rack of the oven. Bake for 30 minutes or until golden. Chicken doesn't brown so do not overcook. Char the tomatoes and use them as a garnish with lemon slices and cilantro. Serve with nan.

Ground Chicken Skewers / *Kabob Naichaee*

GRILLED MARINATED CHICKEN SKEWERS

Kabob Seekhi Morgh

Makes 4 servings

For tender and juicy chicken kabob, breast meat is marinated in spices and vinegar, grilled, and served with plain rice or nan and chutney on the side.

3 pounds boneless chicken
   breasts
1 tablespoon ginger powder
1 teaspoon cayenne pepper
   powder
1 teaspoon ground black
   pepper
1 tablespoon garlic paste
¼ teaspoon ground turmeric
1 tablespoon olive oil
2 teaspoons salt
¼ cup white vinegar
Skewers
Oil for brushing

Cut chicken into bite-size pieces and place in a mixing bowl. Add the ginger powder, cayenne pepper powder, black pepper, garlic paste, turmeric, and olive oil. Mix until well blended. Cover tightly and refrigerate for at least 4 hours.

Add the salt and vinegar to the chicken and mix well. Wait for 10 minutes before grilling. Then divide the marinated chicken into 8 equal portions and thread the pieces onto each skewer. Transfer onto a well-greased preheated grill and brush lightly with oil. Grill for about 6 to 8 minutes, turning from time to time until the meat is golden in color. Serve immediately with chapati bread and any dip or chutney.

ROASTED CUMIN CHICKEN

Kabob Morgh

Makes 6 servings

A whole chicken is marinated in spices and served with lemon slices and lettuce. The outcome is super tender and juicy. Afghans in the suburbs have chicken coops in their backyards and serve their guests organic meat, which is packed with flavor.

1 whole chicken (3 pounds)
¼ cup olive oil
1 tablespoon garlic paste
½ tablespoon ground cumin
  or to taste
Salt and pepper to taste
1 head of green lettuce
3 lemons, sliced

Empty the cavity of the chicken and discard. Then rinse the chicken thoroughly, drain, pat dry with paper towels, and place in a mixing bowl. Rub the chicken inside and out with the olive oil and garlic paste. Then sprinkle generously with the spices, inside and out. Cover the bowl and let the chicken marinate overnight in the refrigerator.

Preheat the oven to 400 degrees F. Transfer the marinated chicken to a roasting pot lined with aluminum foil. Cover and bake for 1½ hours, basting every ½ hour. Chicken is done when the juices run clear and the skin is golden brown. Transfer to a serving plate on a bed of green lettuce leaves. Decorate with lemon slices.

FRIED TURKEY KABOBS

Kabob Lula

Makes 4 servings

Shallow-fried ground turkey ka-bobs are prepared with the in-corporation of mashed potatoes and spices and served with nan and sauces or chutney on the side. Kabob Lula can be kept re-frigerated for one week and are served cool, making them perfect for picnics (mayla). Leftovers can be served whole for breakfast, or crumbled and cooked with eggs and tomatoes, which is called karaee. Great sandwiches are also prepared with this kabob, in combination with tomatoes, let-tuce, and sauces.

½ onion, chopped
½ cup chopped cilantro
4 green chilies chopped
¼ bell pepper, chopped
4 cloves garlic, chopped
2 cooked potatoes (8 ounces),
  shredded finely
1 pound ground dark-meat
  turkey or chicken
½ teaspoon ground black
  pepper
1½ teaspoons salt
1 tablespoon ground
  coriander seeds
Oil for frying
Tomato rose, sliced lemon,
  and cilantro to garnish

Mince the chopped onion, cilantro, chilies, bell pepper, and garlic together and add to the potatoes. Add the ground turkey, pepper, salt, and ground coriander seeds. Massage the potato and meat mixture together for about 5 minutes or until well blended and smooth. With oiled palms, take a portion of the meat mixture the size of a walnut and shape it into an oblong shape. Repeat with rest of mixture.

Heat 3 inches of oil in a large frying pan on medium-high heat. Test the heat by dropping a tiny piece of the meat mixture in hot oil. If it sizzles and quickly floats to the surface, the oil is ready. Add as many kabobs as the pan can hold at the same time and fry. After a minute of cooking, stir for even browning on all sides. Fry for about 3 to 4 minutes or until golden and crispy. Drain on paper towels. Repeat with remaining _kabobs_. Garnish with the tomato rose, sliced lemon, and cilantro.

BAKED MARINATED TILAPIA

Kabob Dashi Mahi

Makes 2 servings

For this dish, fish fillets are marinated in spices, baked in the oven, and served with a drizzle of lemon juice. Freshwater fish caught from rivers have been filling markets in the larger cities of Afghanistan for years. Kokcha River in Badakhshan is known to have the best fish (mahi) in the country. However, farm industries are now booming throughout the country, particularly in Kandahar province. Aquaculture is a source of income through which farmers raise fish in enclosures (an artificial environment) to sell as food.

1 pound tilapia fillets
2 tablespoons olive oil
½ teaspoon salt
½ teaspoon ground black pepper
1 teaspoon ground coriander
seeds
¼ teaspoon ground turmeric
¼ teaspoon ginger powder
Juice of ½ a lemon
Green lettuce leaves to garnish

Arrange the fish fillets in a single layer in an ovenproof dish. In a smaller mixing bowl, place the olive oil, salt, pepper, ground coriander seeds, turmeric, ginger powder, and lemon juice. Stir to mix, and drizzle evenly around the top of the fish, making sure the marinating mixture gets into the bottom of the dish. Let stand 15 minutes.

Preheat the oven to 375 degrees F. Bake the fish for 30 minutes, basting with the marinade in the pan every 15 minutes. The fish is done when all liquids have been absorbed and the fish surface turns golden. Transfer to a bed of green lettuce. Serve warm.

Fried Marinated Trout / *Kabob Mahi Beryan*

FRIED MARINATED TROUT

Kabob Mahi Beryan   Makes 4 to 6 servings

Whole trout are marinated in spices, shallow-fried, and drizzled with lemon juice and dried mint flakes for this traditional dish. Tons of freshwater fish (mahi) are deep-fried in the Afghan markets in preparation for the new year (Nowruz). They are fried in large commercial griddles. The outcome is crispy on the outside and flaky and cooked through on the inside. Afghans some-times prefer to buy uncooked fish for cheaper and deep-fry them in their own kitchens and this is the recipe.

5 whole trout (3½ pounds), scaled
  and cleaned
1 tablespoon garlic paste
1 tablespoon ginger paste
½ teaspoon ground turmeric
Salt and pepper to taste
1 teaspoon ground coriander seeds
Juice of ½ a lemon
Oil for frying
1 cup all-purpose flour
Dried mint flakes

Cut the heads off the fish just before the pectoral fin and discard. Make slight gashes on the trout skin to avoid curling in the hot oil. Slit the trout lengthwise and open the trout as you would a book, by pressing the spines flat.

Mix the garlic paste, ginger paste, and turmeric. Rub the mixture over the flesh side of the whole fish. Sprinkle with salt, pepper, and ground coriander seeds. Drizzle with the lemon juice. Stack the fish in a casserole pan and cover with plastic wrap. Refrigerate for 1 hour.

Heat 1-inch of oil in a griddle on medium-high heat. Coat each fish lightly with flour on both sides and shallow-fry skin-side down, until browned, about 4 minutes. Carefully flip to the other side and fry for about 3 minutes. Drain on paper towels. Sprinkle with mint flakes before serving.

Long-Grain Rice with Lamb and Split Pea Qurma / *Chalow Ladam*

LONG-GRAIN RICE & MEAT DISHES

Palow

Aromatic long-grain rice has a long history of cultivation that goes back thousands of years in Afghanistan. The most famous Afghan rice is Baghlan, similar to Indian basmati rice (sold as Baghlan super basmati sela rice in the U.S.). The cooked grains are dry and fluffy, so they make a nice bed for Afghan stews. Long-grain rice is available as either white or brown rice. Brown rice has more fiber and a stronger flavor, but it takes a considerably longer time to cook. The more aged, the better the rice is and the costlier it is. In Afghan tradition, the look of the rice on the platter is as important as its taste. Afghan long-grain rice, the Afghan cook's pride, is the only rice suitable for *palow* and *chalow*. Basmati rice is a good replacement for Afghan rice. Long-grain rice is usually parboiled, drained, and steamed for better taste and appearance.

Palow is the most popular rice dish in Afghanistan, considered the food of the elite and its national food. It is prepared with meat, fried onion juice for coloring, and four to six distinctive spices: cumin, cardamom, cinnamon, cloves, black cardamom, and black pepper (see Palow Spice Blend, page 319). When used for *palow*, long-grain rice goes through four stages: Soaking for at least four hours; parboiling for two to three minutes; draining; and steaming with meat, spices, vegetable juices, fruits, or fried onions to provide color and flavor. *Palow* has a central place in the Afghan food culture, so it can be regarded as what nutritionists sometimes call a cultural superfood.

Long-grain rice is usually served on decorative platters with the meat buried inside it. In this book, the meat is pictured exposed for a better understanding of the recipe. Nuts, such as skinned almonds, pistachios, and pine nuts, add to the crunchiness of the dish. Carrots and raisins balance the spiciness of rice dishes nicely.

For grand celebrations, large serving platters (*ghouri*) for rice are used to serve guests and extended families. *Ghouri* can hold from 10 to 30 servings of rice and meat. Several platters are loaded with a variety of rice dishes, both long-grain and short-grain rice with colorful toppings, stews, and kabobs on the side. Rice is loaded in a dome shape onto the platter, on top of the meat. Toppings of saffron rice, pistachios, carrots, raisins, and barberries add to the beauty, aroma, and crunchiness of the dish.

Most *chalow* dishes (white plain rice; opposite page) are served with a vegetable or meat stew (*qurma*).

Note: 1 cup of dried rice yields 3 cups of cooked rice.

This photo illustrates the instructions given in many of the recipes in this chapter when steaming rice: Cover the pot with a towel, secure it with the lid, and fold the towel ends up onto the lid.

PLAIN AND SIMPLE LONG-GRAIN RICE

Chalow

This versatile dish is an all-purpose food, served with any stew (qurma) to make a complete meal. Long-grain rice is soaked for at least 4 hours, drained, and parboiled before being steamed with salty water, oil, and whole cumin. The amount of water will determine the fluffiness of the rice. Some Afghans like firmer grains and use less water.

2 cups Baghlan or basmati long-grain rice
2 teaspoons whole cumin seeds (optional)
½ teaspoon ground cardamom (optional)
2 teaspoons salt
¼ cup oil

Place rice in a colander under running water. Rub together in palms of hands to remove any extra starch until water runs clear. Soak rice in a bowl of water for about 4 hours.

In a 4-quart pot bring 4 cups of water to a rapid boil on high heat. Drain the rice and slide gently into the boiling water. Stir and wait for a re-boil. Boil for about 3 to 5 minutes or until the rice grain is tender to the bite. Drain in a colander. Rinse lightly with cool water to remove extra starch and maintain firmness.

Transfer the rice to a pot and sprinkle with the cumin and cardamom. Dissolve the salt in ¾ cup water and pour evenly around the top of the rice. Mix well. Sprinkle with the oil and then pile up the rice in the middle of the pot to form a dome. With a skewer make a few holes through to the bottom of the rice. Place two layers of cloth towels over the pot and secure with the lid and fold the towel ends up onto the lid. Steam on high for about 5 minutes, or until the steam starts to escape through the towel, and then lower heat and simmer for 20 minutes. Serve with any *qurma* and *salata*.

POMEGRANATE RICE WITH CHICKEN

Anar Palow

Makes 4 servings

Sweet and sour pomegranate (anar) rice is combined with a chicken dish pre-pared with pomegranate juices. The best quality pomegranate is produced in many provinces of Afghanistan, particularly the Kandahar and Tagab districts of Kapisa province.

For the chicken:
1 onion, chopped
½ cup oil
4 chicken drumsticks
½ teaspoon ground turmeric
1 tablespoon garlic paste
1 teaspoon salt
1 tablespoon sugar
1 tablespoon lemon juice
5 cracked cardamom pods

Stir-fry the onions in the oil to a golden color. Add the chicken drumsticks, turmeric, garlic paste, and salt. Fry on low heat for about 3 minutes. Add the sugar, lemon juice, and cardamom pods. Add 1 cup of water and stir to mix. Cover and cook gently for about 45 minutes or until the chicken is tender and a thick gravy is formed.

For the pomegranate juice:
2 pounds pomegranate seeds (use the best you can finds, deep in color and rich in sweetness and sourness)
¼ cup sugar (for sour pomegranate); or ¼ cup lemon juice (for sweet pomegranate)

Using a blender liquefy the pomegranate seeds and then filter through a mesh sieve by squeezing the seeds for any extra juices. Discard the residue. Boil the juices gently until reduced to half in volume (about 1½ cups). Taste the juice and adjust the flavor by adding sugar or lemon juice gradually until the desired flavor is obtained. Set aside.

For the rice:
1 tablespoon salt
2 cups Baghlan or basmati long-grain rice, soaked for 4 hours
1 teaspoon ground cardamom
I teaspoon ground cumin
½ cup oil
2 tablespoons pomegranate seeds and parsley leaves for garnish

In a saucepan, add the salt to 8 cups of water and bring to a rolling boil. Drain the soaking rice and stir into the boiling water. Parboil the rice for about 3 to 5 minutes or until tender to the bite. Drain the rice in a colander. Return the rice to the pot. Sprinkle with the cardamom and cumin.

Remove the chicken drumsticks from the sauce and reserve. Measure the sauce to ½ cup and add to the pomegranate juice. Mix well and then pour evenly around the top of the rice in the pot. Stir the rice with the help of a skimmer for even coloring. Drizzle the oil around the top of the rice. Make an opening in the center of the rice and fill it with the reserved chicken. Cover the chicken with rice in a dome shape.

Make holes with the spatula handle through to the bottom of the rice so the steam can escape. Cover the pot with a towel, secure it with the lid and fold the towel ends up onto the lid. Steam on high heat for 5 minutes. Lower the heat and steam for about 20 minutes.

When serving, transfer the meat onto a serving platter and mound rice beside the meat. Garnish with pomegranate seeds and parsley. Serve warm.

SPICY RICE WITH EGGPLANT AND CHICKEN

Badenjan Palow   Makes 4 to 6 servings

Spicy long-grain rice is steamed with fried eggplants and chicken for this dish. The eggplants (badenjan) must be of the best quality for this dish. For seedless, crisp, and young eggplants look for ones with a small, round imprint at the bottom. The softness and juiciness of the eggplants goes well with tender chicken and fluffy rice.

For the eggplant:
2 small (8-inch) Japanese eggplants
Oil for frying
¼ teaspoon cayenne pepper powder
Pinch salt
1 teaspoon garlic paste
Pinch ground turmeric
Pinch dried chili flakes and dried parsley

Peel the eggplants and quarter lengthwise with the stems attached. In a fryer, large enough to hold one eggplant, heat two inches of oil. Fry the eggplants one at a time by turning the quarters occasionally from side to side until they are golden inside and out. Drain on paper towels and let cool. Mix the cayenne pepper powder, pinch salt, garlic paste, turmeric, and ¼ teaspoon water and rub onto the eggplants, making sure all slices are well-coated. Sprinkle with chili flakes and parsley flakes. Wrap loosely in aluminum foil, leaving a large opening on top. Set aside.

For the chicken:
6 chicken drumsticks
½ onion, sliced
1 teaspoon salt

For the rice:
1 large onion, finely chopped
½ cup oil
½ teaspoon ground turmeric
2 teaspoons tomato paste
2 teaspoons salt
3 cups Baghlan or basmati
   long-grain rice, washed and
   soaked for 4 hours
8 cups boiling water
½ teaspoon Palow Spice
   Blend (page 319)

Place the chicken drumsticks in a cooking pot. Add the onion slices and salt. Add 1½ cups water. Cook the chicken until tender. Set aside.

Fry the onions in the ½ cup oil until light brown. Add the turmeric and tomato paste and fry for 1 minute. Add ½ cup water and the salt and simmer for 5 minutes. Set aside.

Drain the soaked rice and add to the pot of boiling water (the water should cover the rice). Cook the rice for about 5 minutes or until tender to the bite. Drain rice in a colander and rinse with cool water.

Place the cooked rice in a big pot. Sprinkle with the Palow Spice Blend. Mix the onion mixture (½ cup) with 1½ cups of the chicken juices and pour over the top of the rice and stir with a spatula.

Then make an opening in the middle of the rice and fill it with the chicken. Cover the chicken with rice in a dome shape. Make holes with the spatula handle through to the bottom of the rice so the steam can escape. Place the eggplant bundle on one side of the rice.

Cover the pot with a towel and secure it with the lid and fold the towel ends up onto the lid. Heat on high for about 5 to 7 minutes until the steam is visible around the lid. Lower heat and simmer for a further 20 minutes.

CHICKEN AND VEGETABLE STEAMED RICE

Dampokht

Makes 6 servings

For this dish, basmati rice is prepared with chicken broth and steamed with chicken, vegetables, and spices. The rice in this dish is not parboiled before steaming. After the chicken is cooked in onion juices, a variety of vegetables and the rice are added to cook together. The outcome is juicy, tender chicken and rice packed with flavor.

3 large onions, finely chopped
½ cup olive oil
6 chicken drumsticks
5 teaspoons salt
¼ teaspoon ground turmeric
1 tablespoon minced garlic
1 tablespoon tomato paste
½ cup thinly sliced carrots
½ cup chopped tomatoes
5 cups boiling water
1 cup chopped cilantro
1 cup sliced bell peppers
1 cup frozen green peas
4 cups Baghlan or basmati long-
  grain rice, washed and soaked
  for 4 hours

In a 6-quart pot, stir-fry the onions in the oil on high heat until golden. Add the chicken, 2 teaspoons of the salt, the turmeric, garlic, tomato paste, carrots, and tomatoes. Reduce heat to medium and stir-fry for about 10 minutes until chicken is golden. Add 1 cup of boiling water. Cover and cook on low heat for 30 minutes or until chicken is just tender.

Add the cilantro, bell peppers, green peas, and the remaining 3 teaspoons salt. Bring to a fast boil on high heat. Drain the soaked rice and slide gently into the boiling juices. Wait for a re-boil. Reduce heat to medium and boil uncovered for about 5 minutes or until the water on the rice surface is reduced to bubbling holes.

Cover with a kitchen towel, secure with the lid, and fold the towel ends up onto the lid. Cook for a further 5 minutes, until the steam escape is visible through the towel. Lower heat and simmer for a further 20 minutes. Serve warm.

DILL RICE WITH CHICKEN

Shebid Palow

Makes 4 to 6 servings

Long-grain rice is parboiled, drained and steamed with chicken and caramelized onion juices. Fresh dill (shebid) and fennel (badyan) are added just before steaming. Shebid Palow is not only a tasty meal but is consumed by Afghans for the dill and fennel's traditional therapeutic properties such as controlling blood pressure and gastrointestinal problems.

For the chicken:
2 onions, finely chopped
½ cup olive oil
1½ pounds chicken drumsticks
3 teaspoons salt
½ teaspoon ground turmeric
1 tablespoon garlic paste
1 tablespoon tomato paste

Stir-fry the onions in the olive oil until golden. Add the chicken, 1 teaspoon of the salt, the turmeric, garlic paste, and tomato paste. Reduce the heat and fry the meat for 3 to 5 minutes. Add 2½ cups water. Cover and cook on low heat until the chicken is tender, 30 to 45 minutes. Remove the chicken and reserve. Add the remaining 2 teaspoons of salt to the juices and stir to mix and set aside.

For the rice:
2½ cups Baghlan or basmati long-grain rice, presoaked for about 4 hours
1 cup well-packed chopped fresh dill
½ cup chopped fresh fennel

Bring some water to a boil in a medium-side pot. Drain the rice and slide gently into the boiling water. When rice grains are tender but firm to the bite drain in a colander. Rinse with cool water. Mix the rice with half of the dill and all of the fennel. Place in a pot and add the reserved chicken juices. Bury the chicken drumsticks inside the rice. Cover the pot with a towel and secure it with the lid and fold the towel ends up onto the lid. Steam on high for about 5 minutes. Continue to steam on very low heat for a further 30 minutes. Mix the rice with the remaining dill and serve.

MUNG BEAN AND CHICKEN RICE

Mash Palow

Makes 6 servings

Tender, fluffy rice and mung beans (mash) are the result of parboiling, drain-ing, and then steaming the rice and beans in onion juices and spices. This recipe recommends the incorporation of chicken meat into the rice and serv-ing salad on the side. Mash Palow *is traditionally prepared with dates and apricots instead of chicken.*

For the chicken:
1 onion, finely chopped
¼ cup oil
1½ pounds chicken drumsticks
   and thighs, chopped into 2
   pieces each
1½ teaspoons salt
½ teaspoon ground turmeric

Stir-fry the onions in the oil until light brown. Add the chicken, salt, and turmeric. Stir-fry on low heat until chicken turns golden. Add 3 cups of water. Cover and cook on low heat until chicken is tender. Set aside.

For the mung beans and rice:
1½ cups mung beans, soaked for
   about 4 hours
2½ cups Baghlan or basmati
   long-grain rice, soaked for
   about 4 hours
3½ teaspoons salt
½ teaspoon Palow Spice Blend
   (page 319)
¾ cup melted butter or oil
1 tablespoon garlic paste

Bring 8 cups of water to a rolling boil. Drain the mung beans and add to the water. Boil until just tender, about 25 minutes.

Drain the rice and add to the beans. Parboil for about 3 to 5 minutes or until tender to the bite. Drain the rice and beans in a colander, then return to the cooking pot. Sprinkle the rice with the Palow Spice Blend.

Spoon out the oil from the surface of the chicken juices. Then measure the juices to 2¼ cups and stir in the 3½ teaspoons of salt and pour evenly around the top of the rice and beans. Fold into the mixture well for even coloring. Make a hollow in the center of the rice and fill it with the chicken. Using a spoon handle, make evenly spaced holes through to the bottom of the rice. Cover the pot with a towel slightly larger than the pot diameter and secure with the lid and fold the towel ends up onto the lid. Cook on high heat for about 5 minutes or until the steam starts to escape through the towel. Lower the heat and simmer for about 30 minutes.

Heat the butter or oil below the smoking point in a saucepan. Fry the garlic paste until it starts to change color. Pour evenly around the top of the rice. Transfer to a serving platter and serve warm with chutney or salad on the side.

RUBY RICE WITH CHICKEN

Yaqut Palow   Makes 6 servings

"Yaqut" means "ruby." This fancy, sweet and sour palow dish is prepared with long-grain rice steamed with sour cherry juices and tender meat and drizzled with nuts and saffron rice. Cherries (alubalu) grow in higher altitudes like Kabul, where it snows in winter. Sour cherries taste good with a sprinkle of salt to balance the tanginess. However, in culinary uses, sugar is added for the sweet and sour taste. The cherries give the rice a vibrant red color. Note that the cherries need to sit overnight before making the sauce.

For the chicken:
1 onion, finely chopped
½ cup olive oil
1½ pounds boneless chicken
    drumsticks, skinned
1½ teaspoons salt
1 teaspoon saffron powder

Stir-fry the onions in the olive oil on medium heat until a light golden color. Add the chicken and stir-fry briefly to remove the pink color. Add 1 cup of water, and the salt and saffron powder. Cover and cook gently until the chicken is tender and the sauce is reduced to a thick gravy, about 30 minutes. If needed, boil uncovered to reduce any extra liquid. Separate chicken from the gravy and reserve both.

For the cherry sauce:
2 pounds sour cherries, seeds
    and stems removed
1½ cups sugar
3 teaspoons salt
Reserved chicken gravy
½ cup lemon juice

In a large bowl, sprinkle the cherries with the sugar and allow to sit overnight. Cook the cherries in their juices on a low flame for about 15 to 20 minutes. Drain well, reserving cherries and juices separately. Measure the cherry juices to 2 cups, adding water if necessary. Add the salt, reserved chicken gravy, lemon juice, and ½ cup water and gently stir.

For the rice:
4 cups Baghlan or basmati
    long-grain rice, soaked for
    least 4 hours
8 cups boiling water
1 teaspoon Palow Spice Blend
    (page 319)

Heat oven to 400 degrees F. Drain the soaked rice and add it to the boiling water. Wait for a re-boil and then boil the rice for 3 to 5 minutes or until the grains are tender to the bite but still firm. Do not overcook. Drain the rice in a colander and rinse immediately with cool water to stop the cooking process. Transfer the rice to a roaster keeping 1 cup aside. Sprinkle the Palow Spice Blend over the rice and mix. Pour the cherry sauce evenly around the top of the rice, and using a skimmer, mix well. Make a few holes through to the bottom of the rice.

For the garnish:
1 teaspoon sugar
1 tablespoon oil
¼ teaspoon saffron
 powder dissolved in
 ¼ cup warm water
2 tablespoons skinned
 pistachios

To prepare the garnish, sprinkle the 1 cup reserved rice with the sugar and oil. Then add the saffron solution and mix in. Add the pistachios and mix in. Wrap the garnish loosely in a foil packet. Place the packet on one side of the rice in the pot.

Cover the pot and bake the rice for 30 minutes or until steaming hot and there is no liquid at the bottom of the pot (steaming times will depend on the thickness of the pot).

Remove the rice from the oven and lower oven temperature to 200 degrees F. Remove the garnish packet and set it aside. Mix the rice well. Then make a hollow in the middle of the rice and fill it with the reserved chicken. Cover the chicken with rice. Sprinkle on the reserved cherries and mix gently with the rice around the meat. Then mound rice in the middle of the pot. Using a wooden spoon handle make holes through to the bottom of the pot. Place the garnish packet back in the pot. Bake for a further 20 to 30 minutes. Transfer onto a platter with the meat covered with rice and decorate with the garnish in the packet.

BARBERRY TOPPED RICE WITH CHICKEN

Zerishk Chalow

Makes 4 to 6 servings

Plain long-grain rice (chalow) is prepared with dried barberries (zerishk), pistachios, and saffron rice for toppings, and is served with tender and juicy chicken, slow-cooked in onion juices, tomatoes, and spices. Barberries give this plain rice color and tart flavor. Barberry bushes grows abundantly in the wild on the terrains and semi-desert zones of Afghanistan and Afghans grow them domestically in their backyards for hedges as well.

For the chicken:
1 onion, finely chopped
½ cup oil
6 chicken drumsticks, skin
  removed
1 teaspoon ground turmeric
1 teaspoon salt
1 tablespoon tomato paste
½ teaspoon ground cardamom

Sauté the onions in the oil until they start to change color. Add the chicken and turmeric. Gently stir-fry to a golden color. Add the salt, tomato paste, and cardamom. Fry briefly. Add 1 cup of water. Cover and cook on a low heat for about 30 minutes or until the chicken is tender and the juices are reduced to a thick gravy. Set aside.

For the rice:
4 cups Baghlan or basmati
  long-grain rice, washed and
  soaked for 4 hours
3 teaspoons salt
½ cup oil

Bring 8 cups of water to a boil. Drain the rice and add to the boiling water. Parboil for about 5 minutes or until the rice grains have expanded and are tender to the bite. Drain in a colander and rinse with cool water. Return rice to the pot. Dissolve the salt in 1½ cups water and pour evenly around the top of the rice. Drizzle the oil on top of the rice. Cover the rice tightly by placing a towel on top, securing it with a lid and folding towel ends onto the lid. Steam for about 5 minutes on high heat. Reduce the heat and steam for 20 more minutes.

For the garnishes:
1 cup dried barberries, soaked in
  water for 10 minutes
1 tablespoon butter or oil
1 tablespoon pistachios
1 teaspoon sugar
Pinch saffron powder dissolved
  in 4 tablespoons water

Drain the barberries and pat dry. Stir-fry the barberries in the butter for about 2 minutes. Add the pistachios and stir-fry for 1 minute. Mix in the sugar.

Transfer the rice to a serving plate, setting 1½ cups aside. Mix the saved portion with the saffron solution and mix. Add the barberry and nut mixture to the saffron rice and use it to decorate the white rice. Arrange the chicken to one side of the rice and serve.

TOMATO RICE WITH CHICKEN

Badenjan Rumi Palow

Makes 6 servings

Basmati rice soaked, parboiled, and steamed in tomato sauce and meat gives fluffy, tender results. The dish is flavored with black pepper and Palow Spice Blend. This palow is usually prepared in late summer when tomatoes (badenjan rumi) are in season and plentiful. Most Afghans prepare this dish for guests at parties or feasts.

For the chicken:
6 chicken drumsticks
1 cup chopped onions
1½ teaspoons salt

Place the chicken, onions, salt, and 2 cups of water in a pot and cook over a low heat until the meat is tender. Remove the chicken from the broth and reserve both separately.

For the tomato sauce:
2 large tomatoes
1 cup oil
2 teaspoons salt
1 (8-ounce) can tomato paste

Place the tomatoes in boiling water for 1 minute. Drain, peel, and finely chop. Heat the oil in a saucepan over low heat. Add the chopped tomatoes, salt, and tomato paste. Cook the tomatoes for 20 minutes, stirring occasionally until the oil turns red. Add 1½ cups of water. Transfer the cooked chicken to the tomato sauce. Simmer for 5 minutes. Set aside.

For the rice:
4 cups Baghlan or basmati long-grain rice, washed and soaked for 4 hours
2 teaspoons salt
1 teaspoon Palow Spice Blend (page 319)
¼ teaspoon ground black pepper
¼ bell pepper, sliced
Tomato and lettuce leaves to garnish

Preheat the oven to 450 degrees F. Drain the rice and place in a pot with boiling water 2 inches above the rice. Boil the rice for 3 to 5 minutes or until tender to the bite. Drain in a colander and rinse with cool water. Put the rice in a roasting pot.

Measure out 1½ cups of the reserved chicken broth. Mix in 1½ cups of the tomato sauce. Mix in the 2 teaspoons of salt and pour evenly around the top of the rice and mix. Cover and bake for 20 minutes or until the juices are absorbed and the rice is dryer and steaming hot (some pots may take longer). Remove the rice from the oven. Sprinkle with the Palow Spice Blend. Mix well.

Make a large opening in the center of the rice and place the reserved chicken inside it. Then sprinkle the chicken with the pepper and bell pepper slices. Cover the chicken by piling up the rice in the center (rice grains will stick to the walls of the pot if not mounded). With a wooden spoon handle make holes through to the bottom of the rice in the spaces between the chicken pieces. Cover and bake for 15 minutes.

Reduce heat to 200 degrees F, and bake for 20 more minutes. Transfer the rice and chicken to a serving platter with the chicken placed inside the rice. Garnish with lettuce and tomato. Serve warm.

Variation:

TOMATO RICE WITH LAMB

You can substitute 1½ pounds 3-inch pieces of lamb shanks for the chicken drumsticks.

LONG-GRAIN RICE WITH LAMB AND SPLIT PEA STEW

Chalow Ladam

Makes 6 servings

Basmati rice is parboiled and drained and then steamed with a layer of split pea and lamb qurma *and spices. Saffron and cardamom aromas make this dish unique. Although chicken and veal could be incorporated into the recipe, lamb on the bone remains the best choice.*

For the lamb and split pea stew:
½ cup dried yellow split peas
3 cups finely chopped onions
¾ cup olive oil
2 pounds lamb with bone, cut into small chunks
2½ teaspoons salt
1 tablespoon ground coriander seeds
Pinch saffron powder
10 whole cardamom pods, cracked
4 mini sweet peppers

Cook the split peas in 2 cups of water for 20 minutes. Drain and rinse with cool water. Cover and set aside.

Stir-fry the onions in the olive oil to a golden color. Add the lamb and sear for about 5 minutes. Reduce the heat to medium. Add the salt and coriander. Stir-fry for about 1 minute. Add 2 cups of water and the saffron and cardamom pods. Mix well and then cover and cook on low heat for about 2 hours, or until the lamb is tender and a thick sauce is formed. Add the cooked split peas and sweet peppers. Cover and simmer for 7 minutes.

For the rice:
2 cups Baghlan or basmati long-grain rice, washed and soaked for 4 hours
2 teaspoons salt

In a 4-quart pot bring 4 cups of water to a rapid boil on high heat. Drain the rice and slide gently into the boiling water. Stir and wait for a re-boil. Boil for about 3 to 5 minutes or until the rice grains are tender to the bite. Drain in a colander. Rinse lightly with cool water to remove extra starch and maintain firmness.

Transfer half of the rice to a cooking pot. Place the lamb and gravy on top of the rice in the pot. Cover the lamb with the remaining rice. Dissolve the 2 teaspoons salt in 1 cup of water and drizzle evenly around the top of the rice in the pot.

With a skewer or wooden spoon handle make a few holes through to the bottom of the rice. Cover the pot with a cloth towel and secure it with a lid and fold the towel ends up onto the lid. Steam on high for about 5 minutes or until the steam starts to escape through the towel. Reduce heat and simmer for 20 minutes.

Long-Grain Rice & Meat Dishes

LAMB SHANKS WITH SPICY RICE

Maheecha Palow   Makes 10 servings

This is the national dish of Afghanistan and is loved by Afghans for its delicious flavors. Long-grain rice is soaked, parboiled, drained, and steamed with cooked lamb shanks (maheecha), caramelized onions, meat juices, and spices and served with the tender lamb buried inside the rice.

For the lamb:
2½ pounds lamb shanks, cut into 10 pieces
½ onion, sliced
1½ teaspoons salt

For the rice:
1 large onion, finely chopped
1 cup oil
½ teaspoon ground turmeric
2 teaspoons tomato paste
5 teaspoons salt
6 cups Baghlan or basmati long-grain rice, washed and soaked for 4 hours
Boiling water
1 teaspoon Palow Spice Blend (page 319)

In a cooking pot, place the lamb in 3 cups of water. Add the onion slices and salt. Cover and simmer the lamb until tender, about 1½ to 2 hours depending on the meat quality (meat of young lamb cooks faster). Set aside.

Fry the onions in the 1 cup oil until light brown. Add the turmeric and tomato paste and fry for 1 minute. Add 1 cup of water and the salt and simmer for 5 minutes. Set aside.

Drain the soaked rice and place in a pot with enough boiling water to cover. Cook the rice for about 5 minutes or until tender to the bite. Drain rice in a colander and rinse with cool water. Place the rice in a big pot. Sprinkle with the Palow Spice Blend.

Mix the onion mixture with 3 cups of the meat juices and pour around the top of the rice. Stir the rice with a spatula. Then make an opening in the middle of the rice and fill it with the lamb. Cover the lamb with rice in a dome shape. Make holes with the spatula handle through to the bottom of the rice so the steam can escape. Cover the pot with a towel and secure it with the lid and fold the towel ends up onto the lid. Heat on a high for about 5 to 7 minutes until the steam is visible around the lid. Lower the heat and simmer for a further 20 minutes.

UZBEK SESAME RICE WITH LAMB

Qabeli Uzbeki

Long-grain rice is layered and steamed in the meat juices with lamb, carrots, and raisins. This palow *is prepared with sesame oil which gives the rice a fragrant, nutty aroma and distinguishes it from other rice dishes. As the name indicates, the northern provinces of the country with predominantly Uzbek or Turkman populations are home to this delicious and unique* palow.

¾ cup sesame oil
1 large onion, sliced
2 pounds bone-in lamb shoulder,
   cut into 8 pieces
3 teaspoons salt
2 large (6-inches long) carrots
1 tablespoon sugar
¾ cup raisins
3 cups basmati rice, washed and
   soaked for 2 hours
1 teaspoon Palow Spice Blend
   (page 319) or ground cumin

Heat the sesame oil in a 6-quart pot on moderate heat. Add the onion slices and stir-fry until they start to change color (for golden or brown rice fry more). Add the lamb to the onions and stir-fry for about 3 minutes. Add 1 teaspoon salt and 2 cups of water. Cover and cook on a gentle heat until the lamb is tender, about 1½ to 2 hours.

Meanwhile, scrape the carrots and cut them in half crosswise. Slice each half lengthwise into narrow strips the thickness of shoelaces. Once the lamb is tender, add the carrots to the pot with the lamb. Sprinkle the sugar and raisins over the carrots. Drain the soaked rice and pour gently over the raisins. Sprinkle the Palow Spice Blend or cumin around the top of the rice.

Mix the remaining 2 teaspoons of salt in 3 cups of boiling water. Pour the boiling water around the top of the rice until the water stands ⅛ of an inch above the rice level. Cover the pot with a kitchen towel and secure it with the lid and fold the towel ends up onto the lid. Steam the rice on medium-high heat for about 5 minutes. Lower the heat to low and steam for a further 30 minutes. Remove the pot cover and fluff up the rice to mix with the lamb, carrots, and raisins. Transfer to a serving platter.

ORANGE AND LAMB RICE

Narinj Palow

Makes 10 servings

Long-grain rice is parboiled and drained and then steamed with onion juice, meat broth, meat, and spices. It is drizzled with orange peel (narinj), crunchy almonds, and pistachios before serving. The citrusy aroma of the orange peel and cardamom make this dish unique. Narinj Palow, being fancy, is prepared for festive gatherings and parties. The orange peel can be prepared ahead of time and stored in a refrigerator for later use.

For the orange topping:
½ cup sugar
1 cup julienned sour orange peel
¼ cup skinless almonds
⅓ cup slivered pistachios
Pinch saffron powder dissolved in
   1 tablespoon warm water
1 tablespoon oil
½ teaspoon ground cardamom

Simmer sugar and ½ cup of water together for 4 minutes and let cool. Boil the orange peels in 1 cup water, drain and rinse with cool water. To the cooled sugar syrup, add the orange peels, almonds, and pistachios. Set aside. Save the saffron water, cooking oil, and cardamom for later.

For the lamb:
1 large onion, finely chopped
1 cup oil
2 pounds lamb shanks, cut into
   10 pieces
½ teaspoon ground turmeric
2 teaspoons tomato paste
1 tablespoon garlic paste
2 teaspoons salt

Fry the onions in the oil until light brown. Add the lamb shanks and stir-fry on moderate heat for about 5 minutes. Add the turmeric and tomato paste and fry for 1 minute. Add the garlic paste and stir-fry until you smell the garlic. Add 4 cups of water and the salt and cook covered until lamb is just tender, about 1½ to 2 hours depending on the shank quality. Separate the lamb shanks from the juices and reserve both.

For the rice:
6 cups Baghlan or basmati long-
   grain rice, washed and soaked
   for 4 hours
Boiling water
1 teaspoon Palow Spice Blend
   (page 319)
3 teaspoons salt

Drain the soaked rice and add to a pot of enough boiling water to cover the rice. Cook the rice for about 5 minutes or until tender to the bite. Drain rice in a colander and rinse with cool water. Setting 1½ cups of rice aside, place the remaining rice in a big 8-to-10-quart pot. Sprinkle the rice in the pot with the Palow Spice Blend.

Add the remaining 3 teaspoons of salt to the lamb juices and pour around the top of the rice. Stir the rice with a spatula. Then make an opening in the middle of the rice and fill it with the lamb. Cover the lamb with some of the rice in a dome shape. Make holes with the handle of a wooden spoon through to the bottom of the rice so the steam can escape.

Mix the reserved 1½ cups rice with the reserved saffron water, and add the orange peel mixture. Sprinkle with the oil and cardamom. Place in a foil packet, leaving a crack open on top, and place the packet on one side of the rice in the pot.

Cover the pot with a towel and secure it with the lid and fold the towel ends up onto the lid. Heat on high for about 5 to 7 minutes until the steam is visible around the lid. Lower the heat and simmer for a further 20 minutes.

Transfer the lamb to a serving platter and pile the rice on top of the meat. Sprinkle with the toppings in the foil packet.

SAVORY STEAMED LAMB AND RICE

Qabeli Palow

Makes 8 servings

Qabeli Palow is one of the national dishes of Afghanistan. Long-grain rice is soaked, parboiled, drained, and steamed with lamb, caramelized onions, meat juices, and spices, and served with the tender pieces of lamb buried in the rice. A drizzle of fried carrots, raisins, and nuts crowns the dish. Unlike its Uzbeki counterpart, Qabeli Uzbeki (page 165), which is cooked and steamed in the meat juice and spices, Qabeli Palow is parboiled and drained before steaming, for a crumblier and cleaner look.

For the topping:
½ pound carrots
4 ounces raisins
2 tablespoons oil
1 tablespoon sugar
2 tablespoons slivered almonds
1 tablespoon split pistachios
½ teaspoon ground cardamom

Scrape the carrots and then slice lengthwise into narrow strips the size of shoelaces and cut those into 2½-inch-long pieces. Fry the raisins in the oil for 1 minute until puffy. Remove with a slotted spoon onto a plate. Add the carrots, sugar, and 2 tablespoons of water to the same oil. Cover and cook for about 10 minutes on moderate heat. Remove from heat. Add in the raisins, almonds and pistachios. Sprinkle with cardamom. Mix well. Wrap the carrot mixture in an aluminum foil packet, leaving a crack open at the top. Set aside.

For the lamb:
2 pounds lamb shanks, cut into 8 pieces
½ onion, sliced
1½ teaspoons salt

Place the lamb shanks in a cooking pot. Add the onion slices, salt, and 3 cups of water. Cook on moderate heat until lamb is tender, about 1½ to 2 hours depending on shank quality. Set aside.

For the rice:
1 large onion, finely chopped
1 cup oil
½ teaspoon ground turmeric
2 teaspoons tomato paste
5 teaspoons salt
6 cups Baghlan or basmati long-grain rice, washed and soaked for 4 hours
1 teaspoon Palow Spice Blend (page 319)

Fry the onions in 1 cup oil until light brown. Add the turmeric and tomato paste and fry for another minute. Add 1 cup of water and the salt and simmer for 5 minutes. Set aside.

Drain the soaked rice and add to a pot of boiling water (the water should cover the rice.) Cook the rice for about 5 minutes or until tender to the bite. Drain rice in a colander and rinse with cool water. Place the rice in a big 8- to 10-quart pot. Sprinkle with the Palow Spice Blend.

Mix the onion mixture with 3 cups of the lamb juices and pour around the top of the rice. Stir the rice with a spatula. Make an opening in the middle of the rice and fill it with the lamb. Cover the lamb with rice in a dome shape.

Make holes with the spatula handle through to the bottom of the rice so the steam can escape. Place the packet of toppings on one side of the rice so it steams together with rice. Cover the pot with a towel and secure it with the lid and fold the towel ends up onto the lid. Heat on high for about 5 to 7 minutes until the steam is visible around the lid. Reduce heat and simmer for a further 20 minutes.

Transfer lamb and rice to a serving platter piling the rice on top of the meat and sprinkle with the toppings in the foil packet.

EMERALD SPINACH AND LAMB RICE

Zamarud Palow

Long-grain rice is steamed in spinach sauce, meat juices, and spices, and then served with tender lamb. The dish is called Zamarud (emerald) Palow for its vibrant green color. Like most rice dishes Zamarud Palow is served with salad, chutney, or pickles on the side.

For the lamb:
1½ pounds lamb shoulder chops
1 teaspoon salt
2 cups finely chopped onions

Place the lamb, 2 cups water, salt, and onions in a pot and simmer until meat is tender, about 1½ to 2 hours. Remove the lamb from the broth and set aside separately.

For the spinach juice:
1½ pounds fresh chopped spinach
1 cup oil
1½ tablespoons salt

Boil the spinach in ½ cup water, covered, on medium heat for about 5 minutes or until most water is absorbed and the spinach is wilted. Cool and then puree in a blender until smooth. Return to skillet. Add the oil and stir-fry the spinach puree on medium heat for 7 minutes, or until the oil turns green (use a spatter screen to prevent spatter). Pour in 1½ cups of the lamb broth and add the salt. Stir and set aside.

For the rice:
4 cups Baghlan or basmati rice, soaked for 4 hours
1 teaspoon ground cardamom
1 teaspoon Palow Spice Blend (page 319)

Bring 8 cups of water to a rolling boil. Drain the rice and add to the boiling water. Parboil the rice for about 3 to 5 minutes or until tender to the bite. Drain in a colander and rinse with cool water. Place the rice in a roaster pot. Sprinkle with the cardamom and Palow Spice Blend.

Measure the prepared spinach juice and lamb broth juice to 2 cups and pour evenly around the top of the rice. Preheat the oven to 450 degrees F. Stir the rice with the help of a skimmer for even coloring. Make a large opening in the center of the rice and fill it with the reserved lamb. Cover the lamb with some of the rice. With a long wooden spoon handle make a few holes through to the bottom of the rice. Cover and cook for 20 minutes in the preheated oven or until the rice is steaming hot. Reduce heat to 250 degrees F and cook another 30 minutes. Serve warm.

BEEF AND PINE NUT RICE

Jalghoza Palow

Makes 6 servings

Long-grain rice is soaked and steamed in the juices of ground beef, pine nuts (jalghoza), and spices. Pine nuts are edible kernels of pine trees grown in the forests of eastern Afghanistan. Due to time-consuming and costly harvesting, pine nuts are pricey. This expensive nut is versatile in cooking due to its mild, nutty flavor. This palow *is prepared when pine nuts are in season.*

2 brown onions, finely chopped
¾ cup oil
2 pounds ground beef
2 teaspoons ground turmeric
5 teaspoons salt
2 tablespoons tomato paste
3 cups basmati rice, washed and
   pre-soaked for 4 hours
1 teaspoon Palow Spice Blend
   (page 319)
6 cups boiling water
1 cup pine nuts
2 tablespoons pistachios

In a 6-quart pot, fry the onions in the oil to a golden color. Add the ground beef and stir-fry on moderate heat for about 3 to 5 minutes. Add the turmeric, 2 teaspoons of the salt, and tomato paste. Stir-fry for 1 minute. Add 4 cups of water. Cover and cook for about 20 minutes or until the liquid is reduced in half.

Drain the rice and add to the meat sauce along with the Palow Spice Blend and the remaining 3 teaspoons salt. Mix well. Add the 6 cups of boiling water gradually until the rice mixture is barely covered. Cook on moderate heat for about 5 minutes or until bubbling steam holes appear on the rice surface. Cook further for about 30 seconds or so. Cover the pot with a towel and secure with the lid and fold the towel ends up onto the lid. Steam the rice for about 20 to 30 minutes on a very low heat.

Roast the pine nuts briefly in a pan and add to the rice, mix by fluffing up the rice using a spatula. Transfer onto a serving plate and decorate with the pistachios. Tastes great with a side vegetable dish.

Rice and Mung Beans with Lamb / *Shoula Goshti*

SHORT-GRAIN RICE & MEAT DISHES

Shoula

Afghans have a unique way of mixing short-grain rice with mung beans to prepare various delicious dishes served with colorful *qurmas* of meats, vegetables, fruits, and pulses. The final cooked dish is called *shoula*. Short-grain rice meals are said to be the favorite food of Afghans in cold weather since they tend to preserve heat longer than long-grain rice due to the preservation of water in the rice grain. Freshly served platters of *shoula* steaming on a cold table are indeed tempting after a hard workday in the rain.

Short-grain rice in Afghanistan is produced through rain-fed farms and irrigation. Unlike the long-grain rice that has a long, slender kernel, four to five times longer than its width, short-grain rice has a short, plump, almost round kernel. The cooked grains are sticky and cling together, while the cooked grains of the long-grain rice are separate, light, and fluffy.

Some *shoula* recipes are prepared plain and served with a stew topping as with *Shoulé Ghorbandi* (page 178) and *Kichri Qurut* (page 180), while other recipes call for the incorporation of the meat and beans into the cooking rice, such as *Shoulé Goshti* (page 174) and *Mastawa* (page 175).

Mung beans (*mash*) are a good counterpart to short-grain rice in *shoula* cookery. These tiny green beans are soaked and boiled until tender. Afghans use whole mung beans with the skin on for *shoula* cooking.

The plain version of short-grain rice without the use of beans is called *bata*. The rice is cooked with just water, salt, and oil. A *bata* is served with a variety of *qurma* dishes, particularly ones made with spinach, eggplants, and turnips.

When short-grain rice is used without beans for preparing various desserts, sugar and milk are added to the cooking process. Cardamom, saffron, and rosewater give these rice puddings a unique flavor. Nuts add crunchiness to the soft texture of most puddings. Fruits like strawberries add color and freshness to these dessert which are still called *shoula* (see Pudding chapter, page 273).

Some *shoula* dishes require the incorporation of bulgur and cracked wheat instead of rice, but the texture will come out quite the same, and for that reason the last two recipes of this chapter are made with wheat instead of rice.

RICE AND MUNG BEANS WITH LAMB

Shoulé Goshti

Makes 6 servings

This winter meal is traditionally prepared with cured, dried meat called lan-di. *However, beef and lamb shanks also taste great in* Shoulé Goshti. *Short-grain rice and mung beans are cooked in the meat juices with the addition of garbanzo beans, bell peppers, and spices. Fresh dill and black pepper are the signature spices for this meal.*

2 cups chopped onions
½ cup oil
1½ pounds bone-in lamb, cut into 3-inch
  pieces
1 tablespoon minced garlic
½ teaspoon ground turmeric
3½ teaspoons salt
1 tablespoon tomato paste
½ cup mung beans, soaked for 2 hours
2½ cups short-grain rice, soaked for 4 hours
½ cup chopped fresh dill
1 teaspoon ground black pepper
¼ bell pepper, sliced
½ cup cooked garbanzo beans

Stir-fry the onions in the oil over high heat until golden. Add the lamb, garlic, turmeric, and 1 teaspoon of the salt. Stir-fry for 4 minutes on medium heat. Add the tomato paste and fry for 1 minute. Add 2 cups of boiling water and stir. Cover and simmer on low heat for about 1 to 1½ hours or until meat is just tender.

Preheat the oven to 400 degrees F. When lamb is tender, remove from pot and reserve. Drain mung beans and add to the lamb juices in the pot along with 8 cups boiling water. Cover and boil for 20 minutes until the mung beans are just tender. Add the rice and cook for about 25 more minutes or until the rice grains are tender and the consistency is similar to cooked oatmeal. Mix in the reserved lamb. Mix in the dill, black pepper, bell pepper slices, garbanzo beans, and remaining salt.

Transfer the *shoula* to a roasting pot. Cover and bake in the middle rack of the oven for 20 minutes. Reduce heat to 250 degrees F and cook for 20 more minutes. Serve on a platter.

ORANGE LAMB & RICE

Mastawa

Makes 6 servings

To make this delicious rice dish, short-grain rice and lamb are cooked with orange peel, black pepper, bell peppers, and garbanzo beans. Badakhshan province, north of Kabul in the foothills of the Hindukush Mountains, is home to this dish. Mastawa in Kabul is referred to as the "mushy shoula rice" and is prepared with dried meat (gosht qaq), garbanzo beans, and qurut and spiced with black pepper and orange peel.

For the lamb:
2 cups chopped onions
½ cup olive oil
1½ pounds lamb with bone and
   fat attached, cut into 3-inch
   pieces
½ teaspoon ground turmeric
1 tablespoon garlic paste
1½ teaspoons salt

For the rice:
2½ cups short-grain rice,
   washed and soaked for 4 hours
2 teaspoons salt
8 cups boiling water
½ bell pepper, sliced
½ cup cooked garbanzo beans
1 cup grated sour orange peel or
   regular orange peel
3 cups chaka (page 318)
2 teaspoons ground black
   pepper

In a non-stick pot fry the onions in the oil over high heat until onion edges turn golden. Add the lamb, turmeric, garlic paste, and salt. Stir for 3 minutes. Add 2 cups of water. Cover and cook on low heat until lamb is tender, about 2 hours. Remove the lamb and reserve, leaving the juices in the pot.

Add the rice to the lamb juices in the pot and add the salt and boiling water. Simmer covered on low heat for 20 to 25 minutes, stirring occasionally. Turn the heat off. Preheat the oven to 400 degrees F.

Add the reserved lamb to the rice, along with the bell pepper slices, garbanzo beans, orange peel, and *chaka*. Sprinkle with black pepper and then gently fold with a spatula. Transfer the rice to a well-greased roasting pot. Bake in the oven for 15 minutes. Reduce the heat to 250 degrees F, and bake for a further 15 minutes. Serve hot.

Rice with Spinach and Lamb Stew / *Sabzi Bata*

RICE WITH SPINACH AND LAMB STEW

Sabzi Bata

Makes 6 servings

Spinach (sabzi) and lamb are stewed and served on a bed of short-grain rice (bata). Afghans love a platterful of this healthful meal in winter since the bata *stays steaming hot longer. Spinach, imported from the warmer districts east of Kabul, is available in the shops and stalls of the cities of higher altitudes such as Kabul.*

For the spinach and lamb stew:
1 cup finely chopped onions
⅓ cup olive oil
1½ pounds lamb, cut into bite-
   size pieces
2 teaspoons ground coriander
   seeds
2 teaspoons garlic paste
1½ teaspoons salt
3 green chilies, sliced
2 pounds fresh spinach
¼ cup chopped fresh dill
2 cups finely chopped gandana
   or leeks, sautéed in
   1 tablespoon oil

Fry the onions in the oil until onions start to brown. Add the lamb and stir-fry on medium heat until golden, about 5 to 7 minutes. Add the coriander and garlic paste and stir-fry on low heat for about 1 to 2 minutes. Add the salt and 2 cups water. Cover and cook on low heat until the lamb is tender, about 1½ to 2 hours.

Check the lamb as it cooks and when it is just starting to tenderize (with about 20 minutes of the cooking process left) add the chilies, spinach, dill, and leeks. The stew is done when the juices are reduced to a thick gravy. Boil uncovered on high heat to rid of extra water if necessary.

For the rice:
3 cups short-grain Jasmine
   rice, washed and soaked for
   4 hours
3 teaspoons salt
½ cup oil

In a 6-quart non-stick pot bring 10 cups of water to a rapid boil. Drain the soaked rice in a colander and then slide gently into the boiling water. Add the salt and cooking oil. Stir well. Cover and cook on medium heat for about 15 minutes, stirring occasionally, until the rice forms a thick mixture with the consistency of cooked oatmeal.

Place two layers of cloth towels on top of the pot. Then secure with the lid and fold the towel edges up onto the lid. Reduce heat to simmer and continue to steam for about 15 to 20 minutes.

Serve the rice warm with the spinach and lamb stew.

RICE AND MUNG BEANS WITH LAMB AND SPLIT PEA STEW

Shoulé Ghorbandi

Makes 6 to 8 servings

*This dish is a spicy lamb and split pea stew made with dried sour plums (*alu Bokhara*) and spices and served on a bed of short-grain rice and mung beans (the* shoula*). Like other* shoula*, Afghans love this meal in winter. This stew was traditionally served with long-grain rice. It is believed that serving it on* shoula *was invented in Ghorband, north of Kabul, when the lady of the house realized she was out of long-grain rice to serve to her uninvited guests.*

For the lamb and split pea stew:
3 cups finely chopped onions
⅓ cup olive oil
1½ pounds lamb, cut into small chunks
2½ teaspoons salt
1 teaspoon cayenne pepper powder
1 tablespoon ground coriander seeds
½ teaspoon ground turmeric
2 tablespoons minced garlic
½ cup chopped tomatoes
Pinch ground saffron
½ cup dried yellow split peas
10 dried sour plums

Stir-fry the onions in the oil to a golden color on medium heat. Add the lamb and stir-fry for about 5 minutes. Add the salt, cayenne pepper powder, ground coriander seeds, turmeric, and garlic. Stir for a minute. Add the tomatoes and fry until dissolved. Add 2 cups water and saffron. Mix well, and then cover and cook over low heat for about 2 hours or until meat is tender and a thick sauce is formed.

Meanwhile cook the split peas in 2 cups of water for 20 minutes. Drain and rinse with cool water. Cover and set aside. When the lamb is cooked, add the dried plums and the reserved split peas and fold in gently. Cover and simmer for 7 minutes.

For the rice:
3 cups finely chopped onions
1 cup olive oil
1½ cup mung beans, washed and soaked for about 4 hours
3½ cups short-grain rice, washed and soaked for about 4 hours
5 teaspoons salt
Pinch turmeric
1 tablespoon dried mint flakes

Stir-fry the onions in the oil to a light golden color. Drain the mung beans and add to the onions with 4 cups water. Cover and cook for about 20 minutes.

Drain the rice and add to the beans. Add the salt, turmeric, and 6 cups water. Cover and cook over low heat for about 15 minutes, stirring occasionally, until rice and beans are tender and the mixture has thickened to the consistency of cooked oatmeal.

Cover the pot with a towel, secure it with a cover and fold edges of towel up onto cover. Simmer for an additional 20 minutes.

Serve the rice with the stew on top. Sprinkle with the dried mint flakes.

RICE WITH MEATBALLS AND QURUT

Kichri Qurut

Makes 4 to 6 servings

This dish is a shoula, *prepared with short-grain rice and mung beans. Spicy meatballs in sauce serve as one topping, along with the tangy qurut, flavored with a drizzle of sizzling hot butter and garlic. Compared to long-grain rice dishes,* shoulas *can remain steaming hot longer, and therefore they are the favorite dishes of cold seasons. Traditionally this winter dish is eaten by 4 to 6 people scooping the meal using their hands and dipping the* shoula *into the* qurut. *However, the modern way of serving the dish involves the use of a spatula for slicing the* shoula *and transferring it to individual plates and then spooning on the* qurut.

For the meatballs:
1½ pounds lean ground beef
1 cup minced onions
½ cup minced tomatoes
1 tablespoon garlic paste
1 teaspoon ground black pepper
1½ teaspoons salt
1 egg

Place the ground beef in a large bowl. Add the onions, tomatoes, garlic paste, pepper, salt, and egg. Knead the ingredients until sticky. Shape the beef mixture into egg-sized balls with wet hands. Set aside.

For the sauce:
2½ cups finely chopped onions
⅓ cup olive oil
2 tablespoons tomato paste
½ teaspoon ground turmeric
1 teaspoon salt
1 tablespoon ground coriander
  seeds

Stir-fry the onions in the olive oil to a golden color. Add the tomato paste, turmeric, salt and coriander. Fry for another 2 minutes on medium heat. Add ¼ cup water and stir to mix with the sauce. Lower the heat to simmer.

Lower the meatballs into the sauce one at a time in a single layer. Arrange any remaining meatballs over the spaces between the meatballs in the first layer. Cover and simmer for about 30 minutes on a gentle heat. Once cooked, stir gently and then let stand for 5 minutes for the oil to form on the surface of the *qurma*. Keep warm.

For the rice:
2 cups finely chopped onions
½ cup oil
3½ teaspoons salt
¼ teaspoon ground turmeric
10 cups boiling water
1 cup mung beans, washed and
  soaked for 4 hours (separate
  from rice)
2½ cups short-grain rice,
  washed and soaked for
  4 hours

In a 6-quart non-stick pot, brown the onions in ½ cup oil. Add the salt, turmeric, and boiling water. Drain the mung beans and add. Cover and cook over medium-low heat for 20 minutes. Drain the soaked rice and add to the mung beans. Stir well, cover, and cook for another 30 minutes, stirring occasionally, until the rice has thickened to an oatmeal consistency.

Preheat the oven to 400 degrees F. Transfer the rice and bean mixture to a roasting pot, cover, and bake in the oven for 10 minutes. Lower the heat to 250 degrees F, and bake for an additional 15 minutes.

For the qurut and garnishes:
2 cups qurut (see page 319) or
  chaka (drained yogurt, page
  318), mixed with salt and garlic
  puree to taste
1 tablespoon powdered mint
2 tablespoons butter
Green and red chilies to garnish

Mound the rice on a large platter. Place the *qurut* in a small bowl and press the bowl into the center of the rice. Sprinkle 2 tablespoons of the *qurut* around the top of the rice. Arrange the meatballs around the *qurut* bowl. Then spoon the meatball sauce on the rice and sprinkle with the powdered mint. Heat the butter and pour evenly over the *qurut*. Decorate with chilis. Serve warm by cutting into wedges containing one or two meatballs.

RICE WITH BEEF AND TURNIP STEW

Shalgham Bata

Makes 6 servings

This form of plain shoula, *without mung beans, is the most popular dish to serve with a stew prepared with beef shanks and turnips (*shalgham*). Ginger is added for flavor and to control the high uric acid levels triggered by beef protein. Brown sugar makes the cooked turnip slices more desirable to eat.* Shalgham Bata *is scooped up by spatula onto individual serving plates.*

For the beef and turnip stew:
3 cups finely chopped onions
½ cup oil
1 pound boneless beef, cut into
  2-inch chunks
1½ teaspoons salt
½ teaspoon ground turmeric
½ tablespoon ground coriander
  seeds
2 teaspoons tomato paste
2 teaspoons minced garlic
1 teaspoon minced ginger
½ cup chopped tomatoes
2 medium turnips, peeled and
  chopped into bite-size pieces
2 tablespoons brown sugar
2 green chilies, chopped
2 tablespoons finely diced red
  peppers

Stir-fry the onions in the oil to a golden color on moderate heat. Add the beef and sear until golden. Add the salt, turmeric, and coriander and stir for 1 minute. Add the tomato paste, garlic, and ginger and stir on low heat until the garlic becomes aromatic. Stir in the tomatoes until dissolved. Add 2 cups water. Stir and cover to cook on low heat for about 45 to 60 minutes or until the beef is just tender.

Stir the stew and add the turnips. Cover and cook on low heat for about 30 more minutes or until the turnips are tender and transparent. Gently fold in the brown sugar, chilies, and red pepper and simmer for 5 minutes.

For the rice:
3 cups short-grain Jasmine rice,
  washed and soaked for 4 hours
3 teaspoons salt
½ cup oil

In a 6-quart non-stick pot bring 10 cups of water to a rapid boil. Drain the soaked rice in a colander and then slide gently into the boiling water. Add the salt and oil. Stir well. Cover and cook on medium heat for about 15 minutes, stirring occasionally, until the rice forms a thick mixture with the consistency of cooked oatmeal.

Place two layers of cloth towels on top of the pot. Then secure with the lid and fold the towel edges up onto the lid. Reduce heat to simmer and continue to cook for about 15 to 20 minutes. Serve the rice warm with the stew.

BEEF AND BULGUR WHEAT

Burghul Palow

Makes 6 servings

Ground beef and bulgur wheat are slowly cooked and steamed with sweet peppers, onions, and spices. Although this dish is prepared with parboiled, dried, and crushed wheat (burghul), the texture categorizes it as shoula *that is prepared with short-grain rice.* Burghul Palow *is an old recipe, popular with the people of Kabul, and adopted from the kitchens of the elite.*

2 large onions, finely chopped
½ cup olive oil
1 pound ground beef
½ teaspoon ground turmeric
2 teaspoons salt
3 tablespoons tomato paste
1 tablespoon garlic paste
1 teaspoon cayenne pepper
  powder (optional)
7 cups boiling water
3 cups #1-grain bulgur wheat
  (fine)
2 cups sliced bell peppers (any
  colors)
½ teaspoon Palow Spice Blend
  (page 319)

Fry the onions in the olive oil until lightly golden. Add the ground beef, turmeric, and salt. Stir-fry on moderate heat for about 5 minutes, breaking up any meat chunks with a spatula. Add the tomato paste, garlic paste, and cayenne pepper powder and stir-fry for about 1 minute. Add 2 cups of boiling water. Cover and cook on a gentle heat for about 20 minutes or pressure-cook for 5 minutes.

Add the bulgur wheat, bell peppers, Palow Spice Blend, and 5 cups of boiling water. Stir well. Cover and boil gently for about 5 minutes or until the bulgur is tender and the water is reduced to bubbling holes. Reduce the heat to just the boiling point. Cover the pot with a kitchen towel and secure it with the lid and fold towel edges up onto lid. Continue to cook for 15 minutes. To serve, mound the bulgur mixture onto a decorative platter or mold in a bowl and unmold on a platter.

Lamb Stew with Wheat and Beans / *Dalda*

LAMB STEW WITH WHEAT AND BEANS

Dalda

Makes 6 servings

Cracked wheat, bulgur wheat, kidney beans, and mung beans are cooked together, folded in with lamb stew, and topped with chaka. Dalda *is protein-rich, filling, and healthful. A simpler form of* Dalda *is prepared with cracked wheat and meat by the farmer families who decorate the dish with home-made yogurt from the milk of their livestock.*

For the lamb stew:
1 onion, finely chopped
¼ cup oil
1½ pounds lamb meat on the bone, cut into chunks
½ teaspoon ground turmeric
1 tablespoon minced garlic
1 tablespoon ground coriander seeds
1½ teaspoons salt
1 tablespoon tomato paste
2 large roman tomatoes, chopped

In a pot stir-fry the onions in the oil until golden. Add the lamb and turmeric. Stir-fry for 2 minutes. Add the garlic, coriander, salt, and stir-fry for 1 minute. Add the tomato paste. Stir-fry for about 1 minute. Add the tomatoes and cook until the tomatoes are dissolved. Add 2 cups of water. Cover and cook on moderate heat for about 2 hours or until the meat is tender and falls off the bone. Remove the meat from sauce and remove the bones and shred the meat. Add back into the reserved sauce.

For the wheat and beans:
1 cup coarse bulgur
1 cup cracked wheat
1 cup mung beans
1 cup kidney beans, soaked for 4 hours
2 teaspoons salt
1½ teaspoons ground black pepper

Wash, rinse and drain the bulgur, cracked wheat, and mung beans together, and place in a medium pot. Add the salt, pepper, and 8 cups of water. Bring to a boil and cook on medium heat for about 40 minutes or until grains are tender and most water is absorbed.

For the garnish:
2 cups chaka (see page 318)
Cilantro leaves
Red dried chilis
2 teaspoon dried mint flakes
½ teaspoon chili flakes

Add the prepared stew to the wheat mixture and mix well. Cover and simmer for about 10 minutes. To serve, transfer the *dalda* to a platter. Decorate with the *chaka*, cilantro, and chilies and sprinkle with the mint flakes and chili flakes. Serve warm.

Butter Bread / *Nan Roughani*

BREADS
Nan

Nan is a staple food in Afghanistan. This basic flatbread accompanies most dishes, especially kabobs. Afghan nan is now well-known outside the country. It is used for flatbread sandwiches and a wide variety of pizzas.

Other varieties of Afghan bread that are prepared with oil and sometimes eggs are suitable for breakfast. Breakfast breads such as *komach*, *waraqi*, and *roughani* mostly come from the north of the country. They are tasty and filling.

When the breads are the food of the poor, they are consumed with sweetened tea. Bread with grapes is also consumed by construction workers when tiredly leaning against a half-built structure during their lunch breaks with a cluster of the yellow grapes in one hand and a loaf of bread in the other, daydreaming about going home to their wives and children at the end of exhausting hours of work.

In the countryside, wheat is harvested in late summer and then converted to flour in the local mills before it is consumed throughout the year by the people of the villages. The fine texture of chapati flour sold in Indian groceries is a better choice for making Afghan bread than regular Western whole wheat flour, which is considerably coarser, so the outcome may not be identical to the authentic Afghan flatbread.

For preparing dough, a fermented, sour-smelling small leftover from the previous day's dough is used as a leavening agent. Powdered yeast could be substituted for the fermented live starter. Most village households have a clay oven called a *tandoor* in their backyards, installed in the ground in an area shaded by a grapevine patio. The heat used for baking the dough in a *tandoor* is considerably higher than the maximum 500 degrees F on most domestic ovens. *Tandoor* bread bakes fast in high temperatures, before losing any moisture which is common in domestic ovens. The bread comes out super soft, fluffy, and easy to break. When pre-heated to the highest temperature, domestic ovens could achieve similar results, but not quite the same. For the *Nan Taba-ee* (page 196), a special cast-iron concave pan is used.

BASIC AFGHAN FLATBREAD

Nan   Makes 2 nan

Basic Afghan nan is prepared with very fine wheat flour and a fresh leavening agent, khamir tursh yeast. Afghans garnish their bread with nigella seeds and sesame seeds. Whether homemade or commercial, nan is baked in a clay ground oven called a tandoor *that could reach 700 degrees F. Nan is the basic daily food served with breakfast, stews, and soups. Nan served with sweetened tea is the poor man's meal.*

1 teaspoon active dry yeast
¼ cup warm water (100 to 105
   degrees F)
½ cup plain yogurt
½ cup boiling water
2½ cups chapati flour (available in
   Indian groceries) or whole wheat
   flour
1 tablespoon olive oil
1 teaspoon salt
¼ cup sesame seeds
1 tablespoon nigella seeds

In a bowl, dissolve yeast in warm water. In a bowl, dissolve the yogurt in the boiling water and let sit until tepid, about 105 degrees F.

Pour the yeast mixture into the yogurt mixture and mix well. Gradually add in half the flour and then, stirring in the same direction, rapidly mix until smooth, about 3 minutes. Cover with plastic wrap and leave in a warm place for 30 minutes or until frothy.

Add the olive oil to the frothy dough. Mix the remaining flour and the salt and pour gradually on the frothy dough while kneading until the ingredients are well incorporated, about 7 minutes. Cover and let stand in a greased bowl for another 75 minutes, until doubled in size. Preheat the oven to 500 degrees F.

Punch the dough down and split it into two portions. Cover and let rest for 15 minutes. Using a rolling pin, shape each into a rectangle 7 by 14 inches long on a lightly dusted surface. Pull one end to make a heart shape. Transfer onto the back side of a large baking sheet. Dip your fingers in water and press groove lines lengthwise from top to bottom of the bread. Sprinkle with the seeds and transfer the baking sheet to the oven. Bake for 7 to 10 minutes or until the bread starts to turn golden. Remove from oven and transfer the bread from the sheet onto a large kitchen towel. Cover with another towel. When cool, store the bread by wrapping it in plastic bags. Reheat using a toaster.

BUTTER BREAD

Nan Roughani

This Afghan butter bread is prepared with nigella seeds that give the bread a nutty and toasted flavor. It is served with sweetened milk or tea during breakfast. Nan Roughani *has a long shelf life, about a week, and for that reason it was prepared in the old days for farmers to have as snacks in their fields or travelers packed them to take along on horseback. The butter prevents the nan from drying faster.*

4½ cups all-purpose flour
3 teaspoons instant yeast
3 teaspoons salt
1 tablespoon nigella seeds
1 cup melted butter (oil can be
  substituted)
1¾ cups warm milk
3 eggs, beaten
Vegetable oil
1 egg yolk mixed with 2 teaspoons
  milk
Sesame seeds and nigella seeds
  for garnish

In a mixing bowl, mix the flour, yeast, salt, and nigella seeds. Heat the butter and milk separately to 120 degrees F and gradually add to the flour while mixing. Add the eggs and mix well. Then transfer the dough to a floured smooth surface and knead well for about 5 minutes with floured hands until homogenized.

Divide the dough into 4 equal portions and form them into smooth balls. Grease two 17-by-12-inch baking sheets well. Place two dough balls on each baking sheet leaving space for expansion. Brush the balls with oil liberally and cover with plastic wrap. Set aside to rise for about 2 hours.

Preheat the oven to 375 degrees F. Working with your hands, press on the center of the dough balls to flatten the center of each dough ball into a disc 5 inches in diameter leaving a 1½-inch rim around the bread. Do not deflate the rim by touching it. Decorate the center with circles using a bottle cap. Brush with egg wash and sprinkle with seeds. Bake for about 30 to 35 minutes or until golden. Serve warm or cold with breakfast.

Walnut & Egg Bread / *Nan Komach*

WALNUT & EGG BREAD

Nan Komach

Makes 2 nan

This nan has its home in the northern cities of Afghanistan. Walnuts, eggs, and milk are the main components of this rich bread. Being nutritious and having a longer shelf life, this nan used to be prepared for travelers in the old days when modern transportation such as cars and buses were not available.

1 teaspoon active dry yeast
2 teaspoons sugar
2 eggs
½ teaspoon salt
2 cups all-purpose flour
1 cup whole wheat flour
2 tablespoons sugar
1 teaspoon ground cardamom
1 teaspoon nigella seeds
2 tablespoons oil
½ cup milk
½ cup chopped walnuts

Mix the yeast and sugar with ½ cup water and set aside to get frothy for about 15 minutes. Mix the eggs and salt and set aside.

In a bowl mix the flours, sugar, cardamom, and nigella seeds. Add the oil and massage into the flour. Add the milk and walnuts. Add the yeast mixture and massage to mix. Add the egg and salt mixture and massage until a sticky dough is obtained. Dust the dough and your hands with flour and knead the dough for about 5 minutes to homogenize.

Divide the dough into 2 portions and form into balls. Brush with oil and cover with cling wrap. Place on a greased cookie sheet and set aside in a warm place for 2 to 3 hours until doubled in size, depending on the room temperature.

Flatten each ball into a disk 6 inches in diameter. Cover and let rest for 30 minutes. Heat the oven to 480 degrees F. Decorate the dough disks with circle imprints and bake for about 15 minutes or until well-risen and golden. Cover with a towel and leave to cool.

ONION BREAD

Nan Pyazi

Makes 4 nan

Onions, cilantro, and flaked chilies are used to prepare this Afghan onion bread. This nan is often slapped to the walls of a hot tandoor for baking. Domestic ovens produce similar results. The high heat of the tandoor oven causes the red onions to go from having an intense, pungent flavor to having a mild aroma and sweet, appetizing flavor.

2 cups thinly sliced red onions
½ cup chopped cilantro
1 teaspoon chili flakes
¾ teaspoon salt
1½ cups all-purpose flour
½ teaspoon active dry yeast
¾ cup warm water
Vegetable oil for greasing
¼ cup melted butter
1 egg white, beaten

Mix the onions, cilantro, chili flakes, and ¼ teaspoon salt in a bowl. Divide the mixture into 4 portions and set aside.

Mix the flour with ½ teaspoon salt in a separate bowl. Dissolve the yeast in the warm water and gradually add to the flour. Using your hands knead well to form a soft dough. Form the dough into a smooth ball and grease with oil. Cover the bowl with plastic wrap and leave to rest for about 15 minutes.

Preheat the oven to 400 degrees F. Divide the dough into 4 portions. Form the portions into smooth balls. Cover and let rest for 5 minutes. Working with one ball at a time, use a rolling pin to spread it into a thin round 11 inches in diameter. Brush some of the melted butter evenly around the top of the dough circle. Sprinkle one portion of the onion mixture on the prepared dough circle. Roll the dough away from you to form a cylinder. Then, form the cylinder into a round spiral. Pinch the end to secure against the spiral. Dust the spiral with flour and using your hands flatten the bread into 7 inches in diameter. Transfer to a baking sheet. Repeat the process with the remaining dough balls.

Place the baking sheet on the middle rack of the oven and bake for about 20 minutes or until golden and crisp. Remove from oven and cover with kitchen towels.

Onion Bread / *Nan Pyazi*

Hot and Spicy Pancakes / *Nan Roughani Masaladar*

The Best of Afghan Cooking

HOT AND SPICY PANCAKES

Nan Roughani Masaladar

Makes 6 nan

These hot and spicy pancakes are made with onions, chilies, and cilantro mixed with flour. It is prepared in Hindu and Sikh Afghan homes and is also popular in the adjacent cities of Hindu and Sikh communities, namely Kabul, Kandahar, Ghazni, and Nangarhar.

½ cup all-purpose flour
½ cup whole wheat flour
½ teaspoon salt
½ teaspoon ground turmeric
2 teaspoons ground coriander seeds
½ teaspoon ground cumin
½ teaspoon ground black pepper
½ cup plain yogurt
1 tablespoon oil
1 small onion, finely chopped
1 green chili, finely chopped
½ cup cilantro, finely chopped
Oil for frying

In a small mixing bowl, place the flours, salt, turmeric, ground coriander seeds, cumin, and black pepper. Whisk the dry ingredients well. Add the yogurt, 1¼ cups water, and the 1 tablespoon oil. Mix well with the help of a fork. Add the onions, green chilis, and cilantro. Mix well.

Place a nonstick pan over medium heat and cover with a thin film of oil. Take a ladle full of the batter and gently pour it into the center of the pan. The size of the ladle will determine the size of the pancake. Then with the backside of the ladle spread the batter into a thin larger circle. Wait for the batter to set and get transparent. Turn over to the other side and cook until crisp on the edges and cooked through on the inside.

Drain on paper towels. Serve with breakfast or as a snack anytime.

THIN GRIDDLE BREAD

Nan Taba-ee

This delicate, thin round of nan is leavened by natural yeast (khamir tursh) which is saved in a warm place to ferment from the previous day's leavened dough. To preserve moisture and softness, this bread needs to be cooked on high heat, which will cause the dough to bubble in seconds, before losing any moisture. Sometimes a round pillow called a rafeeda is covered by this dough and then the dough is slapped to the wall of a hot tandoor for baking. This version is called nan paraki *or* nan pastay. *This bread tastes great with fried or grilled meat. A soaked version with soup comes out delicious due to its high absorbency.*

1½ cups all-purpose flour*
½ cup whole wheat flour*
½ teaspoon salt
1 tablespoon khamir tursh (fresh yeast),
  or 1 teaspoon active dry yeast
2 tablespoons oil, warmed
1 cup warm water

** You can replace the two flours with
  2 cups chapati flour.*

Mix the two flours, salt, and yeast in a bowl. Add the warm oil and massage into the mixture. Gradually add the warm water and mix until a soft, sticky dough is obtained. Transfer the dough to a floured surface and knead well with clean, flour-dusted hands for 5 minutes to homogenize.

Divide the dough into 10 equal portions (for larger breads divide into 9 portions). Dusting the dough and your hands with flour as needed, shape each portion into a ball. Brush the balls with oil and cover with plastic wrap. Leave to rise at room temperature for 60 minutes.

Dusting the dough and your hands with flour as needed press each ball into a patty 3 inches in diameter. Dust the patties with flour and cover and let rest for 15 minutes.

Using a rolling pin, roll out one dough patty into a circle 10 inches in diameter. Dust lightly with flour, cover and set aside. Work with the remaining dough portions until all the rounds are finished in a stack.

Place a non-stick pan or a cast-iron griddle on high heat and wait until it smokes. Pick up each dough round in turn, between two hands, and pat it gently to shake off excess flour. Then slap it onto the hot pan. The flat dough disc must start to bubble in 3 to 5 seconds. Make sure that the nan surface gets bubbly and puffs evenly in 15 to 20 seconds, pressing down the uncooked spots with tongs for bubbles. Turn on the other side and cook for a further 5 to 7 seconds or until bubbles start turning color. Remove to a plate and cover the cooked bread with a cloth towel while you cook the remaining dough.

LAYERED FLAKY BREAD

Nan Waraqi

Makes 4 nan

This nan, as the name indicates, is layered (waraqi) and flaky and is loved by everyone for its buttery, flaky, yeasty, and chewy quality. Nan Waraqi originated in the northern provinces of Afghanistan. A cup of sheer chai tea tastes great with this and nigella seeds add to the flavor and aroma, as well as the look of this nan.

6 cups all-purpose flour
2 teaspoons active dry yeast
1½ teaspoons salt
3¼ cups warm water
3 tablespoons oil
½ cup melted butter
1 egg white, beaten
Nigella seeds as needed

Mix the flour, yeast, and salt in a bowl. Add the warm water gradually and mix until a sticky, soft dough is obtained. Transfer the dough onto a flour-dusted board and knead for about 5 minutes until homogenized. Divide into 4 portions and form into smooth balls. Brush the balls with oil and cover with plastic wrap. Let the dough rest for 10 minutes.

Working with one ball at a time, on a flour-dusted surface spread it into a circle ⅛-inch thick using a rolling pin. Brush the dough circle with some of the butter. Starting at the dough edge nearest you roll away from you into a 1½-inch thick and 15-inch long roll. Then start with one end of the dough roll and roll into a spiral, tucking the very end inside the bottom of the dough. Cover the dough spiral and work with the rest of the dough balls. Cover and let rest for 20 minutes.

Preheat the oven to 480 degrees F. Transfer one roll onto a large greased baking sheet. Flatten the dough to an 8½-inch round using your hands. Prick the center with a fork in multiple places and glaze with the egg white. Sprinkle some nigella seeds in the center and bake on the middle rack of the oven for 15 to 17 minutes or until golden. Work with the rest of the dough the same way to finish all 4 nans. Transfer onto paper towels, and cover with a cloth towel to maintain tenderness and warmth. Serve immediately.

Sweet and Sour Pepper Chutney / *Chutney Morch Sorkh*

CONDIMENTS

Turshi & Chutneys

The appetizing taste and aroma of *turshi* and chutneys make them a must on an Afghan table. *Turshi* are condiments made with fruits or vegetables spiced up with spices and preserved in vinegar. Most *turshi* are prepared with vegetables such as eggplants, carrots, turnips, cauliflower, peppers, onions, and squash. The most common spices used in *turshi* are garlic, fenugreek, mint, cumin, coriander seeds, and onion extract. *Turshi* are also prepared with fruits such as peaches, apricots, and figs, and sugar is added for a sweet and sour flavor. The fruit *turshi* are mostly served with long-grain basmati rice dishes, while the vegetable *turshi* are suitable for the short-grain rice *shoula* dishes.

This chunky appetizer was invented long ago as a salad replacement during winter. When fruits and vegetables were plentiful after the summer harvest, the *turshi* were prepared in large quantities and then stored in huge clay jars called *khum*. The *khum* lids were then sealed with dough against rotting. The *turshi* were then left in a cool, dark spot for the flavors to fuse, normally about a month. Then the big jars were given away by the grandmother to the heads of each extended family. Only a trusted family member of each household was designated to open the jars in a certain way for daily supplies to guarantee the freshness of the *turshi*. With fruits and vegetables available in all seasons in today's Afghanistan, condiments are enjoyed more for their nutritional benefits and the medicinal benefits of vinegar for food digestion.

The pureed version of *turshi* is called chutney. Chutney is believed to be consumed more in the provinces with grapevines in the north of Kabul. The intense sweetness of grapes and mulberries is indeed pleasant after a meal with hot chutney. Chutneys make great dips with snacks such as *pakowra* and *bolani*. Chutneys are served immediately after preparation as compared to *turshi* that requires weeks of wait for the flavors to fuse. In today's Afghanistan, when the howling wind of the blizzards discourage families from stepping outside to shop for fruits and vegetables, *turshi* and chutneys come to the rescue as they did in days of old and put smiles on the faces of the lunchtime crowd as the mouth-watering aromas of the garlic and vinegar of the colorful *turshi* or chutneys touch the nostrils.

TURNIP AND CARROT PICKLE

Awry Turshi

Makes 10 servings

Turnips and carrots are mixed with spices and crushed mustard seeds and set aside to ferment for this turshi. *Awry Turshi is served alongside most rice dishes. Unlike most Afghan* turshi *that use vinegar as a fermentation agent, this* turshi *is allowed to ferment in crushed mustard seeds (awry) that turn sour. A variety of other vegetables, such as cauliflower and eggplant, can be used to prepare* Awry Turshi, *depending on what you have on hand. Afghans love* Awry Turshi *for its mild and less intense flavor compared to the vinegar-based condiments.*

2 large carrots, peeled and sliced
2 large turnips, peeled and diced
1 red bell pepper, sliced
2 green chilis (optional)
1 tablespoon garlic paste
1 tablespoon crushed dried mint
1 tablespoon dried red pepper flakes (optional)
1½ teaspoons salt (or as needed)
1 cup fresh mint leaves
2 tablespoons coarsely chopped mustard seeds
Small green bell pepper, chopped, for garnish
Lukewarm water previously boiled

Place the carrots and turnips in a small pot. Add the bell pepper slices and chilis. Add enough water to cover the vegetables. Bring to a rolling boil and cook until fork-tender, about 5 to 7 minutes. Drain in a colander. Transfer to a mixing bowl and allow to cool.

Add the garlic paste, dried mint, red pepper flakes, salt, and fresh mint to the vegetable mixture. Sprinkle with the crushed mustard seeds and then mix well with a spoon. Add the green peppers. Cover the *turshi* and set aside for about 2 days for the flavors to fuse and the seeds to ferment.

Once fermented, transfer the *turshi* to a glass jar large enough to hold the vegetables. Fill the jar with lukewarm water previously boiled. Cover the jar and leave it to stand at room temperature for another week.

202   **The Best of Afghan Cooking**

Turnip and Carrot Pickle / *Awry Turshi*

STUFFED EGGPLANT PICKLE

Badenjan Shekampor   Makes 2½ pounds

Indian eggplants or baby eggplants (badenjan) are parboiled in water, stuffed with spices, and soaked in a combination of distilled water and vinegar to ferment. The "stuffed belly" (shekampor) turshi is served with most rice dishes. Good quality, seedless eggplants must be chosen for this turshi (see Glossary, page 318). Sometimes the Indian term achar is used for this particular turshi.

1 tablespoon fenugreek seeds
1½ pounds Indian or baby
  eggplants, stems removed
2 red bell peppers, sliced
1½ cups white vinegar
½ cup sliced garlic
½ cup fresh mint sprigs
Salt and pepper
½ pound red and green sweet bell
  peppers, stem and seeds removed
  and minced
1 teaspoon salt
1 teaspoon crushed dried chilies
1 teaspoon nigella seeds
½ tablespoon dried crushed mint
1½ cups distilled water

Boil the fenugreek seeds in 1 cup of water until the seeds expand and the water turns yellow, about 2 minutes. Drain and reserve. Boil the eggplants and bell pepper slices in the vinegar for 5 minutes. Drain, reserving the vinegar, and set aside to cool.

Take one eggplant. Make a slit through the pulp half an inch deep. Open slit by pushing in the ends of eggplant simultaneously. Fill the opening with a slice of garlic and a mint leaf, and sprinkle with salt and pepper. Work with the rest of the eggplants to complete the process.

Place the stuffed eggplants and bell pepper slices in a mixing bowl. Add the minced bell peppers, and any leftover garlic slices and mint leaves. Sprinkle with salt, dried chilis, nigella seeds, and crushed mint. Add the distilled water and reserved vinegar. Stir gently to mix. Transfer to a 1-quart jar and seal tightly. Let the *turshi* stand at room temperature for a week to fuse. This *turshi* tastes great with any rice dish.

PEARL ONION PICKLE

Turshi Pyaz

Makes 6 cups

Parboiled pearl onions (pyaz) are marinated here in vinegar, fenugreek, and spices, and served with short-grain rice. Like other condiments, this turshi *is an essential part of Afghan food. Not having* turshi *on the table or* destarkhwan *is embarrassing to most Afghans.*

10 ounces white pearl onions
1½ cups white vinegar
1 tablespoon fenugreek seeds
1½ teaspoons salt
5 cloves garlic, crushed
½ cup fresh mint sprigs
1 teaspoon dried mint flakes
2 teaspoons dried red pepper flakes

Chop off the heads and tails of onions and peel. Place in a saucepan with the vinegar. Cook over medium heat for about 5 minutes. Let cool completely.

Meanwhile, boil the fenugreek seeds in 1 cup of water for about 5 minutes. Drain and rinse. Pat dry with paper towels and add to the cooled onions and vinegar. Add the salt, garlic, mint sprigs, dried mint, and red pepper flakes. Mix well. Store the *turshi* in an air-tight jar. Let stand for one week before serving. Serve with rice dishes.

BUTTERNUT SQUASH PICKLE

Turshi Kadu

Makes 6 servings

This turshi *is prepared with parboiled butternut squash (kadu) that is mixed with fenugreek and nigella seeds, chilies, garlic, and mint, and soaked in a combination of distilled water and vinegar. It is served with most rice dishes. Squash, which grow in most regions of Afghanistan, are also utilized for preparing other foods such as soups,* sambosa, borani, *and* bolani.

¼ cup fenugreek seeds
1 pound butternut or banana squash
1½ cups vinegar
1 tablespoon salt
¼ cup sugar
½ cup small whole red chilies
1 teaspoon nigella seeds
6 cloves garlic, sliced
1 teaspoon dried mint
½ teaspoon cayenne pepper powder
½ cup fresh mint sprigs

Boil the fenugreek seeds in 1 cup of water for about 2 minutes. Drain and set aside. Peel the squash and cube into 1-inch pieces.

Mix 1½ cups water with the vinegar and place in a pan over medium heat and bring to a boil. Add the squash and cook for about 15 minutes or until fork tender. Mix in the salt and sugar. Let cool.

Once cool, mix in the chilies, nigella seeds, garlic, dried mint, cayenne pepper powder, and fresh mint. Store in a sealed, sterilized jars at room temperature. Allow one week for the flavors to fuse.

LEMON PICKLE

Turshi Post Limo

The peel of the lemon (limo) is soaked in salt water then boiled and rinsed several times to rid of bitterness. Crushed chilis, mint sprigs, dry mint, and fresh peppers are mixed with the lemon peel and soaked in a combination of lemon juice and vinegar. After the turshi *fuses in about a week, the fresh and mouthwatering aroma of the lemon becomes stronger and more appetizing. This* turshi *is served with rice dishes.*

10 large lemons
Salt water
1 cup vinegar
½ cup fresh ornamental red
  peppers
1 tablespoon crushed dried
  chili flakes
1 teaspoon dried crushed
  mint
½ cup fresh mint sprigs
2 teaspoons salt

Quarter the lemons. Squeeze the juices by hand into a bowl. Measure the juice to 1 cup and reserve. Scoop out the inside of the lemon quarters and discard, leaving the white lining intact. Soak the peel quarters in salt water for 3 days by which time the white inner lining should appear transparent.

After the 3 days, drain and boil the lemon peels in fresh water for 20 minutes, changing the water every 5 minutes to rid of the bitterness and hardness. Add the ornamental peppers in the last 5 minutes of boiling. Drain. Add the vinegar to the peels, together with the reserved lemon juice and simmer for 5 minutes. Let cool completely.

Once the lemon mixture is cool, add the crushed dried chili flakes, dried and fresh mint, and salt. Stir to mix. Store the *turshi* in an air-tight jar. Let stand at room temperature for a week to fuse. This *turshi* is delectably refreshing with rice dishes.

MIXED VEGETABLE PICKLE

Turshi Makhlut   Makes 3½ quarts

Mixed (makhlut) vegetable turshi is the most popular condiment in Afghanistan, prepared in all seasons. A variety of vegetables such as carrots, cauliflower, squash, and turnips, and herbs are parboiled and soaked in distilled water, spices, and vinegar, and left to fuse at room temperature.

½ pound turnips, peeled and
  chopped
3½ cups white vinegar
1 pound carrots, scraped and cut
  into ⅛-inch thick slices
6 ounces cauliflower, cut into
  florets
4 ounces red and green chili
  peppers
1½ tablespoons salt
1 cup distilled water
6 cloves garlic, sliced
1 teaspoon nigella seeds
1 teaspoon dried mint leaves
1 cup well-packed fresh mint
  leaves

Cook the turnips in the vinegar on low heat for 10 minutes. Add the carrots and cook for 10 minutes. Add the cauliflower and peppers, and cook for a further 10 minutes. Let cool completely.

Mix the salt with the distilled water and pour over the cooked vegetables. Add the garlic slices, nigella seeds, and dried mint. Sprinkle with fresh mint leaves. Mix gently. Transfer to a sterilized jar. Cover and let stand at room temperature for at least a week before serving. This type of *turshi* tastes great with rice dishes. It can be stored in the refrigerator for up to three months.

BELL PEPPER PICKLE

Turshi Morch Sherin

Makes 1 quart

Unlike other vegetable turshi *that goes through the parboiling process first, this condiment recommends charring peppers before peeling and slicing them. The grilled peppers are then mixed with spices and vinegar and left to fuse at room temperature. This bell pepper (*morch sherin*) turshi is served with short-grain rice dishes (*shoula*).*

2 green bell peppers
1 red bell pepper
1 yellow bell pepper
3 cloves garlic, sliced
1 tablespoon salt
1 teaspoon cayenne pepper
  powder
½ tablespoon sugar
1 tablespoon garlic paste
½ cup white vinegar

Heat a grill on high heat and grill the bell peppers until blackened and blistered evenly on all sides. Remove from the grill and place in a container with a tight lid. Set aside for 10 minutes to sweat.

After 10 minutes, rub off the charred skin of the peppers and cut each pepper in half lengthwise. Remove the seeds, and trim off the membrane and stem. Then slice into ½-inch-wide strips and place in a mixing bowl. Add the garlic slices. Mix together the salt, cayenne pepper powder, sugar, garlic paste, and vinegar and pour evenly around the top of the peppers.

Place the peppers in a one-quart sterilized jar and cover tightly. Let the *turshi* stand for a week before serving. This is a great *turshi* to serve with the short-grain rice dishes.

MANGO PICKLE

Turshi Am   Makes 2 cups

Mango (am) is first sliced and cooked in water for this sweet, sour, and spicy condiment, and then brown sugar, vinegar, and spices are added and the turshi *is set aside for the flavors to fuse. This* turshi *is served with most rice dishes. Mint sprigs add color, aroma, and freshness to the condiment.* Turshi Am *lasts for a month.*

2 cups white vinegar
1 ripe firm mango, peeled, pitted, and sliced
¼ cup brown sugar
1 cup distilled water
½ tablespoon minced garlic
2 teaspoons salt
½ teaspoon nigella seeds
½ tablespoon crushed dried chilies
¼ cup chopped walnuts
¼ cup fresh mint sprigs

Bring the vinegar to a boil on moderate heat. Add the mango slices and simmer for about 60 minutes until the mangos are tender. Set aside to cool. Once cool, fold in brown sugar, distilled water, garlic, salt, nigella seeds, chilies, walnuts, and mint sprigs. Mix well. Transfer into a sterilized jar. Seal tightly and leave at room temperature to ferment for about 4 days. Serve with rice dishes, especially plain rice with stew on the side.

PEACH PICKLE

Turshi Shaftalu

Makes 6 cups

Utilizing peaches (shaftalu) to prepare turshi *is very popular. Firm peaches are picked fresh from the tree and sliced for this sweet and sour condiment. Garlic, fenugreek seeds, nigella seeds, and spices are mixed with the peaches that are then soaked in distilled water and vinegar containing salt and brown sugar to fuse.* Turshi Shaftalu *is served with most rice dishes.*

2 pounds firm peaches
1 cup white vinegar
1 cup fresh whole chili peppers
½ red bell pepper, sliced
2 tablespoons fenugreek seeds
1 tablespoon garlic paste
1 tablespoon cayenne pepper
  powder (optional)
1 teaspoon crushed dried mint
1 teaspoon nigella seeds
¼ cup sliced garlic cloves
1 tablespoon salt
¾ cup well-packed brown sugar

Peel the peaches. With a sharp knife, slice each peach into 6 equal wedges discarding the pit. Bring 1 cup of water and the vinegar to a boil. Toss in the peaches and cook gently for about 5 minutes or until just tender, depending on the fruit quality.

Remove peaches and transfer to a mixing bowl to cool. Add the chili peppers and bell pepper slices to the water and vinegar solution and boil for about 5 minutes. Remove peppers from the juices and add to the peaches. Set aside the juices to cool.

In a small saucepan, boil the fenugreek seeds in ½ cup water for about 2 minutes. Drain, rinse, and add to the peaches. Add the garlic paste, cayenne pepper powder, mint, nigella seeds, and garlic slices to the peaches. Mix the salt and brown sugar with the reserved juices and pour on top of the peach *turshi*. Mix gently with a wooden spatula. Store the *turshi* in sealed, sterilized jars and let it fuse for a week before serving.

CILANTRO CHUTNEY

Chutney Gashniz

Makes 6 servings

Ground cilantro (gashniz) is mixed with ground walnuts and spices, soaked in vinegar, and served with fried dishes. Chutney Gashniz makes a good dip for bolani (savory pastries) and Pakowra (Potato Fritters, pages 36 & 37) snacks as well as French fries and potato chips. A tablespoon of this chutney also serves as a delicious dressing for any salad.

**4 cups coarsely chopped cilantro
  (about 3 bunches)
1 large red chili pepper
½ cup walnuts
1½ cups vinegar
1 teaspoon salt
1½ tablespoons sugar
1 teaspoon garlic paste**

Place the cilantro in a food processor. Cut off the stem of the chili pepper and then cut it in half. Remove the seeds and coarsely chop. Add to the cilantro along with the walnuts. Pulse into a coarse puree. Transfer the puree into a mixing bowl. Stir in the vinegar, salt, sugar, and garlic paste. Serve as a dip for kabobs, vegetables, and chips.

SWEET AND SOUR PEPPER CHUTNEY

Chutney Morch Sorkh

Makes 4 cups

This sweet and sour hot sauce is a combination of red chilies (morch sorkh) and red bell peppers cooked into a thick sauce that is flavored with spices and mixed with nigella seeds. This versatile chutney has many uses when served with snacks and the main course. It makes a delicious condiment for rice dishes. As a dip, it can be served with most fried foods such as bolani, pakowra *(potato fritters), French fries, and potato chips. A drizzle of this condiment in sandwiches packs them with freshness and flavor.*

2 pounds red chili peppers
1 red bell pepper
3½ cups vinegar
½ cup packed brown sugar
1 tablespoon salt
1 tablespoon garlic paste
1 tablespoon nigella seeds

Remove the seeds and stocks from the chili peppers and bell peppers and place them in a blender. Add the vinegar and process the peppers into a puree. Transfer the puree to a saucepan. Add the brown sugar, salt, and garlic paste. Place the saucepan on low heat and cook until the chutney is thick and shiny and the foam has disappeared from the surface, about 45 minutes. Let cool and add the nigella seeds. Mix with a spatula. Serve as a dip with your favorite snack.

Kheta Butter Cookies / *Kulché Kheta ee*

PASTRIES

Sherini Ardi

Pastries have been prepared in Afghanistan since ancient times when cars were non-existent and long, rough terrains required carrying long-lasting sweets like *Kulché Tandoori* and *Khajur* on horseback. Once made, *Kulché Tandoori*, also known as *Kulché Rah* or travel cookies, last for days. This tasty *kulcha* along with roasted wheat and hard-boiled eggs used to be stored in a sack made from camel wool (*khorjeen*) that the travelers carried on horseback in the past. *Khajur* served the same purpose because the fried pastry could endure long trips.

This cookbook serves as a pioneering publication by introducing these and other rare, much-sought-after Afghan recipes such as a Walnut Butter Cookies (*Kulché Chaharmaghzi*) that take their name from walnuts (*chaharmaghz*). These melt-in-your-mouth cookies are baked in tandoor ovens in the north of the country, particularly Badakhshan province where walnuts grow abundantly.

While Afghanistan is home to a great array of pastries, the origin, background, and history of some Afghan cakes and cookies involve a variety of culinary influences. Pastries such as Afghan baklava and rolls are adopted from other countries with an added touch of Afghan ingredients such as cardamom and pistachios and have been around for at least the past half century.

Most commercial and homemade pastries are considered a delicacy in Afghanistan, particularly in Kabul, and are prepared for special occasions such as Eid celebrations and feasts. Feasts called *Asrya* are prepared for grand occasions like engagement parties where various cookies, cakes, and fried dough rolls embellish the tables, along with enticing kabobs and *qaimaq chai* (green tea brewed in milk to a peach color). When pastries are commercially prepared, they are available for consumption in large quantities. During Eid celebrations, Afghans stock up on their pastry supplies to welcome a multitude of extended family members, neighbors, and friends into their homes. On New Year's Eve (Nawruz) the delicate rose-flavored *Kulché Berenji* (Nawruzi Rice Cookies) are prepared to celebrate the arrival of the first day of spring. It marks the beginning of the Afghan lunar year. For other occasions, pastries are always available on the shelves of local shops to be purchased for guests showing up during between-meals hours.

Simple tools are used to decorate Afghan pastries. The rim of a drinking glass embellishes the *rout* (sweet breads), thimbles are used for imprinting smaller circles on cookies—soda caps are a good replacement for a thimble—and large wire strainers or metal drains are used to leave imprints on *Khajur* (Deep-Fried Pastry Shells). The crisscross lines of *Kulché Berenji* (Rice Cookies) materialize from the blunt edge of a knife or from bottle lids. A light sprinkle of either sesame seeds, nigella seeds, poppy seeds, or ground pistachios completes the look of each unique finished pastry.

There are various methods used to prepare pastries. Some pastries like *khajur*, *paratha*, and *qatlama* are deep-fried, while other pastries, such as cookies and routs, are baked. Similar to the western world, baking takes place in a domestic oven in Kabul and other large cities. However, in villages, a *tandoor* is utilized to bake pastries. A fermented dough starter, leftover from the previous day, is used to leaven the dough. For the recipes in this book, commercial dry active yeast is substituted.

Afghans have retained the tradition of preparing pastries with freshly harvested ingredients. On the outskirts of Kabul and most villages, flour is ground in the neighborhood mills. Cows are milked daily, and the milk is then processed into fresh butter. Doughs, prepared from the fresh ingredients, are shaped into beautifully crafted cakes and cookies that are then baked in a pre-heated *tandoor* clay oven. The rich aroma of spices and the crispiness of roasted nuts, combined with fresh milk and wheat, create unique desserts that require simple preparation but deliver mouth-watering results.

Afghan Baklava / *Baghlawa*

AFGHAN BAKLAVA

Baghlawa

This is the Afghan version of baklava. Filo pastry sheets are lightly coated with butter, layered with ground almonds and walnuts, and baked. Sugar syrup is used to saturate the baklava before sprinkling with chopped pistachios. The aroma of cardamom and rose water makes Afghan Baklava unique. Baghlawa *is served with plain tea.*

For the syrup:
1½ cups sugar
1 tablespoon lemon juice
4 tablespoons rose water

In a small saucepan mix the sugar, lemon juice and ¾ cup water. Bring to a boil over moderate heat and boil until sugar dissolves and the syrup turns clear. Mix in the rose water and set aside to cool.

For the pastry:
3 sticks (12 ounces) unsalted butter
1 cup whole almonds, finely ground
2 cups walnuts, finely ground
2 tablespoons ground cardamom
3 tablespoons sugar
1 pound (about 20 sheets) frozen filo pastry (also called phyllo), thawed
2 tablespoons ground pistachios

Preheat oven to 400 degrees F. In another small saucepan cook the butter over moderate heat. As the foam appears on the surface, keep skimming it off and discard until the butter turns clear. Set aside. Mix the ground almonds, ground walnuts, cardamom, and sugar in a bowl. Set aside.

Layer six of the filo sheets in a pan the size of the pastry sheets, brushing each sheet thoroughly with butter. (Keep the remaining sheets covered to prevent drying.) Spread the nut mixture evenly over the layered pastry. Brush one filo sheet with butter and place on top of the nuts, buttered side down. Then layer all but 3 of the remaining filo on top of the nuts brushing with butter between layers. Brush the 3 last sheets liberally with all the remaining butter as you layer them on top. Cut the pastry through to the bottom of pan into diamond-shaped pieces.

Place the *baghlawa* on the middle rack of the oven and bake for about 25 minutes or until it is golden. Remove from oven and pour the cool sugar syrup over the hot *baghlawa* evenly. Let cool. Cut the pastry through to the bottom of the pan for easy serving. Decorate with ground pistachios and serve with plain tea or coffee.

BAKLAVA ROLLS

Baghlawa Loula

Makes 40 pieces

This is another version of baghlawa. *Filo pastry sheets are coated with butter, sprinkled with nuts, and then rolled. The filo rolls are baked, then cut into smaller rolls, and finally bathed in sugar syrup. Chopped pistachios add beauty and crunch to the finished* baghlawa. Baghlawa Loula, *which is served with plain tea, is prepared for festive occasions. Stored covered,* baghlawa *lasts for weeks.*

For the syrup:
1½ cups sugar
1 teaspoon lemon juice
4 tablespoons rose water

In a small saucepan mix the sugar, lemon juice, and ¾ cup water. Bring to a boil over moderate heat and boil until sugar dissolves and the syrup turns clear. Mix in the rose water and set aside to cool.

For the pastry:
1½ cups unsalted butter
1 cup coarsely chopped
  pistachios
1 cup coarsely chopped
  walnuts
½ cup powdered sugar
2½ teaspoons ground
  cardamom
1 pound (about 20 sheets)
  frozen filo pastry (also
  called phyllo), thawed
Ground pistachios for
  garnish

Cook the butter over moderate heat in a saucepan. As the foam appears on the surface, keep skimming it off and discarding until the butter turns clear. Set aside.

Preheat oven to 375 degrees F. Mix the pistachios, walnuts, powdered sugar, and cardamom. Divide the mixture into 10 equal portions. Place one sheet of the filo pastry on a smooth surface. Coat liberally with butter and sprinkle with one portion of the mixed nuts. Place a stick ½ inch in thickness on one short end of the sprinkled pastry and roll the pastry away so that the nuts trap inside and the roll is complete.

Coat a second sheet of filo with butter. Place the prepared roll with the stick still inside on the short end of the filo sheet and roll away from you so that there are two layers of filo on the same roll. Take the roll from both sides and push gently towards the center until the roll is 9 inches long. Remove the roll from the stick and place it in a 9x13 inch ovenproof dish, and coat the top with butter. Work with the rest of the filo dough to finish 9 more rolls. Once all the rolls are in the pan, bake in the pre-heated oven for 30 to 35 minutes or until golden.

Remove pastry from the oven and leave to cool for 5 to 7 minutes. Cut the rolls into 4 equal portions while still in the pan and saturate with the cooled syrup. Sprinkle with pistachios and let cool completely.

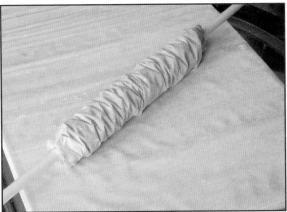

Baklava Rolls / *Baghlawa Loula*

CREAM ROLLS

Kerim Roul

Makes 24 rolls

Brittle rolls are prepared with leavened dough and filled with homemade cream to make these delicious little pastries. Pistachios and powdered sugar add color to the rolls. These pastries are available commercially in Afghan cities and they are served for festive and celebratory events, usually with plain tea. To make these pastries at home you will need forms/tubes used for making cannolis that are available online.

For the cream:
1½ cups heavy whipping cream
1 cup confectioner sugar

Place a metal mixing bowl and the mixer beaters in the refrigerator for 3 hours to get cold. Using the cold bowl and beaters, beat the cream for 1 minute on low until foamy. Beat on medium speed for about 2 to 3 minutes or until the cream reaches the consistency of pea soup. Add the sugar and beat on high until soft peaks form. Cover and refrigerate until ready to use.

For the pastry:
2½ cups all-purpose flour
1½ teaspoons active dry yeast
Pinch salt
½ tablespoon sugar
1 teaspoon ground cardamom
1 egg
3 tablespoons oil
¾ cup warm milk
12 cannoli forms
1 egg white, beaten
1 tablespoon melted butter
Powdered sugar and ground
  pistachios to garnish

In a mixing bowl, mix together the flour, yeast, salt, sugar, and cardamom. Beat the egg separately and add to the mixture. Add the oil and massage into the flour. Add the milk and keep massaging until a sticky dough is obtained. Wash and dry hands and dust them with flour. Knead the dough for 5 minutes until homogenized. Cover and leave to rise for about 60 minutes, depending on the room temperature.

Preheat the oven to 375 degrees F. Divide the dough into 4 equal portions. Cover the portions, and working with one portion at a time, spread into a rectangle 4 inches wide by 12 inches long. Then, cut the rectangle into 6 ribbons lengthwise. Wrap one ribbon around one cannoli tube in an overlapped manner pinching the beginning and end to secure. Brush with

the egg white and place on a cookie tray. Repeat with all the dough until the tray is full. Bake the rolls for 12 to 15 minutes or until crisp and baked through.

Gently remove the hot rolls from the tubes by twisting them with gloved hands against the molds. Work with the remaining batches of dough until all rolls are ready. Allow pastries to cool.

Pipe the whipped cream into the cooled rolls from both sides until filled. Dot the top of the roll with melted butter and sprinkle with powdered sugar and pistachios.

ELEPHANT EAR PASTRIES

Goush Feel

**Makes 10 servings
(4 pieces each)**

"Goush" means "ear" and "feel" means "elephant." These delicate 'elephant ear' egg yolk brittles are fried and coated with ground pistachios and powdered sugar and served with tea on the side. They are usually prepared for festive occasions such as Eid, or celebratory parties such as graduations, engagements, and weddings. This pastry is a great make-ahead as they last for weeks.

2 cups all-purpose flour
1 teaspoon ground cardamom
Pinch salt
1 teaspoon baking powder
1½ tablespoons oil plus additional
 for frying
½ cup whole milk
3 egg yolks
1 cup powdered sugar
Ground pistachios for garnish

In a mixing bowl mix flour, cardamom, salt, and baking powder. In a separate bowl mix the 1½ tablespoons oil, milk, and egg yolks until smooth. Add the flour mixture to the milk mixture and mix and knead for 7 minutes until homogenized and smooth. Cover the dough and leave it at room temperature for 60 minutes.

Roll the dough into an oblong shape and cut it into 12 portions and keep them covered as you work. Set 2 portions aside for the flower and then working with one portion at a time use a rolling pin to spread a portion into a paper-thin circle. Cut the circle into 4 equal quarters. Pleat one straight side of the quarter and pinch so the pleats will not open during frying. Form the rest of the dough in the same way (except for the 2 reserved portions) until all leaves are prepared, keeping the leaves covered after you form them.

To make the flower (*as pictured in center of plate*)**:** combine the two reserved portions of dough and spread into a paper-thin sheet. Cut the sheet into smaller rounds about 2 inches in diameter using a cookie cutter. Arrange the dough rounds in an overlapped manner. Moisten between the contact areas and press gently so they stick together. Brush the top of the connected rounds with oil and fold lengthwise with the greased side in. Then role loosely and pinch the ends to finish the flower. Cut the bottom of the flower and pinch so it will not open during frying.

Heat 3 inches of oil in a small pot and fry a few leaves at a time. Remove the leaves from the oil when they start to change color. Drain the fried pastry on paper towels. Fry the flower in the same manner. Let cool, then sprinkle liberally with powdered sugar on both sides and sprinkle ground pistachios on the top. Arrange leaves and flower on a serving dish as pictured.

Pastry Flowers / *Qatlama*

The Best of Afghan Cooking

PASTRY FLOWERS

Qatlama

Delicate fried pastry flowers are sweetened with powdered sugar, decorated with ground pistachios, and served with tea on the side. This pastry comes from the northern provinces of Afghanistan where predominantly Uzbek and Turkman Afghans reside. These mild and crumbly pastry flowers are prepared with 3 dough sheets that are layered with melted butter and rolled. The roll is then cut into rounds and shallow-fried.

2½ cups all-purpose flour
1½ tablespoons active dry yeast
½ teaspoon salt
3 tablespoons sugar
5 tablespoons oil, plus oil for frying
¾ cup warm water
4 tablespoons butter, melted
Powdered cardamom
Powdered sugar and ground
  pistachios for garnish

In a mixing bowl whisk together the flour, yeast, salt, and sugar. Add the 5 tablespoons of oil and rub in with your hands. Add the warm water and knead until elastic and homogenized. Cover the dough and leave it at room temperature for 2 hours to rise.

Divide the dough into 3 equal portions. Shape each portion into a ball and cover. Spread each ball into a paper-thin circle with the help of a rolling pin, dusting the board and dough with flour from time to time. Brush one side of each circle with the butter and sprinkle with cardamom and some flour. Stack the 3 circles on top of each other and then role loosely into a log shape. Cut the log crosswise into 1-inch-thick slices. Lay the slices flat on a cutting board and flatten slightly with the help of a rolling pin. Secure the ends of the dough with a toothpick before frying.

Add 3 inches of oil to a frying pan and heat over medium heat. Oil is ready when a tiny dough portion dropped in sizzles and floats to the surface. Fry the flat rolls until they are puffy and start to change color. Drain on a paper towel. Remove the toothpicks and sprinkle with powdered sugar and pistachios. Serve.

LAYERED PASTRIES

Paratha

Makes 24 *paratha*

Aromatic, mild pastry brittles are sweetened with a sprinkle of powdered sugar and garnished with ground pistachios. "Paratha" in India means "lay-ered dough." The dough in this recipe is layered with butter and shaped into cookies. This layering technique is also used for paratha *bread and nan stuffed with meat and vegetables. The Afghan* paratha *may have been ad-opted from Hindu and Sikh Afghans.*

4 cups all-purpose flour
1 teaspoon baking powder
½ teaspoon salt
¼ cup sugar
1½ cups warm water
½ cup butter, melted
Oil for frying
Ground pistachios, powdered sugar,
  and ground cardamom for topping

Mix the flour and baking powder. Dissolve the salt and sugar in the warm water and gradually add to the flour. Knead the dough on a flour-dusted surface for 5 minutes to homogenize. Cover the dough and let rest for about 30 minutes.

Divide the dough into 6 equal portions and shape each portion into a ball. Working with one ball at a time cover the rest. With a rolling pin spread the ball into a ⅛-inch-thick round. Brush the round with some of the melted butter and sprinkle lightly with flour. Once the first 3 circles are finished, stack them on top of each other and roll up loosely into a log shape. Then cut the log into 1-inch-thick disks (you will have 12 disks). Lay the disks on the flat side and gently spread them by pressing with the palm of your hand. Secure the ends of the dough with toothpicks. Work with the remaining three dough balls the same way.

Add 3 inches of oil to a frying pan and heat on medium-low heat. The oil is ready when a small lump of dough dropped in it sizzles in 10 seconds and comes to the surface. Fry the *parathas* on both sides. Remove with a slotted spoon when they start to change color. Adjust heat if they become brown too quickly. Drain on paper towels and sprinkle with pistachios, powdered sugar, and cardamom.

Layered Pastry / *Paratha*

DEEP-FRIED PASTRY SHELLS

Busraq / Khajur

Makes 6 servings

These melt-in-your-mouth deep-fried pastry shells are prepared with a yeast dough that is not allowed to leaven before frying. Otherwise, the shells will open and lose their shape. This ancient pastry with mild sweetness was often prepared for travelers since they stay fresh for a long time. They were stored in sacks and carried on horseback along the rough and wild terrains of Afghanistan when modern-day transportation was not feasible. In India the word "pekhraj" means "yellow ruby" and the term was Arabized to busraq to describe this pastry. They are also sometimes called khajur.

2¼ cups all-purpose flour
¼ teaspoon salt
2 teaspoons ground cardamom
¼ cup hot oil, plus more for frying
¾ cup sugar dissolved in ¼ cup hot
  water, then cooled
1½ teaspoons active dry yeast,
  dissolved in ¼ cup lukewarm
  water

Mix the flour, salt, and cardamom. Add the ¼ cup hot oil and massage into the flour. Add the sugar mixture and the yeast solution to the flour and massage to homogenize. Knead the dough on a floured surface until smooth.

Divide the dough into walnut-size balls. For the shell texture, press one ball against a surface with holes or raised design, until you obtain a patty 2 inches in diameter. Then curl in the patty edges loosely to form a shell with the textured side out. Insert a teaspoon handle inside the shell and press the middle of the seam against the teaspoon handle to seal. Slip the shell off the spoon handle and place on a tray and cover. Repeat with the rest of the balls.

Heat 3 inch of oil in a large pot on medium-low heat. Oil is ready when a small dough lump dropped in it sizzles and rises to the top slowly. Lower a few shells into the oil at a time, seam side down. Turning the shells for even browning, fry for about 2 to 3 minutes or until crisp and golden on the outside and cooked through on the inside. Drain on paper towels. Serve warm or cool. When stored in a covered container these last for about two weeks.

Deep-Fried Pastry Shells / *Busraq*

Pastries

FIG AND WALNUT PASTRIES

Sambosa Sherin

Makes 16 *sambosa*

Puff pastry triangles are filled with dried figs and walnuts and served with tea or milk. This pastry is prepared for special occasions like Eid celebrations and celebratory gatherings such as engagement parties or graduations. Figs are grown in many provinces of Afghanistan, such as Herat, Balkh, Farah, Zabul, and Jawzjan, but the southern Kandahar province is known as the center of fig production.

8 ounces soft dried brown figs
½ cup finely chopped walnuts
2 teaspoons ground
   cardamom
8 (5 inch x 5 inch) puff
   pastry sheets, thawed until
   bendable
1 egg beaten with 1 teaspoon
   water
Powdered sugar

Cut the figs in half and chop finely. Add the chopped walnuts and cardamom. Mash together until well-blended. Divide into 16 equal portions.

Preheat the oven to 375 degrees F. Take one pastry sheet and cut diagonally into two triangles. Place on a cutting board with a long edge towards you. Brush some of the egg wash around the edges. Place one portion of the fig mixture on the right half of a pastry triangle, leaving ⅛ inch of a margin on the dough. Fold over the other half to cover the fig mixture and make a smaller triangle. Press the two open edges with the back of a fork to seal. Brush with the egg wash. Repeat process with the remaining dough.

Place the prepared pastries on a baking sheet lined with parchment paper, leaving 1-inch of space between them. Bake the *sambosa* for about 15 to 20 minutes or until well-risen and golden. Sprinkle with powdered sugar immediately and cool on a wire rack.

AFGHAN CREPES

Eshel

Makes 12 servings

Eshel, another form of the French crepe, are a traditional sweet treat prepared with egg, flour, and water or milk and salt. Powdered sugar and ground pistachios are sprinkled over the rolls. Eshel are prepared in large quantities for weddings and are served along with maleeda *(wedding cake) after dinner, or the morning of the wedding with breakfast. In today's Afghan kitchens, eshel are often stuffed with sweet or savory filling.*

½ cup all-purpose flour
¼ cup sugar
1 teaspoon ground cardamom
Pinch salt
1 egg
¼ cup plus 2 tablespoons milk
Pinch saffron powder
   dissolved in ¼ cup hot water
   and cooled
1 tablespoon melted butter,
   plus more for brushing on
   the finished crepes
1 tablespoon chopped
   pistachios
2 tablespoons powdered sugar

In a mixing bowl, whisk together the flour, sugar, cardamom, and salt. Beat the egg in a separate bowl and add to the flour. Gradually add in the milk and saffron water, stirring to combine. Add the 1 tablespoon melted butter and mix.

Heat a non-stick 9-inch griddle or a frying pan over low heat. Scoop about 3 tablespoons of the batter and pour onto one side of the pan. Tilt the pan quickly with a circular motion so that the batter coats the surface evenly. Cook the crepe for about 2 minutes, or until it starts to bubble and the bottom is lightly browned. Loosen with a spatula, turn and cook the other side. Roll the crepe and place on a plate, seam side down. Repeat with the rest of the batter.

Cut any irregular ends off of the rolled crepes and then cut each roll in the middle into two rolls. Brush the tops of the rolls liberally with melted butter and sprinkle with the pistachios and powdered sugar.

ORANGE & NUT ROLLS

Loulè Muraba

Makes 24 rolls

Crumbly pastry shells are prepared with all-purpose flour. Rolls are filled with aromatic orange marmalade, usually homemade, and a variety of nuts, including pistachios, walnuts, and almonds. These rolls are more modern and healthful version of the traditional cream rolls. Homemade rolls take their place on breakfast destarkhwan *when oranges are in season. To make these pastries at home you will need forms/tubes used for making cannolis that are available online.*

For the rolls:
2½ cups all-purpose flour
1½ teaspoons active dry yeast
Pinch salt
½ tablespoon sugar
1 teaspoon ground cardamom
1 egg
3 tablespoons oil
½ cup plus 1 tablespoon warm
  milk
24 cannoli forms
1 egg white, beaten
Powdered sugar and ground
  pistachios

Place the flour, yeast, salt, sugar, and cardamom in a bowl. Beat the egg with a fork in a separate bowl and add to the flour mixture along with the oil. Add the warm milk and massage into a soft sticky dough. Transfer the dough onto a board. Dust clean, dry hands with flour and knead the dough for 5 minutes to homogenize. Cover and leave at room temperature to rise for about 60 minutes.

Preheat oven to 375 degrees F. Divide the dough into 4 portions and cover with a towel. Working with one portion of dough at a time, roll out into a 12- by 4-inch rectangle. Cut the dough lengthwise into 6 ribbons. Wrap each ribbon around a cannoli form, pinching the beginning and end to secure. Transfer to a cookie sheet and brush with egg white. Repeat with all the dough until the tray is full. Bake for 12 minutes. Gently remove the hot rolls from the forms by twisting and pulling gently. Let cool.

For the filling:
16 ounces orange marmalade
2 cups coarsely chopped
  walnuts
½ cup coarsely chopped
  pistachios

Mix the filling ingredients. Using the handle of a teaspoon put some filling in the cooled rolls until the rolls are full. Sprinkle with powdered sugar and ground pistachios.

RAISIN AND WALNUT CAKE

Kaykè Kishmishi

Makes 8 servings

This moist and fluffy raisin (kishmish) and walnut cake is served with tea on the side. Organic wheat flour, mixed with walnuts for crunch and raisins for extra sweetness, results in a scrumptious cake packed with the aroma of cardamom. This particular cake is prepared commercially and sold in the late afternoon when guests show up at homes between meal hours. A variety of raisins are produced in Afghanistan and walnut trees are grown in the northern and eastern districts of the country.

2 cups all-purpose flour plus
  1 tablespoon flour
2 teaspoons ground
  cardamom
3 teaspoons baking powder
¾ cup chopped walnuts
½ cup raisins
1½ cups sugar
4 large eggs
½ cup milk
½ cup oil

Preheat the oven to 350 degrees F.

In a bowl mix the 2 cups flour with the cardamom and baking powder. In a separate bowl mix the walnuts and raisins with 1 tablespoon flour. Set aside.

Place the sugar in a bowl. Add the eggs and using a mixer beat the egg mixture until pale in color. Add the milk and oil and beat for 1 minute. Add the flour mixture gradually to the egg mixture and beat until well-combined. Fold in the walnuts and raisins.

Transfer the batter into a well-greased 9- by 5-inch loaf pan lined with parchment paper. Bake for about 60 minutes or until golden brown and crisp on the outside and when a toothpick inserted in the cake center comes out clean. Remove the cake from the oven and immediately cover it with a kitchen towel and leave it to cool completely. Un-mold, slice, and serve.

CARDAMOM RICE CAKE

Kaykè Berenji

Makes 24 portions

This gluten-free simple cake is prepared with rice (berenj) flour, sugar, milk, and eggs and spiced up with ground cardamom. It is coated with honey and almond flakes and served with plain tea. The culinary uses of rice are not limited to savory dishes only. Puddings, cakes, and cookies are prepared with Afghan short-grain rice. Like wheat, rice is a main food source in Afghanistan. According to the Afghan Ministry for Agriculture, Irrigation, and Livestock, the country is moving towards achieving self-sufficiency in rice production.

1 cup rice flour
1 cup sugar
1 teaspoon baking powder
2 teaspoons ground
   cardamom
2 large eggs
1 cup whole milk
¼ cup oil
½ cup honey
½ cup flaked almond

Preheat the oven to 375 degrees F. In a mixing bowl, whisk together the flour, sugar, baking powder, and cardamom. In a separate bowl, whisk the eggs until smooth and add to the flour mixture. Whisk in the milk and oil.

Grease the bottom and sides of a 12-by-8-inch casserole dish with shortening. Sprinkle lightly with flour. Mix the batter again and pour gently into the pan. Bake for 35 to 40 minutes.

Let the cake cool and then cut into 24 equal squares. Spread honey on individual squares and press the almonds on top. Serve with plain tea.

CARDAMOM CORN CAKE

Kaykè Jawari

Makes 6 to 8 servings

This crumbly yellow cornmeal (jawari) cake is prepared with milk, eggs, sugar, and oil and spiced up by ground cardamom. Whipped cream and tea are served on the side. A simpler, traditional version of this cake called douda *is prepared with water. It is formed into a large patty the size of a plate and is slapped to the wall of the heated ground oven (tandoor) for baking. Douda is served with yogurt or a yogurt drink (doogh), or with sweetened tea. Corn is the third most important cereal crop in Afghanistan (after wheat and barley) and is cultivated throughout the country in different ecological zones, particularly in the Paktia and Nangarhar provinces.*

1¼ cups yellow cornmeal
1½ cups whole milk
½ cup all-purpose flour
3 teaspoons baking powder
½ teaspoon baking soda
½ teaspoon salt
¾ cup sugar
1 tablespoon ground cardamom
2 eggs
¼ cup oil
Icing or whipped cream

In a bowl, mix the cornmeal and milk. Set aside to rest for 30 minutes. In a separate mixing bowl, whisk the all-purpose flour, baking powder, baking soda, salt, sugar, and cardamom. Add the eggs and oil and beat the mixture using a fork until a creamy mixture is achieved. Set aside to rest until the 30-minute timing for the cornmeal is over.

Preheat oven to 400 degrees F. Add the cornmeal mixture to the flour mixture and whisk until well blended. Grease the bottom and sides of a 7-by-11-inch cake tin with shortening. Sprinkle lightly with flour. Mix the batter again and pour gently into the pan. Bake for 30 minutes.

Remove the cake from the oven. Cover with a cloth kitchen towel and let cool completely. Slice and serve with whipped cream topping.

Syrup-Soaked Corn Cake / *Kayké Sharbati*

The Best of Afghan Cooking

SYRUP-SOAKED CORN CAKE

Kaykè Sharbati

Makes 6 servings

Kaykè Sharbati is drizzled with ground nuts and served with tea. This cake is prepared for festive occasions like Eid, and celebratory parties such as engagements, weddings, graduations, childbirth, and circumcisions. The cake, which is prepared with homegrown organic corn (jawari), is soaked in sugar syrup (sharbat).

For the syrup:
2 cups sugar
¼ cup rose water
1 teaspoon ground cardamom

In a small saucepan dissolve the sugar in 1½ cups water and bring to a boil over medium heat. Boil for about 7 minutes or until a film of syrup forms on the surface of a spoon when dipped in the syrup. Mix in the rose water and cardamom and set aside.

For the cake:
2 cups yellow cornmeal
1 cup sugar
2 teaspoons ground cardamom
1 tablespoon baking powder
4 eggs
1 cup plain yogurt
1 cup oil
½ cup chopped walnuts and pistachios

Heat the oven to 375 degrees F. In a mixing bowl combine cornmeal, sugar, cardamom, and baking powder. Add the eggs, yogurt, and oil. Mix well with a fork until smooth. Pour the batter into a 13x9x2-inch cake pan and bake for about 30 minutes or until golden and crisp on top and bottom.

Remove the cake from the oven and cut it into diamonds while still in pan. Leave in the pan to cool completely. Saturate the cake with the prepared syrup by pouring the syrup on top and between the cuts. Decorate with the chopped nut and let stand for 4 to 5 hours before serving.

FLUFFY CARDAMOM SWEET BREAD

Rout Pashan

Makes 6 servings

Rout *has a place between cake and bread. Sesame and nigella seeds add nutty flavor and aroma to this fluffy, crumbly sweet bread.* Rout *is traditionally made to rejoice in the first steps taken by a child. Relatives are invited and the* rout *is distributed among guests, after a ritual of rolling the* rout *behind the toddler's steps. It is believed that by doing so, the child will not be running to procure food for his family one day; instead, it will be the food following the future breadwinner. Traditional* routs *are prepared at home and then taken to bakeries for baking.*

4 cups all-purpose flour
2½ cups sugar
2 teaspoons baking powder
½ teaspoon baking soda
½ teaspoon salt
2 tablespoons ground cardamom
¾ cup oil plus 1 tablespoon
1 cup milk
4 whole eggs
1 egg white, beaten
Nigella seeds and sesame seeds

In a bowl, whisk together the flour, sugar, baking powder, baking soda, salt, and cardamom. In another bowl whisk together the ¾ cup oil, milk, and 4 whole eggs. Add to the dry ingredients. Whisk to the consistency of fudge. Cover and let rest for 20 minutes. Preheat the oven to 350 degrees F.

Transfer the dough into a 17- by 11-inch baking pan lined with well-greased aluminum foil. Spread the batter across the pan with the help of a spatula. Then sprinkle the surface with the remaining 1 tablespoon oil and smooth out with the palms of your hands. Drizzle on the egg white and spread with your palms until the surface of the dough is shiny and smooth. Sprinkle the batter with the seeds. Bake for 40 to 45 minutes or until the rout is golden brown and crispy on top, and the edges have started to separate from the pan.

Remove the *rout* from oven and let cool for about 10 minutes. Cover with kitchen towels and let cool completely. Cut and serve with tea.

TRADITIONAL CARDAMOM SWEET BREAD

Rout Khanagi

Makes 1 large disk

Made with yeast and allowed to rise overnight, this is the traditional way of making rout. This sweet bread is prepared with baking powder and yeast as leavening agents, drizzled with white poppy seeds and nigella seeds, and served with milk or tea. This sweet bread with mild sweetness and crumbly texture is traditionally prepared to celebrate the first steps of a child.

3¼ cups all-purpose flour
1¼ cups sugar
1½ teaspoons baking powder
1 tablespoon ground cardamom
2 eggs, beaten, at room
  temperature
½ cup warm oil
1 teaspoon active dry yeast
  dissolved in 2 teaspoons
  lukewarm (110° F) water
2 tablespoons warm milk
1 egg beaten with 1 teaspoon
  water
White poppy seeds and nigella
  seeds to garnish

In a bowl, whisk together the flour, sugar, baking powder, and cardamom. Hollow the center and add the eggs. Beat the eggs with a fork and massage with the flour. Add the oil and rub into the flour until breadcrumb consistency is reached. Add the yeast solution and mix well. Add the milk and knead the dough well to form an homogenized, firm dough. Transfer to a plastic bowl with a cover. Place the bowl inside two layers of plastic bags, covering tightly. Wrap in kitchen towels. Let the dough stand overnight at room temperature.

Preheat the oven to 300 degrees F. Cover a large pizza pan with well-greased aluminum foil. Form the dough into a smooth ball and transfer it onto the center of the pan. With your palms, flatten the dough into an 11-inch disk. Decorate the round by pressing the lid of a jar and the blunt end of a skewer randomly into the dough. Brush the dough lightly with the egg wash and sprinkle with poppy and nigella seeds. Bake for about 35 minutes or until well risen and golden. Cover with kitchen towels and leave to cool before serving.

EASY CARDAMOM SWEET BREAD

Rout Sada

Makes 6 servings

Sweet and fluffy bread, with the aroma of cardamom, is served with tea or milk on the side. This simple and easy rout is prepared in minutes. Unlike the traditional rout which requires yeast and overnight resting time, this cake is prepared with baking powder and simple ingredients such as flour, eggs, oil, and milk with the addition of some sugar.

3 cups all-purpose flour
1¼ cups sugar
3 teaspoons baking powder
1 tablespoon ground
  cardamom
2 eggs
½ cup oil
3 tablespoons milk
Poppy seeds and sesame
  seeds to garnish

In a bowl, whisk together the flour, sugar, baking powder, and cardamom. Break the eggs into a small bowl and reserve 1 teaspoon of the egg white for glazing before beating. Hollow the center and add the beaten eggs and massage with flour. Mix in the oil and milk. Knead well to form a firm dough. Cover and let rest for 20 minutes.

Preheat the oven to 350 degrees F. Form the dough into a smooth ball and transfer it to a greased pizza pan dusted with flour. Spread into a 10-inch round shape. Decorate with the imprints of overlapped circles using the lid of a jar or rim of a glass. Prick the entire surface with the flat end of a wooden skewer, leaving an inch between the holes. Glaze the *rout* with the reserved egg white and sprinkle with the seeds. Bake for 25 to 30 minutes or until well risen and golden. Leave to cool before serving. Store covered.

CORNMEAL CAKE

Hawasi

Makes 16 servings

"Hawasi" means "the desireable." Traditionally, hawasi *is a street food loved by school children and passersby. It is sold in all the Afghan markets when corn is in season.* Hawasi *is a cake with a crumbly texture made with a combo of yellow cornmeal (jawari) and all-purpose flour. Nigella seeds are sprinkled over the cake for decoration and their nutty flavor. The addition of flour to this cake balances the coarseness of the cornmeal texture. This cake is usually served with tea on the side.*

2 cups yellow cornmeal
1 cup all-purpose flour
1 cup sugar
1 teaspoon baking powder
1 tablespoon ground cardamom
1½ cups whole milk
½ teaspoon yellow food coloring
3 eggs, beaten
½ cup oil
1 tablespoon nigella seeds

Preheat the oven to 375 degrees F. Grease a 15- by 10-inch baking pan and sprinkle lightly with flour.

In a mixing bowl whisk the cornmeal, flour, sugar, baking powder, and cardamom. Add the milk, food coloring, eggs, and oil. Whisk until a thick, creamy batter is obtained. Pour the batter into the prepared pan and spread evenly. Sprinkle with the nigella seeds. Place on the middle rack of the oven and bake for about 45 minutes or until lightly brown on top and bottom and when a toothpick inserted in the cake comes out clean.

Cut with a sharp knife or cookie cutter into desired shapes and sizes. Cover and let cool completely before serving.

CARDAMOM BUTTER COOKIES

Kulché Bazaari

Makes 16 cookies

These crumbly, crisp cookies (kulcha) are prepared with a combination of butter, oil, and powdered sugar. Cookie stores in shopping areas (bazaars) usually carry them, thus their name. The aroma of cardamom gives these cookies uniqueness. Kulché Bazaari are served to guests with tea on the side. When prepared at home the overall timing takes less than 30 minutes.

3 cups all-purpose flour
1½ cups powdered sugar
**1 tablespoon ground
  cardamom**
1 teaspoon baking powder
1 cup melted butter
¾ cup canola oil
**1 tablespoon ground
  pistachios**

Preheat the oven to 400 degrees F. Whisk the flour, powdered sugar, cardamom, and baking powder together. Add the melted butter and canola oil and gradually massage into the flour mixture to form a soft dough. Divide the dough into 16 equal portions.

Roll one portion of dough into a smooth ball and place it on a cookie sheet lined with parchment paper. Make an imprint in the center of the ball with your thumb. Repeat with the rest of the cookies, leaving a 2-inch space between them for expansion. Bake the cookies for about 15 minutes or until the bottoms of the cookies change color by which time the cookies should have flattened to 4 inches in diameter.

Sprinkle cookies with ground pistachios. Cool cookies on the pan until crispy before serving.

KHETA BUTTER COOKIES

Kulché Kheta ee   Makes 12 cookies

These melt-in-your-mouth butter cookies are served with tea. Kheta, a land in old Turkestan, may be home to this delicious butter cookie that is associated with Turkmans in the northern zones of Afghanistan. The preparation is easy and simple as well as time-saving. Kulché Kheta ee is prepared both commercially and domestically in Afghanistan.

¾ cup powdered sugar
1½ cups all-purpose flour
2 teaspoons ground cardamom
1½ teaspoons baking powder
¼ teaspoon baking soda
¾ cup plus 1 tablespoon
   clarified unsalted butter
1 tablespoon finely chopped
   pistachios

Preheat the oven to 375 degrees F. In a mixing bowl whisk the powdered sugar, flour, cardamom, baking powder, and baking soda. Add the ¾ cup of clarified butter gradually while massaging the mixture for about 5 minutes, until the dough softens and the sugar dissolves. If a ball of dough cracks when pressed down gently, add the remaining clarified butter gradually and knead. Divide the dough into 12 portions. Leave to rest for 15 minutes.

Shape each portion of dough into a smooth ball and place them on a baking sheet lined with parchment paper leaving 1-inch of space between them for expansion. With your knuckle, make a hollow imprint in the center of each cookie. Bake the cookies for about 15 minutes or until they crack and expand and the bottoms of the cookies change color.

Sprinkle with the ground pistachio. Allow to cool on the pan at room temperature and then refrigerate for 4 hours before serving. Transfer cookies to a serving plate using a turner or cake server.

NAWRUZI RICE COOKIES

Kulché Berenji Nawruzy

Makes 30 cookies

These mild, aromatic rice (berenj) cookies are crisp on the outside and soft on the inside. They are decorated with ground pistachios and served with tea. Powdered short-grain rice, which commonly has culinary uses in shoula cooking, is utilized for these in combination with all-purpose flour. These cookies are traditionally prepared to celebrate the first day of the year, Nawruz, which falls on the spring equinox.

1 cup all-purpose flour
2½ cups rice flour
2 cups sugar
2 teaspoons baking powder
1 tablespoon freshly ground
  cardamom
3 eggs
1 cup canola oil
3 tablespoons rose water
3 tablespoons milk
Ground pistachios to garnish

Mix the flours, sugar, baking powder, and cardamom. Beat the eggs in a separate bowl and mix with the dry ingredients. Mix in the canola oil, rose water, and milk. Dust your hands and a board with flour and place the dough on the board and knead the mixture to make a soft, shapeable dough.

Heat the oven to 375 degrees F. Line two baking sheet with parchment paper (you might need a third baking sheet depending on their size). Divide the dough into 30 equal portions with greased hands. Take one portion and roll it into a ball and then place it onto one corner of the baking sheet. Press gently with the palm of your hand to flatten slightly. Decorate with the lid of a jar. Do the same with the rest of the dough leaving enough room between cookies for spreading.

Bake for 12 to 15 minutes or until the cookies start to change color. Cool before removing from baking sheet. For softer cookies cover with a towel as they cool. Decorate with pistachios.

TANDOORI COOKIES

Kulché Tandoori

These mildly sweet, crumbly cookies are traditionally baked in a tandoor, a clay ground oven constructed in most homes in the Afghan suburbs. While meat dishes and shourba soups are lowered on the glowing embers of the pit for a long, slow-cooking process, tandoori cookies are baked on the walls of the tandoor simultaneously. This cookie was often packed for travelers in the old days due to its long shelf life.

2¼ cups all-purpose flour
1 cup whole wheat flour
1 cup sugar
1½ teaspoons baking powder
1 tablespoon ground cardamom
½ cup oil, warmed
1 teaspoon active dry yeast dissolved in
  2 teaspoons lukewarm (110°F) water
2 room temperature eggs, beaten; plus
  1 egg beaten with 1 teaspoon water
5 tablespoons milk, warmed
2 teaspoons nigella seeds
2 teaspoons sesame seeds

Whisk together the flours, sugar, baking powder, and cardamom in a bowl. Add the warm oil and yeast solution and massage together with your hands until well blended. Add the 2 beaten eggs and massage with the flour. Add the warm milk. Then knead the dough, dusting lightly with flour, for about 5 minutes. Divide the dough into 6 portions and form each portion into a smooth ball. Using two baking sheets, place 3 balls on each sheet, evenly spaced. Brush the balls lightly with oil and cover with plastic wrap and let rise at room temperature for about 2 hours.

With your thumb flatten the center of each ball into a round so center is 2½ inches in diameter with ¼-inch thickness. Do not flatten the rim. Cover the cookies with a towel and let them stand for about 15 minutes. Heat the oven to 350 degrees F.

Without touching the top of the cookie's edge reshape the cookies by pushing on the inside wall of the edge so the inside is 5 inches in diameter. Then decorate the center with overlapped circles using a soda bottle cap. With the help of the same cap imprint curved lines around the outer edges of the cookies. Brush the cookies lightly with the egg wash and sprinkle with the seeds. Bake cookies for 20 to 25 minutes or until golden. Transfer the cookies onto a wire rack. Cover with kitchen towels and let cool completely.

SALTED BUTTER COOKIES

Kulché Namaki

These crumbly, salted butter cookies with a sprinkling of sesame and cara-way seeds are traditionally served with sweetened milk or tea. These cookies have a special place with savory dishes, fancy sweets, and qaimaq chai *on Afghan tables or* destarkhwans *for the Asrya feasts that take place in the late afternoon hours. Asrya is not a dinner party where rice and meat dishes are served but rather it is a fancy snacks and sweets arrangement that includes special treats (hawasana). Asrya feasts are often arranged for engagement parties.*

1½ cups all-purpose flour
1 teaspoon salt
½ teaspoon ground cardamom
1 teaspoon baking powder
½ teaspoon active dry yeast
1 egg
¼ cup plain yogurt
½ cup plus 3 tablespoons
  unsalted clarified butter
1 egg white, beaten
Sesame seeds and caraway
  seeds for garnish

Mix the flour, salt, cardamom, baking powder, and yeast in a mixing bowl. Whisk the egg in a separate bowl and add to the dry ingredients. Add the yogurt and massage it in with your hands. Add ½ cup of butter and mix well. Then add the rest of the butter and knead the dough until a homogenized, shapeable dough is obtained. Cover the dough and leave it to rise at room temperature for about 3 hours, depending on room temperature.

Preheat the oven to 375 degrees F. Divide the dough into 20 equal portions for 10 cookies. Shape the portions into balls and then roll each ball into a 6½-inch oblong. Twist two portions around each other to form a rope and bring the two ends of the rope together and lock by pinching. Repeat with remaining pieces. Place the cookies on a baking sheet lined with parchment paper, leaving spaces between them. Brush with the egg white and sprinkle with seeds. Place on the middle rack of the oven and bake for 25 minutes or until golden. Serve with *Qaimaq Chai* (page 311).

WALNUT BUTTER COOKIES

Kulché Chaharmaghzi

Makes 20 cookies

Chopped walnuts (chaharmaghz) add to the crunch of these mildly sweet butter cookies and compliment the sweet cardamom spice. "Chaharmaghz" means "four brains," referring to the shape of walnuts inside the shell. A touch of salt marries well with the addition of powdered sugar on the surface of these cookies and chopped pistachios add color and crunch.

1½ cups all-purpose flour
¼ cup sugar
1 tablespoon ground cardamom
¼ teaspoon salt
¼ cup finely chopped pistachios,
  plus ½ cup crushed pistachios
  for garnish
2 cups finely chopped walnuts
2 teaspoons rose water
6 ounces (12 tablespoons)
  unsalted butter, softened
½ cup powdered sugar

Preheat the oven to 300 degrees F. In a mixing bowl mix together the flour, sugar, cardamom, salt, finely chopped pistachios, and walnuts. Add the rose water and mix. Add the butter gradually, saving 2 teaspoons for later. Massage with hands until the mixture forms a soft, lumpy paste.

Divide the dough into 20 equal portions. Shape each portion into a ball and place on a baking sheet lined with parchment paper, leaving ½-inch space between them. Bake for 25 minutes.

Sprinkle cookies immediately with the powdered sugar and leave to cool completely. Melt the reserved 2 teaspoons of butter and dot centers of cookies with the butter and press the crushed pistachios on the butter. Transfer the cookies onto a serving plate with a flat spoon. Refrigerate for 4 hours before serving.

Carrot Fudge / *Sherini Zardak*

SWEETS

Sherini Ha

Afghan sweets comprise two main categories: commercial and homemade. *Halwaé Suhanak* (Pistachio and Walnut Brittles), *Jelabi*, and *Noqul* (Sugar-Coated Almonds) are prepared in large quantities for commercial purposes. During the school year, stalls are loaded with crisp *Halwaé Suhanak* ready to be sold to school children. Other commercial sweets are traditionally prepared for national celebrations such as Nawruz and Eid. On the eve of New Year's Day (Nawruz) men and women, with their children tagging along, shop the busy food markets for *jelabi*, mounded on the stalls of shops resembling crystal bangles, the color of gold.

The eve of Eid is another joyous occasion when even the most modest families fork out their few Afghani bills for a pound of *noqul* to sweeten their guests' mouths. Commercial *noqul* is prepared both with almonds and roasted garbanzo beans. The almond *noqul* is considerably more expensive than the bean *noqul*.

Homemade sweets vary from home to home. They are prepared by appointed experts in each extended family and represent various regions of the country. *Chukida* (Black Mulberry and Walnut Squares) come from the mulberry villages of northern Kabul. Various kinds of mulberries (*toot*) are harvested and then dried and stored for winter snacks when fruits become scarce. *Halwaé Safidak*, on the other hand, originates in the snowy high altitudes of the north, particularly Badakhshan. If consumed in warmer climates, this melt-in-your-mouth *halwa* must be kept refrigerated. *Abreshum Kabob* (Egg Thread Dessert, page 86), the indulgence of the elites, comes from the heart of the capital. The preparation of this delicious egg thread dessert is elaborate and requires practice. The delicate egg threads constituting the kabobs are referred to as the silk threads, the *abreshum*. Why it is called *kabob* is not known since *kabobs* always involve the use of meat rather than eggs.

Other colorful and tasty varieties of regional desserts such as *rasgula* and *ladu*, were originated by Hindu and Sikh Afghans. *Jelabi, shirpera* (fudge-like desserts), and *Rasmalai* (Sweet Cheese Balls) are the most common Hindu-Afghan sweets adopted by Kabul natives and other larger cities where Hindu and Sikh communities exist. *Gulab Jamun* (Rose-Scented Sweets) are another Hindu-Afghan sweet popular in the Afghan culinary world.

To Afghans, sweets are never complete without cups of plain green or black tea brewed to perfection. From village slums to the upscale neighborhoods of Kabul, tea is simply a necessity to go along with sweets.

249

BLACK MULBERRY AND WALNUT SQUARES

Chukida

Makes 16 pieces

Chukida is a sweet treat prepared with dried black mulberries (toot) and walnuts. A small number of dates are also used as a binding agent. A sprinkle of crushed pistachio and walnuts adds to the color and crunch of this sweet. "Chukida" means "pounded." After the mulberries have dried, they are placed in a mortar, together with the walnuts, to be pounded by a pestle into a shapable paste. Dried mulberries are available online in the US.

2 cups dried black mulberries, coarsely ground
  (see page 320)
1½ cups walnut halves, coarsely ground
8 Medjool jumbo dates
Chopped pistachios and walnuts to garnish

In a mixing bowl, stir together the dried mulberries and walnuts. Skin the dates and remove the seeds (for dried dates, soak the date in hot water for 10 minutes and then peel). With the help of a fork, mash the dates until smooth. Add the dates to the berries and walnuts, and massage well until smooth and well-mixed into a firm paste. Transfer the paste into a 6-by-4-inch dish and gently press to set. Using a sharp, wet knife cut the mixture into equal squares. Press a walnut and some pistachios in the center of each square. Keep refrigerated. Serve with tea or coffee.

WHITE MULBERRY AND WALNUT BALLS

Chukida Toot Safayd

Makes 20 balls

This version of Chukida uses white mulberries that have a milder flavor than black. Walnuts, dried white mulberries, and a touch of dates are pounded into a paste and then rolled into smooth balls for dessert. Whole pistachios add to the color and crunch of this sweet. During the Soviet occupation of Afghanistan, the opposing Mujahidin snacked on this filling, nutritious sweet while stationed on hard terrain and difficult-to-pass mountains after long and exhausting walks from their villages. Chukida tastes great with plain green tea.

**2 cups dried white mulberries
  (see page 320)**
1¼ cups walnut halves
1 cup jumbo Medjool dates
1 tablespoon split pistachios

Place the mulberries in a food processor and grind into a breadcrumb consistency. Transfer the ground mulberries to a mixing bowl. Pulse the walnuts coarsely in the food processor and add to the mulberries. Peel the dates and remove the seeds (for drier, hard to peel dates, soak them in hot water for about 10 minutes before removing the skin). With the help of a fork, mash the dates until smooth. Add the mashed dates to the mulberry mixture. Massage the mixture until a shapeable paste is obtained.

Transfer the paste onto a tray or cutting board and divide it into 10 equal portions. Shape each portion into a smooth ball by rolling in your palms. Decorate with the split pistachios. Refrigerate overnight before serving with coffee or plain tea. Keep covered.

SAFFRON AND ROSE-SCENTED TREATS

Gulab Jamun

Makes 8 servings

These aromatic sweets are prepared with flour, cream, and milk, saturated with saffron syrup, and served with tea. "Gulab" means "rose" in Pashtu and Dari and jamun *is a fruit berry in India.* Gulab jamun *smells like roses and resembles the* jamun *fruit—thus its name. Hindu and Sikh Afghans prepare this delicious treat during their festive holidays and share it, along with other colorful sweets, with their fellow Muslim Afghans. Today* gulab jamun *is also popular in Muslim Afghan homes.*

1½ cups sugar
¼ teaspoon powdered saffron
½ cup all-purpose flour
1 cup powdered milk
¼ teaspoon baking soda
1 teaspoon ground cardamom
½ cup heavy whipping cream
Oil for frying
1 tablespoon rose water

Dissolve the sugar and saffron in 2½ cups water in a medium saucepan. Bring to a boil over medium heat. Reduce heat to simmer.

Meanwhile, whisk together the flour, milk, baking soda, and cardamom. Gradually add the whipping cream while mixing until a soft dough is obtained. Wash and dry your hands and then oil your palms. Roll the dough into balls the size of marbles. Cover to prevent drying.

Heat 3 inches of oil in a medium-size saucepan to 250 degrees F (medium). Submerge half of the balls into the hot oil, one at a time. Stir gently with a spatula for even browning for about 5 to 7 minutes. Remove with a large slotted spoon and submerge in the simmering syrup. Repeat the procedure with the second batch of balls. Let cool. Mix in the rose water and let stand for at least 4 hours before serving.

SPICY NUT BALLS

Gur Masaladar

Makes 12 2-ounce portions

Spicy (masaladar) gur is prepared by forming brown sugar, walnuts, pistachios, and ginger into crumbly balls. Decorate these with pistachios and serve them with tea. Gur is a sweetener obtained from the juice of sugarcane, which is abundantly grown in the tropical climate of eastern Afghanistan in Nangarhar province. Tons of spicy gur are exported from the eastern districts to other parts of the country each year.

½ cup chopped walnuts
½ cup chopped pistachios
1½ teaspoons ginger powder
½ tablespoon ground cardamom
3 cups well-packed light brown
   sugar dissolved in ¾ cup water
1 tablespoon ground pistachios

Mix the walnuts and pistachios with the ginger and cardamom. In a small saucepan, boil the brown sugar solution gently, stirring occasionally to avoid overflowing. When the candy thermometer* registers 235 degrees F (softball stage), remove syrup from the heat.

Mix the walnut mixture into the syrup. Let sit until it solidifies into a soft, shapeable paste, 10 to 15 minutes depending on room temperature. Divide the paste into 12 equal portions and quickly form each into a ball. Sprinkle with pistachios. Let cool and store in an air-tight container.

If you do not have a candy thermometer use this method to test the syrup: After 7 minutes of cooking on moderate heat drop a tiny portion of syrup on a cool surface; if the syrup forms a clear ball it is ready.

PISTACHIO CANDY

Halwaé Maghzi

Makes 12 pieces

This chewy candy is prepared with sugar, egg white, and pistachios, and is usually served with tea on the side. To Afghans, halwa means a variety of sweet puddings prepared with flour, sugar, and oil, and not a chewy candy. The name may be derived from the Arabic "halu" that means "sweet." "Maghzi" means "having nuts." Almost every Afghan growing up in Afghanistan will remember this commercial candy sold at the stalls by their schools.

½ cup plus 3 tablespoons
   honey
½ cup plus 1½ tablespoons
   sugar
1 egg white, room temperature
Pinch salt
½ teaspoon rose water
2 cups whole pistachios
Cornstarch for dusting

Place the honey and sugar in a heavy saucepan. Stir over medium heat until the sugar dissolves. Simmer for 30 minutes, stirring occasionally. The mixture becomes pale and smooth. Turn the heat off while you beat the egg white.

Beat the egg white in a mixer for 2 to 3 minutes until puffy. Heat the honey again and whisk the egg white gradually into the hot honey. Simmer the mixture for about 45 minutes, stirring occasionally. The mixture should thicken, leaving grooves when stirring that last for 6 seconds.

Turn the heat off. Mix in the rose water and pistachios. The mixture should have thickened to a soft dough consistency. Transfer to an 8x12 rectangular dish lined with aluminum foil. Place another piece of foil on top and press to level. Set aside to cool.

Using a heavy kitchen knife, cut into squares. Sprinkle with cornstarch to prevent stickiness.

CHICKPEA AND CARDAMOM CANDY

Sherini Nakhodi

Makes 24 pieces

This crumbly chickpea (nakhodi) sweet is prepared with simple ingredients in less than 30 minutes. It is served with plain tea.

1½ cups powdered sugar
1¼ cups melted unsalted butter
1½ cups chickpea flour
½ teaspoon fresh ground cardamom
Ground pistachios for garnish

Using a mixer beat the powdered sugar and butter until well incorporated.

Place the flour in a pan on moderate heat and stir for 6 to 7 minutes until it smells roasted and slightly changes color. Set aside to cool.

Add the cardamom and the butter mixture gradually to the cooled roasted flour while stirring with your hands, until a soft shapeable dough is obtained. Transfer the dough quickly onto a greased pan (the thickness of the sweet and number of pieces will depend on the size of the dish used) and press with your palms to smooth the surface. Cut to desired shapes with a sharp knife. Press the pistachios on the top center of the shapes while the sweet is still warm. Cover and store for up to a week.

WHITE WALNUT HALWA

Halwaé Safidak

Makes 3 pounds

This melt-in-your-mouth flour and butter sweet is served with nan, or shaved and used as a spread on Afghan nan for breakfast. Badakhshan province, northeast of Afghanistan, is home to this delectable sweet. Halwaé Safidak is prepared in regions with harsh winters. Also known as handmade Halwaé dast, *this sweet is filling, delectable, and could last for a month.*

1¼ pounds (5 sticks) unsalted butter
3 cups all-purpose flour
2 cups powdered sugar
1 tablespoon ground cardamom
2½ cups chopped walnuts
1 tablespoon chopped pistachios

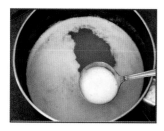

In a small saucepan, melt the butter over medium heat. Stir for about 3 minutes, removing foam from the butter surface as it forms and discarding. Transfer the clear portion to another larger non-stick pan, discarding the milky residue at the bottom of the pan.

Heat the clarified butter for 1 minute. Add the flour and stir-fry on low heat for about 7 minutes, until the flour smells toasted but does not turn color and resembles a soft dough. Remove from the heat. Mix in the powdered sugar and cardamom. Refrigerate for about 2 hours or until solidified.

Remove dough from refrigerator and leave at room temperature for about 30 minutes or until the surface layer of the *halwa* starts to peel off when scraped with a butter spreader. Continue scraping off the surface as the halwa forms into a soft, white paste.

Transfer the *halwa* to a bowl and mix, using an electric mixer on high for about 7 to 10 minutes or until white and fluffy. Add 1½ cups of the walnuts and mix.

Mix the remaining 1 cup of walnuts with the pistachios and sprinkle them in a 7-x-10-inch pan. Transfer the *halwa* into the pan on top of the pistachio and walnut mixture. Press the *halwa* gently with wet hands until set. Refrigerate to solidify for 6 hours. Unmold and cut or shave for serving.

PISTACHIO AND WALNUT BRITTLES

Halwaé Suhanak

Makes 1 pound

These brittles are prepared with roasted flour, sugar, pistachios, and walnuts. Halwaé Suhanak is available commercially in Afghanistan and sold at stalls as snacks, particularly a favorite of school children. Its texture is chewy and walnuts contribute their nutty flavor and pistachios give it color and crunch. Homemade Halwaé Suhanak *comes out tastier, richer, and more aromatic than the stall seller's.*

Pinch ground saffron
2 teaspoons ground cardamom
2 tablespoons warm water
1 cup canola oil
1 cup sugar
1 cup all-purpose flour
1 tablespoon chopped pistachios
½ cup chopped walnuts

Line a small cutting board with aluminum foil and set aside. Mix the saffron and cardamom into the warm water.

Place the canola oil in a saucepan over high heat. Add the sugar and wait until it starts to melt. Lower the heat to medium and stir with a warm spatula until it runs clear and is light brown (338 degrees F on a candy thermometer). Turn the heat to the lowest possible setting. Protecting your hands with gloves, add the flour, and stir vigorously into a creamy mixture for about 1 minute or until it smells toasted. Add the seasoned water and nuts. Stir for another 30 seconds. The mixture will separate from the oil.

With a warm slotted spoon, transfer a portion the size of an egg onto the center of the cutting board lined with aluminum foil. Flatten with the back of the spoon. Place another piece of foil on top. Using a rolling pin spread the *halwa* quickly between the foil sheets into a thin sheet. Leave between the aluminum foil to cool. Repeat the process with the rest of the *halwa* using additional foil sheets.

Peel the *halwa* off once cool. Layer the *halwa* with paper towels until serving.

SWEET CARROT BALLS

Halwaé Zardak

Makes 12 balls

This carrot (zardak) sweet is prepared when the vegetable is plentiful in the market and requires the incorporation of simple ingredients such as sugar and spices for aroma, and pistachios for crunch. This is traditionally prepared without nuts, transferred onto a plate without forming into balls, and then the nuts are sprinkled around the top. However, the balls can be served more easily as individual servings to guests.

2 pounds carrots, chopped
2 cups sugar
1 teaspoon lemon juice
2 teaspoons ground cardamom
1 tablespoon rose water
½ cup crushed pistachios
Slivered pistachios to garnish

Mince the carrots in the food processor. Mix with the sugar and let stand in a bowl for about 15 minutes until the sugar crystals are dissolved on the carrots. Place the carrots in a non-stick pot over medium heat. Add the lemon juice and mix well. Cook the carrots for about 35 to 45 minutes, stirring occasionally, until the carrots reduce in half and turn transparent and start to separate from the pot.

Add the cardamom, rose water, and crushed pistachios to the carrots. Stir well and cook for 5 minutes. Remove from the heat and set aside to cool. Once cool, divide carrot mixture into 12 equal portions and form each portion into a smooth ball. Decorate with slivered pistachios. Serve with tea.

CARROT FUDGE

Sherini Zardak   Makes 2 pounds

Carrots (zardak) are mixed with sugar and set aside to release water then cooked further in their juices until the juices evaporate completely and allow sugar crystallization to form this crumbly sweet. Sherini Zardak is decorated with pistachios and served with tea. Carrot sweets and puddings can be prepared in all seasons in Afghanistan. Carrots are cultivated for human and livestock consumption through the fall season but can also be stored for months in piles of sand for moisture preservation and protection from subzero temperatures.

2 pounds carrots, minced
2 pounds sugar
2 teaspoons ground cardamom
2 teaspoons rose water
Chopped pistachios for garnish

In a mixing bowl mix together the carrots and sugar. Leave to sit for 15 minutes. Transfer the carrots to a non-stick skillet. Cook the carrots on moderate heat for 30 minutes, stirring occasionally. The carrots are ready when they have reduce to half their volume, have turned transparent, and separate from the edge of the skillet. Add the cardamom and rose water and mix well. Transfer to a well-greased rectangular dish and press slightly to set. Cut the sweet in diamond shapes while still warm and press the pistachios on the center top of each diamond. Leave to cool completely. Serve with plain tea.

MILKY WALNUT CARDAMOM FUDGE

Shirpera Roghani

Makes 36 pieces

Sugar syrup is crystallized by the addition of powdered milk and oil into a melt-in-your-mouth sweet. Walnuts are added for flavor and crunch and cardamom and rose water make this a delectable sweet. This oil-based (roghani) shirpera is mostly prepared commercially and is available in the markets of the larger cities such as Kabul, Kandahar, Jalalabad, and Balkh. In the postwar era, markets also offer sweets adopted from neighboring countries, but sadly, the authenticity of most old products are either changed or faded away due to the war.

1½ cups sugar dissolved in 1 cup boiling water
½ cup cooking oil
1½ cups chopped walnuts
1 tablespoon ground cardamom
1 teaspoon rose water
1½ cups powdered milk
1 tablespoon ground pistachios

Grease well an 11-by-9-inch pan and set aside. In a 6-quart pot, boil the sugar solution on medium heat for about 8 minutes. Then test the consistency by dripping a tiny portion of the syrup over a cool saucer every 20 seconds or so until the drop doesn't run and forms a clear solid ball (235 degrees F on a candy thermometer, softball stage). Add the oil to the syrup. Stir and wait for a re-boil. Turn the heat off but leave the pan on the burner.

Add the walnuts, cardamom, and rose water to the syrup. Gradually sprinkle in the powdered milk while stirring until the mixture achieves a soft, sticky consistency that slowly spreads. Transfer the mixture quickly to the greased pan and press evenly across the pan with lightly greased palms as the mixture transforms into a soft paste. With the help of a sharp greased knife first cut strips 1 inch apart. Then cut each strip diagonally to make diamonds. Garnish with pistachios.

Note: To make larger quantities, this recipe must be repeated rather than doubled.

NUTTY FRESH MILK FUDGE

Shirpera Shir Taza

Makes 1 pound 4 ounces

Fresh milk (shir taza) and sugar are boiled together to a fudge-like consistency and set aside to cool in a pan, as it sets and gets ready to be cut into diamond shapes. This sweet may be more readily available in farmhouses and suburbs where Afghans have access to fresh milk. This shirpera is a versatile sweet served with tea for guests and all festive and celebratory events such as Eid, weddings, graduations, childbirth, etc. Shirpera Shir Taza is loved by Afghans throughout the country.

⅓ cup mixture of coarsely
   chopped walnuts and
   pistachios
2 cups sugar
4 cups regular whole milk
1 tablespoon ground
   cardamom

Sprinkle the nuts in a 9-by-7-inch pan and set aside.

In a heavy 6-quart pot, dissolve the sugar in the milk and bring to a gentle boil. Reduce heat and simmer for about 60 minutes stirring occasionally with a flat-ended wooden spatula as it thickens to pea soup consistency.

Add the cardamom and stir to mix. Begin stirring constantly once the milk reaches yogurt consistency. When the milk starts to thicken to fudge, test by dropping a portion the size of a pencil eraser into a glass of cool water. If it solidifies in about 10 seconds into a shapeable paste, it is ready (firm ball stage on a candy thermometer, 242 degrees F).

Pour the hot fudge into the prepared pan and gently spread across. Insert a sharp knife into the fudge. If it leaves a clean solid cut, divide it into squares or diamond shapes. If the fudge is too soft for cutting, wait longer.

Note: To make larger quantities, this recipe must be repeated rather than doubled.

MILKY FUDGE WITH WALNUTS AND PISTACHIOS

Shirpera Pista   Makes 20 pieces

Sugar syrup is crystallized into a crumbly sweet by the addition of pow-dered milk. This pistachio milk sweet is prepared with walnuts for the crunch. Ground cardamom and rose water are added for aroma. Shirpera Pista, a sweet for all occasions, is usually served with tea.

3 cups sugar
2 tablespoons ground
   cardamom
1 tablespoon rose water
2 cups coarsely chopped
   walnuts
4 cups Nido dry milk
   powder
½ cup coarsely chopped
   pistachios

Grease well a springform pan and set aside.

Bring 2 cups water to a rolling boil. Add the sugar and stir to dissolve. Boil on medium heat for about 10 minutes. The syrup is ready when a tiny portion forms a clear ball when dropped on a cool saucer. Turn the heat off and add the cardamom and rose water to the hot syrup. Mix the chopped walnuts with the dry milk powder and gradually add to the syrup while stirring to mix until a soft paste is obtained—you may not use up all the milk powder.

Transfer the mixture into the well-greased springform pan and press with hands until even (the size of the pan will determine the thickness of the sweet). Sprinkle the ground pistachios on top of the *shirpera* and then press onto the warm paste.

Perform a cut test by inserting a sharp, wet knife into the hot fudge—it must come out clean, leaving a solid, clean-cut. If the fudge is still soft, wait for up to an hour for it to solidify before cutting. Release the side clamp of the springform and remove the band. Cut the shirpera into diamond shapes. Serve with plain tea.

SWEET CHEESE BALLS

Rasmalai

Makes 12 servings

In this dessert, cheese is produced by boiling milk with lemon juice. Then the cheese balls are boiled in sugar syrup and dipped in evaporated milk. Hindu and Sikh Afghans traditionally prepare this delicious treat during their festive holidays and share it, along with other colorful sweets such as ladoo, barfi, *and* rasgulla *with their fellow Muslim Afghans. Today,* rasmalai *is also loved by Muslim Afghans who have learned this delectable recipe and now prepare it for their own families.*

For the cheese:
4 cups whole milk
Juice of one lemon
2 cups sugar dissolved in
 3 cups water
Cheesecloth

Bring the 4 cups of milk to a boil. Add the lemon juice and stir. The curd (lumpy milk) will separate from the whey (water). Drain on a cheesecloth in a strainer and rinse lightly with chilled water to avoid firming. Gather together the 4 corners of the cloth and squeeze out any extra water by squeezing the cheese. Transfer the cheese onto a large plate and knead for about 3 to 4 minutes or until smooth and flexible.

Divide the cheese into 12 portions and roll between your palms into smooth balls. Then flatten the balls slightly. Bring the sugar solution to a boil in a large pot. Add the cheese balls and boil, covered, on high heat for about 5 minutes until the cheese balls double in size. Lower heat and simmer for an additional 15 minutes. Remove from heat and allow to cool in the sugar water.

For the milk syrup:
4 cups whole milk
¼ cup sugar
1 tablespoon chopped
 pistachios
1 teaspoon ground
 cardamom
2 teaspoons rose water

Boil the milk until it is reduced to less than half its volume, about 1¾ cups, about 25 minutes on medium-high heat. Mix in the sugar. Add the pistachios, cardamom, and rose water. Stir well. Squeeze out extra syrup from each cheese ball by pressing gently between forefinger and thumb and add to the prepared milk one at a time. Chill before serving.

SWEET CARDAMOM BREADCRUMBS

Maleeda

Makes 1½ pounds

This breadcrumb ceremonial sweet with the incorporation of butter, cardamom, and sugar is served at weddings along with the wedding cake at the end of the ceremony. It is an ancient custom, equivalent to serving a cake at weddings. "Maleeda" means "massaged." Before a wedding, members of the bride's side of the family massage crumbly pieces of bread into breadcrumb consistency, which will then be mixed with sugar, butter, and ground cardamom for the wedding. Food processors have made the preparation of this ancient sweet much simpler.

1½ cups all-purpose flour
1½ cups whole wheat flour
2 teaspoons baking powder
¼ cup unsalted butter, melted, or extra virgin olive oil
1 cup warm water
1 cup clarified butter or oil of your choice
2 tablespoons ground cardamom
1½ cups sugar

Preheat the oven to 375 degrees F. In a mixing bowl, whisk together the flours and baking powder. Add the ¼ cup melted butter or oil and mix. Add the warm water gradually and knead into a smooth dough. Shape the dough into a ball and cover to rest for 15 minutes.

After it has rested, shape the dough into a disk 9-inches in diameter. Place on a cookie sheet. Bake for about 25 to 30 minutes or until it has risen and starts to turn color. Remove from oven and cover with a kitchen towel immediately and let cool. Once cool, break the bread into chunks. Place in a food process and process into fine breadcrumbs.

Gradually massage ½ cup of the clarified butter or oil into the breadcrumbs. Sprinkle the cardamom and sugar onto the breadcrumbs and mix well. Squeeze a handful of the *maleeda* in the palm of your hand. If it does not feel moist, fluffy, and clump when squeezed, add more of the remaining ½ cup butter until right consistency is achieved. Mound the *maleeda* in a decorative dish. Serve with tea and cake.

FRIED DOUGH SPIRALS WITH CARDAMOM SYRUP

Jelabi   Makes 12 *jelabi*

These spirals of fried fermented dough saturated with aromatic syrup are usually served with tea. Jelabi, loved by most Afghans, were adopted from the Hindu and Sikh Afghan communities in larger cities of Afghanistan. Jelabi are a festive sweet for the Hindu and Sikh Afghans. Muslim Afghans celebrate the Afghan New Year (Nawruz) by consuming tons of fish and jelabi that are sold by the same vendors for that special day.

For the cardamom syrup:
1½ cups sugar
½ tablespoon lemon juice
10 cardamom pods
1 teaspoon rose water

Boil the sugar, lemon, and cardamom pods in 1 cup of water on medium heat until the candy thermometer reads just below 224 degrees F (syrup stage). Mix in the rose water and when the candy thermometer reaches 224 degrees F remove from heat. Keep syrup lukewarm.

For the jelabi:
1 cup all-purpose flour
3 drops yellow food coloring
  (optional)
¾ cup warm water (130
  degrees F)
½ teaspoon active dry yeast
  dissolved in ¼ cup warm
  water (105 degrees F)
Oil for frying

Mix the flour, food coloring, and ¾ cup warm water in a non-reactive bowl. Pour the dissolved yeast over the batter. Mix, cover with plastic wrap, and let stand at room temperature until frothy.

Heat 2 inches of oil in a frying pan to 260 degrees F (medium). Pour the batter into a bottle with an applicator nozzle or small opening. Test the oil by dripping a tiny amount of the batter in it. If it sizzles and floats to the top the oil is ready (high temperatures will result in breaking the *jelabi* strands into pieces and low temperatures will cause the *jelabi* to flatten).

Make the first *jelabi* by squeezing the bottle above the hot oil starting at the center and making a spiral of batter the size of a saucer. Cross two straight lines of batter over the spiral to lock the rings. The spiral will bubble in a few seconds. Form as many spirals as the pan can hold. With the help of a fork turn the *jelabi* when they become crispy and start to change color. Fry the other side. Remove from oil and submerge in the prepared syrup. Let stand in the syrup for about 30 seconds or until transparent. Transfer onto a serving platter. Continue making other spirals. Serve with plain tea.

Fried Dough Spirals with Cardamom Syrup / *Jelabi*

GLAZED ALMONDS

Khastè Sherin

Roasted almonds are glazed with melted sugar and sprinkled with cardamom powder. "Khastè sherin," which means "sweet nuts," are prepared in minutes with only three ingredients: almonds, sugar, and cardamom. This sweet is traditionally served with other sweets such as Sugar-Coated Almonds (Noqul; next page) on Eid celebration days.

¼ cup sugar
1 cup whole almonds
1 tablespoon ground cardamom

Pre-heat oven to 375 degrees F. Place the sugar in a non-stick medium-size pan and set aside on a burner without turning the burner on.

Spread the almonds in a single layer on a baking sheet and place on the middle rack of the preheated oven.

After the almonds have roasted for about 3 minutes, start heating the sugar on high heat without stirring. When the sugar starts to turn clear, remove almonds from the oven. Wait for a few seconds until sugar is all melted but has not changed color. Slide the roasted almonds gently into the melted sugar and stir quickly with a warm spatula to coat all almonds with the sugar syrup. Transfer immediately onto an aluminum sheet and spread quickly with the same warm spatula.

Sprinkle cardamom over the top of the roasted almonds while they are still warm. Let sit for about 5 minutes before eating until almonds are cool and crisp. To store, let almonds completely cool off for about 30 minutes and then store in a jar at room temperature. Do not refrigerate.

SUGAR-COATED ALMONDS

Noqul   Makes 1 cup

Sugar-coated crunchy almonds are prepared with sugar syrup and roasted almonds with the addition of rose water and cardamom. The best noqul *is prepared commercially for festive occasions such as Eid, weddings, or engagements since the laborious and long process of coating the almonds with multiple layers of sugar in large quantities require the involvement of more than one person for the preparation process.* Noqul *are also sometimes prepared with roasted chickpeas and called* Noqul Nakhudi.

1 cup almonds
1 cup sugar
½ cup warm water
1 teaspoon cardamom pods
1 teaspoon rose water

Preheat the oven to 350 degrees F. Spread the almonds in a single layer onto a small ovenproof tray and place them on the middle rack of the oven. Roast for about 5 to 6 minutes.

Meanwhile, in a small pot dissolve the sugar in the warm water and place it over medium heat. Bring to a boil. Add the cardamom pods and rose water and then boil for 1 to 2 minutes. Test the syrup by dripping one drop on a cool saucer. If it doesn't run and forms a little ball the syrup is ready. Keep warm.

After the almonds have been roasted, place in a deep preheated saucepan. Drizzle 1 teaspoon of the prepared hot syrup on the roasted almonds and shake the pan vigorously for about 20 to 30 seconds until the almonds are coated with the syrup. Repeat the above procedure until all the syrup has been used and the almonds are coated thoroughly.

Let the *noqul* cool completely until they whiten. Serve with plain tea.

Fruit and Nut Compote / *Haft Mewa*

The Best of Afghan Cooking

FRUIT AND NUT COMPOTE

Haft Mewa

This special dried fruit and nut compote is served on lunar New Year's Day to celebrate the arrival of Nawruz, which means "new day" and falls on the spring equinox. The best quality dried fruits and nuts are offered in the Afghan markets for this ancient treat. Haft Mewa, *which means seven fruits, is served on the morning of Nawruz followed by a special festive lunch or dinner consisting of a spinach dish, chalow rice, chicken, and fish. The celebratory meal is followed by* Jelabi *(Fried Dough Spirals with Cardamom Syrup, page 266).*

1 cup munuqa (or black raisins)
½ cup keshta (or dried apricots)
1 cup black raisins
1 cup green raisins
1 cup gholeng (or dried apricots)
3 quarts (12 cups) boiling water
1 cup walnut quarters
1 cup whole almonds
1 cup whole pistachios plus ¼ cup slivered
 pistachios
½ cup senjid (dried lotus tree fruit; see
 page 320)

Soak the munuqa, apricots, black and green raisins, and gholeng in warm water for about 10 minutes. Drain and rinse. Then place in the boiling water, cover and let stand overnight. Meanwhile, in a separate bowl soak the walnuts, almonds, and pistachios overnight in cool water.

Peel the pistachios and almonds. Remove the walnut skins with tweezers. Rinse the nuts and add to the soaked fruits. Add the slivered pistachios and senjid. Stir well and serve. Store any leftovers in jars and refrigerate them for up to a week.

Yellow Rice Pudding / *Shoulé Zard/Sherin*

Note: *Traditionally the garnish on a great number of milk puddings consists of a light sprinkle of ground pistachios. This book attempts to adopt more creative ways of decorating puddings. The use of fruits, such as raspberries and strawberries, and other nuts in this book for decorating puddings is unconventional and aims at adding color and beauty to the respective dishes.*

PUDDINGS

Halwa & Firni

Afghan puddings are classified into milk puddings, cereal puddings, flour puddings, and simple water puddings. Traditionally organic milk is the basic component of most Afghan puddings. Among the types of milk desserts, *firni* and *quimaq* are the most popular ones, designed to serve multiple objectives. Because of their mild flavor and soft texture, *firni* and *quimaq* are prepared to pamper those stuck in bed due to an illness. They are also fed to infants during the transitional stage from milk to more solid food. Mostly, these cardamom-flavored milk desserts are prepared to bring beauty and elegance to buffet tables on grand occasions. Milk is also incorporated into rice to create a variety of rice desserts like *Daygcha* (Rice Pudding) and *Shoule Zard* (Yellow Rice Pudding).

Flour-based puddings (*halwas*) are prepared with flour, sugar, oil, and water. Cardamom and rose water add to the aroma. These puddings take minutes to prepare and then are ready to achieve various objectives. *Halwa* fulfills a religious rite to bless the souls of the dead. It is offered to a newlywed couple to receive blessings, and to a survivor of injury or illness to acknowledge thanksgiving. In Afghanistan, the ancient tradition of "The Night of the Dead" is observed when millions of *halwa* bowls are given away to the poor and exchanged between neighbors to receive blessing from the souls of the dead. Afghans believe that when preparing for a celebratory holiday such as the Eid celebration, the souls of the dead will watch them closely to see if they are remembered as well. Other times these delectable puddings make a scrumptious dessert served with tea. One type in particular, *Samanak*, is a more complex flour pudding prepared with flour cooked in the juices of wheat sprouts through an elaborate process.

Cereals are converted into a healthy and nutritious pudding for wintertime breakfasts called *haleem*. *Haleem*, prepared with cream of wheat and lamb, is usually made commercially in large quantities. Vendors prepare traditional *haleem* the night before and then carry the heavy pots of steaming cereal to their stalls in the overcast mornings of the cold seasons. Today's food processors and domestic ovens have made the preparation of this delicious and unique morning treat more feasible in the home. A touch of sugar, butter, and cinnamon makes the delicious treat enticing to the senses.

CREAMY PUDDING WITH ALMONDS

Firni

Firni is a creamy milk and almond pudding served for all occasions. Firni is also prepared for babies at the beginning of a transitional stage of going from milk to more solid food. Cornstarch is used as a binding agent for this pudding. Rice flour is used as the binding agent in another version of this recipe (next page). Rosewater and cardamom are added to the firni for aroma. Seasonal fruits and chopped nuts can be used for decoration.

¾ cup cornstarch
8½ cups whole milk
2 cups sugar
2 teaspoons ground
    cardamom
¾ cup slivered almonds
2 tablespoons rose water
    (optional)
6 medium-size strawberries,
    halved
1 tablespoon ground pistachios

Dissolve the cornstarch in 1 cup of milk. Set aside. Bring the remaining milk to a boil in a saucepan. Pour the cornstarch solution in a narrow stream into the boiling milk while stirring vigorously. Continue to stir for about 5 minutes on medium heat until the mixture is smooth and creamy.

Add the sugar and stir until dissolved. Add the cardamom, slivered almonds, and rose water. Stir well for a few more minutes until a thick creamy mixture with a pea soup consistency is obtained. Set aside to cool for about 15 minutes.

Once cool, transfer the pudding to a serving dish and let chill for about 4 to 5 hours. Decorate with the split strawberries and ground pistachios.

CREAMY RICE PUDDING

Firni Berenji

This firni *is prepared with short-grain rice flour (berenj), whole milk, and cream. Slivered almonds are added for a crunchy texture. Rose water and cardamom contribute to the aroma. Unlike regular* firni *(previous page) that requires the incorporation of cornstarch as a binding agent, the rice starch is sufficient to thicken this creamy pudding. Nuts and fruits of the season look beautiful as decoration. Firni Berenji is served on all occasions in Afghanistan and is also fed to babies in their transitional stage of switching to more solid food.*

¾ **cup rice flour**
7 cups whole milk
1½ cups sugar
1 cup half & half
2 teaspoons ground cardamom
¾ **cup slivered almonds**
1 tablespoon rose water
  (optional)
1 tablespoon ground pistachios
9 fresh raspberries
Powdered sugar

Dissolve the rice flour in the milk in a saucepan and place it over low heat. Stir for about 7 minutes until it bubbles and thickens to a creamy mixture. Add the sugar and half & half. Cook the pudding for another 5 minutes while stirring constantly. Add the cardamom, almonds, and rose water. Stir well and cook for about 5 more minutes.

Let the pudding cool for about 10 minutes. Transfer to a decorative dish and let the pudding cool in the refrigerator for 1 hour. Decorate with the ground pistachio and the raspberries. Sprinkle with powdered sugar before serving.

RICE PUDDING

Daygcha

This rice pudding is prepared with milk, sugar, butter, and cream. The incorporation of rose water makes this rice pudding luxurious. Short-grain rice with a sticky consistency is used for this dessert. For the first half of the cooking, the rice is cooked only with water and butter to prevent sticking to the bottom of the pot. The sugar, milk, and cream are added in the second phase of cooking. Daygcha is traditionally prepared for Nazer, making a resolution to God for certain fulfillments. Other times, it is prepared for guests as a dessert after a meal.

1½ cups short-grain rice
½ cup unsalted butter
1 cup heavy whipping cream
4 cups fresh whole milk
1¼ cups sugar
½ tablespoon rose water
  (optional)
2 tablespoons pistachios

Rinse any extra starch from the rice and let soak overnight.

Drain the rice in a colander and place in a 6-quart pot. Add the butter and 6 cups of water. Bring to a gentle boil on low heat. Cover with a lid with a vent hole to prevent overflowing. Cook the rice for about 20 to 25 minutes, until the rice grains are tender and the mixture has thickened.

Add the cream, milk, and sugar. Mix well. Bring to a boil and then lower heat and simmer, covered, for a further 20 to 25 minutes, stirring occasionally. The pudding is ready when the liquid milk evaporates from the surface of the rice and it turns thick and creamy, and the rice starts to separate from the sides of the pot.

Mix in the rose water. Let the *daygcha* cool for about 10 minutes and then refrigerate for at least 4 hours or until completely cold. Decorate with the pistachios. Serve with hot plain tea.

YELLOW RICE PUDDING

Shoulé Sherin/Zard

Makes 8 servings

This pudding is prepared with rice, sugar, oil, and water. Saffron adds color to the pudding and cardamom and rosewater add aroma. Short-grain rice with a sticky outcome is used for this dessert. For the first half of the cooking, the rice is cooked only with water and salt to prevent sticking to the bottom of the pot. The sugar and other ingredients are added in the second phase of cooking. Shoulé Sherin/Zard (sweet/yellow shoula) is traditionally prepared for Nazer, making a resolution to God for certain fulfillments. Tons of shoula are prepared ahead of time in the neighborhoods to be given away on the tenth of Muharram, a Memorial Day for Prophet Mohammad's martyred family.

2 cups short-grain rice,
  presoaked for 4 hours
12 cups boiling water
¼ teaspoon salt
¼ cup oil
2 cups sugar
¼ teaspoon powdered saffron
2 teaspoons ground cardamom
2 tablespoons rose water
  (optional)
Split almonds and ground
  pistachios for garnish

Drain the rice and add to 10 cups of boiling water with the salt and simmer on low heat for about 45 minutes.

Add the oil, sugar, saffron, and cardamom, and 2 more cups of boiling water. Mix well. Continue to cook for 30 more minutes or until the mixture thickens to honey consistency. Add the rose water and mix.

Remove from heat. Then let the pudding cool for about 10 minutes. Transfer to a bowl or platter and set aside to cool completely. Decorate with the nuts. Serve as dessert with plain tea. Refrigerate or store at room temperature for up to two days.

Fenugreek Rice Pudding / *Shoulé Hulba*

The Best of Afghan Cooking

FENUGREEK RICE PUDDING

Shoulé Hulba

Makes 4 to 6 servings

Short-grain rice is used to prepare a variety of sweet dishes in Afghanistan, most of which are prepared with milk. This pudding is perhaps the only sweet shoula *that is cooked with fenugreek seeds (*hulba*). Afghans love this dessert after returning from the public bathing place, the* hamam, *due to its soothing effects. This dessert is also prepared for breastfeeding mothers to increase milk production.*

1½ cups short-grain rice
¼ cup fenugreek seeds
½ cup olive oil
1½ cups brown sugar
¼ teaspoon powdered saffron
Walnuts and pistachios to garnish

Wash and soak the rice for 30 minutes. Boil the fenugreek seeds for 2 to 3 minutes in 1½ cups of water. Drain and dry by pressing between two paper towels. Drain the rice and set it aside.

Place the oil over medium heat in a 6-quart non-stick pot. Fry the fenugreek seeds for about 2 to 3 minutes or until golden. Add the rice and stir-fry for 1 minute until the liquid is absorbed. Add 6 cups of water. Stir and then cover and cook on low heat for 30 minutes or until the water is absorbed and the rice is tender.

Add the brown sugar and saffron and stir well to mix. Cover the pot with a cloth towel and secure it with a lid and fold the towel ends on top of the lid. Steam for 15 minutes on the lowest heat.

Transfer the pudding to a well-greased 8-inch round mold. Let stand at room temperature for about 20 minutes. Unmold on a larger plate and decorate with walnuts and pistachios. Serve warm or cold.

CREAMY FLOUR PUDDING

Quimaq

Makes 4 servings

Quimaq *is a pudding prepared with milk and flour. Green cardamom gives* quimaq *its aroma. Afghans love this creamy dessert in winter. This versatile pudding serves multiple purposes. It is fed to infants at the transitional stage to more solid food. New mothers enjoy a bowl by their bedside as a soothing remedy for stomach cramps and inflammations after childbirth. It also adds beauty and color to dinner tables or* destarkhwans.

¼ **cup all-purpose flour**
1 cup cool water
4 cups whole milk
1 teaspoon ground green cardamom
½ **cup sugar**
1 tablespoon butter
Chopped walnuts and ground pistachios to garnish

Whisk the flour in the cool water in a small mixing bowl. In a saucepan bring the milk to a boiling point. Whisk the flour batter into the hot milk in a narrow stream, and vigorously whisk for about 1 minute. Add the cardamom and sugar. Whisk until the sugar is dissolved and the cardamom is mixed well into the milk. Add the butter and continue to stir for about 15 minutes on medium-low heat until the mixture is thickened to pea soup consistency. Transfer the pudding to a serving bowl and let cool for about 15 minutes. Decorate with the nuts and let cool completely in refrigerator.

SWEET WHEAT PUDDING

Halwa Ardi

Makes 8 servings

Of the many forms that halwa *takes, this is considered the most traditional one. This* halwa *is prepared with wheat flour, stir-fried in oil, and steamed after water is added.* Halwa *is traditionally served on a piece of bread at funerals to receive a blessing for the soul of the dead. This* halwa *is also prepared for the bride's arrival in the groom's house to receive blessings for the newlyweds.*

2 cups dark brown sugar
1 tablespoon ground
  cardamom
4 cups boiling water
1 cup oil
2 cups whole wheat flour
¼ cup rose water
2 tablespoons chopped
  walnuts
2 tablespoons chopped
  pistachios

Dissolve the brown sugar and cardamom in the boiling water.

In a saucepan, heat the oil over medium-high heat for about 2 to 3 minutes. Add the flour gradually and stir-fry for about 5 minutes until the flour smells toasted (lower heat if the flour turns brown too quickly). Protecting your hands from splatter with gloves, pour the prepared brown sugar syrup over the frying flour. Stir vigorously until a thick creamy shiny mixture is obtained, then keep stirring the *halwa* until it starts separating from the side and base of the pot.

Remove the cooked pudding from heat and mix in the rose water. Divide into 8 small plastic molds, 4 inches in diameter. Press tightly to close any cracks or air bubbles. Un-mold the *halwa* while still warm onto saucers. Decorate with walnuts and pistachios. Store covered in refrigerator.

VELVETY WHEAT PUDDING

Kachi   Makes 4 to 6 servings

This soft, velvety pudding is popular in winter in most provinces of Afghanistan, particularly the southeast regions. Kachi is prepared through prolonged, slow cooking of all-purpose wheat flour in water and salt to produce a rich, creamy pudding that is then sprinkled with white or brown sugar and dipped in melted butter or ghee. Sandali, a heating system of a covered table, is the favorite spot for consuming this steaming hot pudding on a snowy day. Being rich in calories, this dish is also served as a main course in certain areas.

**2 tablespoons sugar plus
  ½ cup sugar
2 cups all-purpose flour
4 cups cool water
4 cups boiling water
¼ teaspoon salt
2 tablespoons oil
½ cup melted butter or oil
Walnut halves**

Place the 2 tablespoons sugar in a saucepan over medium heat and wait until the sugar bubbles and caramelizes to a rich brown color. Add ½ cup water to the sugar and stir to mix. Set aside.

In a bowl, whisk the flour gradually into the 4 cups of cool water until creamy and smooth with a honey consistency. Transfer the flour mixture to a medium-size non-stick pot and start the heat on low. Add the caramelized sugar to the flour mixture and stir to mix. Add the boiling water and stir. Add the salt and the 2 tablespoons of oil. While stirring, if the mixture forms a lump at the bottom too soon, the heat must be reduced. Keep stirring until the mixture starts to achieve a honey consistency, about 20 minutes. Once it is a honey consistency, reduce the heat to the lowest point and keep stirring for about 10 to 15 more minutes until the *kachi* leaves tracks at the bottom but quickly covers them over. At this point, cover the pot with a towel and steam the *kachi* for about 10 minutes.

Transfer the hot *kachi* onto a serving plate in a dome shape. Heat the butter or oil and pour in a small bowl. Press the butter/oil bowl into the center of the *kachi*. Decorate with a sprinkle of sugar and nuts. Serve warm using butter as a dip.

RICE AND SEMOLINA PUDDING

Halwaé Berenji

Makes 12 servings

This grainy halwa *is prepared with a combination of rice flour and semolina which are stir-fried and steamed with the addition of water. Pistachios and walnuts add to the crunch and beauty of this fancy dessert. Cardamom and rose water make the* halwa *aromatic and luxurious. This* halwa *is traditionally prepared on Eids and during Ramadan. Most* halwa *desserts are equally popular in different areas of the country.*

1¼ cups sugar
3 cups boiling water
½ cup oil
¾ cup rice flour
¼ cup semolina
1 tablespoon ground cardamom
1 tablespoon rose water
Chopped pistachios and walnuts for
  garnish

Dissolve the sugar in the boiling water.

In a pot, heat the oil until hot. Add the rice flour and semolina. Stir-fry on medium-high heat for about 3 to 4 minutes or until the flour smells toasted and is light beige. Add the prepared sugar water gradually while stirring. Stir for about 5 minutes until it has thickened to a fudge consistency and separates from the side of the pot. Add the cardamom and rose water and mix. Simmer the *halwa*, covered, on low heat for about 10 minutes.

Transfer to a mixing bowl and let cool enough to be handled, about 5 to 10 minutes. Place the *halwa* in a mold 7 inches in diameter. Press well to close any gaps or bubbles. Then unmold onto a serving dish and decorate with the walnut and pistachios. Store the *halwa* covered and refrigerate or leave at room temperature.

SEMOLINA PUDDING 1

Halwaé Suji 1

Makes 4 servings

This pudding is prepared by stir-frying semolina (suji) in oil and steaming it with the addition of water and sugar. Cardamom and rose water add aroma, and nuts are added for crunch and beauty. Compared to flour halwa *with its soft and smooth texture, this pudding is grainier and shinier due to a lack of oil absorbency.* Halwa Suji *is prepared as a dessert for the family to enjoy and is typically not given away to the poor at funerals to receive blessings as other* halwas *are.*

1 cup sugar
3 cups boiling water
½ cup oil
1 cup semolina
1 tablespoon ground
  cardamom
¼ cup sliced almonds
1 tablespoon rose water
  (optional)
¼ cup slivered pistachios

Dissolve the sugar in the boiling water.

Heat the oil in a pot on high heat for about 3 to 4 minutes. Add the semolina and stir-fry for about 2 minutes until it smells toasted. Add the sugar water while stirring with a wooden spatula. Add the cardamom and almonds as the *halwa* thickens to pea soup consistency. Stir for a further 5 minutes or until the *halwa* has thickened and starts to separate from the side of the pot. Reduce heat to the lowest point. Cover the pot with several paper towels and secure them with the lid. Steam the *halwa* for 10 minutes.

Mix in the rose water. Then press the hot *halwa* into the desired plastic mold and let stand for about 5 minutes.

To un-mold, place a flat tray on top of the *halwa* mold and gently turn it upside down. Decorate with the pistachios by pressing around the top of the *halwa* while it is still warm. Serve immediately.

Note: To store the *halwa*, let cool completely and then cover to prevent drying. Re-heat the *halwa* before serving (using a microwave is suitable), or serve cool with plain tea and bread.

SEMOLINA PUDDING 2

Halwaé Suji 2

Makes 4 to 6 servings

This pudding is prepared with semolina (suji) by dry-roasting the cereal in the pan first and then mixing it with a prepared syrup and steaming it. Carda-mom adds aroma and nuts are added for crunch and beauty. This halwa *is prepared with less oil than* Halwaé Suji 1 *(opposite page) due to the dry-roast-ing.* Halwaé Suji *is prepared as a dessert, specifically in the fasting month of Ramadan.*

¾ cup sugar
1½ cups boiling water
¼ teaspoon powdered
  saffron
½ teaspoon ground
  cardamom
½ cup semolina
¼ cup melted butter or
  oil or a combination of
  both
1 tablespoon split
  pistachios
1 tablespoon sliced
  almonds

Dissolve the sugar in the boiling water. Add the saffron powder and cardamom and set aside for about 20 minutes.

Place a saucepan on medium heat. Pour the semolina into the pan and dry-roast, stirring constantly for about 10 minutes or until it smells roasted and the color changes slightly to light beige. Add the butter or oil and stir-fry for 1 minute. Add the prepared sugar water to the roasted semolina and keep stirring for about 10 minutes, until most of the liquid is absorbed and evaporated and the *halwa* is dry and lumpy.

Cover tightly and steam for about 10 minutes on the lowest heat. Transfer to a decorative plate and decorate with the nuts.

TRADITIONAL LAMB AND WHEAT PORRIDGE

Haleem (Traditional)

Makes 12 servings

"Haleem" *means "enduring." The preparation of this ancient porridge that is served for breakfast was time-consuming and painstaking in the absence of modern kitchen utensils. So the porridge was prepared through endurance and patience. In its country of origin, Iraq,* haleem *is called* harrisa. *Through invasions and occupations of the Middle Eastern and Central Asian countries,* harrisa *became popular in those countries and transformed into several variations in India, Iran, Nepal, Pakistan, and Afghanistan. The Afghan version of this porridge is prepared with wheat and lamb through a long cooking process.*

1½ pounds pelted wheat,
  soaked overnight
1 pound lamb shank pieces
1 cup heavy whipping cream
¼ cup melted butter
Sugar to taste
1 teaspoon ground cardamom
1 teaspoon ground cinnamon

The night before: Put the pelted wheat in water to soak. Cook the lamb shanks on low heat in 6 cups of water, covered, for about 2 hours or until the meat is tender and about to fall off the bone. Refrigerate overnight.

In the morning: Cook the soaked wheat in water 5 inches above the wheat's level on low heat for about 1½ hours, until the wheat grain is tender and the water has evaporated.

Remove the animal fat that has solidified on the surface of the lamb and discard. Shred the meat and set aside, reserving the lamb juices separately.

Grind the cooked wheat with the lamb juices in a food processor in batches until smooth. Filter the mixture through a sieve and rub the coarse wheat coat against the sieve to extract all the wheat cream. Place the wheat cream mixture in a saucepan. Stir in the shredded lamb and the heavy cream and place over low heat. Cook for about 10 minutes.

Transfer the *haleem* to a serving dish. Spoon the melted butter on top of the porridge in a swirl shape. Sprinkle with sugar and then the cardamom and cinnamon. Serve warm for breakfast.

INSTANT CHICKEN AND WHEAT PORRIDGE

Haleem (Instant)

Makes 6 servings

Haleem is filling and mostly consumed as a cold-weather treat for breakfast. This porridge is prepared with cooked chicken and Cream of Wheat®. Compared to the traditional Haleem (opposite page) with the time-consuming labor of extracting the wheat cream, this porridge takes minutes to prepare. This healthful meal is prepared both commercially and domestically in Afghanistan.

2 each chicken thighs and drumsticks, skinned and fat removed
1 cup heavy whipping cream
1½ cups Cream of Wheat®
¼ cup melted butter
½ cup sugar
1 teaspoon ground cinnamon
1 teaspoon ground cardamom

Cook the chicken in 5 cups of water on low heat, covered, until it is falling off the bone. Remove the chicken pieces, reserving the juices, and remove the bones and cut the meat into 1-inch pieces. Measure the juices to 4 cups and return to pot.

Shred the chicken pieces further with your hands and return to the measured juices. Add the whipping cream. Bring the cream mixture to a boil. Gradually add the Cream of Wheat while stirring with a whisk for about 5 minutes or until thickened. Simmer for a further 5 minutes. Stir well.

Transfer the *haleem* to a serving dish. Spoon the melted butter on top in a swirl shape. Sprinkle the sugar, then the cinnamon and cardamom evenly around the top of the pudding. Serve warm for breakfast.

ANCIENT WHEAT JUICE PUDDING

Samanak

Makes 12 servings

Samanak is an ancient pudding prepared with flour and the juices of wheat sprouts through a prolonged cooking and steaming process. Samanak has a natural sweetness and extraordinary flavor and is prepared before Nawruz (the Afghan New Year). Wheat is grown in large containers in Afghanistan just so that the sprouts and roots can be used for this pudding. The samanak is then prepared in large quantities in extremely large steaming pots on fires made in backyard gardens. Among a huge gathering of friends and relatives, each takes turns in stirring the samanak. Guests and hosts dance and sing the night away until the samanak is finally ready the following morning. However, samanak prepared in smaller quantities takes a considerably shorter time (about 4 to 6 hours) but it usually takes 2 to 3 people to constantly stir the pudding in the final hours to prevent it from sticking to the bottom of the pot.

7 quarts (28 cups) wheat sprout juices *(see sidebar next page)*
3 pounds whole wheat flour *(for grainy results)***, or all-purpose flour** *(for smoother and lighter-color results)*
6 walnuts in shell, plus ½ cup chopped walnuts
Pistachios for garnish

Place the juices in a large pot. Whisk the flour gradually into the cold juice until dissolved. Bring to a boil. Lower the heat to maintain a gentle rolling boil. Cook, stirring occasionally, for about 2 hours or until the mixture has obtained a pea soup consistency and starts to bubble.

Reduce heat to prevent the *samanak* from spattering. As the mixture thickens, it requires less heat and constant stirring with a flat-ended wooden spatula to prevent it from sticking to the bottom of the pot. Continue to cook for another 2 hours or until the *samanak* turns a rich brown color and is reduced to one-quarter of its original volume and spreads around when poured on a saucer (the consistency is more similar to puree than to a paste).

Add all the walnuts. Steam the pudding by placing a cloth towel between the pot and the lid on very low heat for about 20 minutes. Transfer to a serving bowl. Let cool completely. Sprinkle with pistachios before serving.

How to prepare wheat sprout juices for Samanak:

1. In a bowl, soak 1 pound of unpelted wheat grain in water overnight.

2. With a wooden skewer, poke evenly spaced holes 3 inches apart all through the bottom of a disposable aluminum roasting pan. Drain the soaked wheat and spread it across the bottom of the roasting pan loosely, in a thin layer. Sprinkle with cool water. Dampen a towel and lay it over the wheat. Transfer the roasting pan with the wheat onto a wire rack and place it in a well-lit area at room temperature (avoid direct sun and over-watering). The wheat germination will start the next day. Keep the grains and the towel moist by spraying with water when dry until the wheat germination is complete, about 2 to 3 days.

3. Replace the kitchen towel with a paper towel when light-green sprouts appear on the grains. Keep the grains moist for another 2 days until the green needle-shaped leaves appear and eventually open and are grown 3 inches tall, around the 8th day.

4. Hold the wheat leaves by one corner and lift them. You will notice a 1-inch white layer of roots formed underneath the wheat grains and a 1-inch light green layer of sprouts just above the grains. Above the sprouts is the extension of the bright green blade-like leaves. With the help of kitchen scissors cut the leaves and discard, leaving 1 inch of the light-green sprouts close to the wheat and roots. Transfer the roots, sprouts, and wheat to a  colander and rinse lightly under running water. Then cut into smaller portions for easier grinding.

5. You will need 7 quarts of water (28 cups). To extract the sprout juices, grind 2 cups of the sprouts, wheat, and roots with 1 cup of water in a food processor for about 2 minutes until it forms a paste. Squeeze out the juices from the paste into a large, heavy cooking pot and then return the paste to the processor and grind again, adding 1 more cup of water and then transferring the juices to the cooking pot. Repeat this two more times adding 2 more cups of water. Discard the paste after grinding it 4 times. Continue the process grinding the remaining wheat with water until you have about 28 cups of juices.

Note: When the recipe for *Samanak* is doubled, preparation time and cooking time must be doubled as well.

COOL CARDAMOM PUDDING

Maghut

Maghut *is perhaps the lightest and simplest of all Afghan puddings, prepared with water and cornstarch, colored by saffron and pistachios, and scented with rose water and cardamom.* Maghut *is often made attractive by adding food coloring in addition to the saffron for color. Sometimes it is served un-molded from small containers onto a platter. Afghan children love* maghut.

⅓ cup cornstarch
¼ cup cool water
Pinch saffron powder
1 tablespoon warm water
1½ cups sugar
Seeds of 6 cardamom
   pods
2 tablespoons whole
   pistachios
½ tablespoon rose water

Dissolve the cornstarch in the ¼ cup of cool water and set aside. Dissolve the saffron powder in the warm water and set aside.

Bring 4 cups of water to a rolling boil. Add the sugar and cardamom seeds. Stir to dissolve sugar. Reduce heat to low and add the cornstarch solution gradually in a thin stream while stirring vigorously. Add the saffron solution and stir to mix. Simmer for 5 minutes while stirring, until the pudding turns thick and clear. Turn the heat off.

Add the pistachios. Mix well and let cool for 7 minutes. Add the rose water and mix. Transfer to a serving bowl or divide among 4 serving bowls. Let the *maghut* chill for about 3 hours before serving.

SWEET YOGURT

Mast Sherin

*Mast Sherin is prepared with milk and starter yogurt (*mast*) as a culture to ferment the milk. Sweet (*sherin*) yogurt is served as a dessert with fruit toppings and chopped or sliced nuts. The fermentation process takes from eight to twelve hours depending on room temperature. Yogurt, in general, is prepared with organic milk throughout Afghanistan. Ghazni province is known to have the best dairy products in the country.*

¼ cup plain yogurt
1 quart (4 cups) fresh whole
  milk
2 tablespoons sugar
Fresh strawberries
Sliced pistachios

Whisk the plain yogurt and set it aside. Heat the milk to a boiling point. Then let cool at room temperature until it is 130 degrees F (not burning hot to touch).

Mix the sugar into the milk until dissolved. Fold the yogurt gently into the milk. Then transfer to a decorative dish, and cover with a lid and several cloth towels in a secure place at room temperature. Let stand for 12 hours.

Refrigerate the finished yogurt for 2 hours before serving. Serve the yogurt as a dessert with some strawberries on top and sprinkled with some pistachios.

Snow and Noodles Dessert / *Zhala wa Faluda*

The Best of Afghan Cooking

SNOW AND NOODLES DESSERT

Zhala wa Faluda

Makes 6 servings

Zhala *noodles are prepared with wheat or cornstarch. Rice noodles prepared with cornstarch can serve the same purpose. To prepare the* faluda, *snow is mixed with cold noodles and saturated with a cold lemon syrup. Scoops of ice cream are placed on top of the noodles. Cream and nuts add to the beauty of this cold dessert.* Zhala wa Faluda *is prepared commercially in Afghanistan. Snow is brought from the Salang Mountains, layered with hay, and stored in special, natural storages dug in the mountain of Kabul for later use. Luckily, since most of us don't have access to mountain snow, today's food processors can turn ice into "snow" in seconds.*

2 ounces rice stick noodles
1 cup sugar
1 tablespoon lemon juice
¼ cup rose water
3 cups crushed ice or snow
6 scoops of vanilla or strawberry ice
  cream
Whipped cream for decoration
2 tablespoons ground pistachios

Bring 4 cups of water to a boil. Remove from heat and add the noodles. Soak for about 10 minutes or until tender. Drain the noodles and soak in cool water. Refrigerate in the water for 1 hour.

Bring 1½ cups of water to a boil. Stir in the sugar and lemon juice. Boil the mixture until syrupy. Add the rose water and stir to mix. Refrigerate for 2 hours.

If using crushed ice, grind in a food processor until snowy. Keep in the freezer.

To serve the *faluda*, mix the noodles with the ground ice or snow and divide among serving stemware. Saturate the snow and noodle mixture with the reserved lemon syrup. Top with one scoop of ice cream in each bowl. Pipe the whipped cream on top of the ice cream scoops. Sprinkle with ground pistachio. Serve immediately.

SYRUP AND SNOW

Sheera wa Barf

Makes 4 to 6 servings

Sheera *is a syrup prepared with brown sugar, mint, and lemon juice and then served with snow (barf). Afghanistan's higher altitudes have harsh winters and plenty of snow. This quick and easy dessert is made with* gur *in Afghanistan but in the US we substitute brown sugar. Gur is obtained from sugarcane, abundantly grown in the tropical climate of Eastern Afghanistan in Nangarhar province. Tons of spicy* gur *are exported from the Eastern districts to other parts of the country each year. Spicy* gur *is consumed as a sweet with tea, while plain* gur *is utilized in the culinary field for making desserts such as* halwa *and* laytee.

½ cup mint sprigs
1½ cups light brown sugar
2 tablespoons lemon juice
4 cups snow or powdered ice
Crushed pistachio to garnish

In a small saucepan place the mint sprigs, brown sugar, lemon juice, and 1 cup of water. Using a spoon stir to mix well. Place the solution on moderate heat and bring to a rolling boil. Boil gently for about 8 minutes or until a light syrup is obtained. Filter the syrup through a sieve and discard the mint sprigs. Refrigerate the syrup to cool completely.

To serve, divide the snow into serving bowls. Drizzle the syrup around the top of the snow and sprinkle with pistachios. Serve immediately.

SOOTHING POSTPARTUM DRINK

Laytee

Laytee is prepared by stir-frying whole wheat flour in oil. Enough water and sugar are then added to make a thick liquid. Saffron adds color and cardamom is added for aroma. Walnuts and pistachios are used for crunch and decoration. Some laytee *recipes call for ginger. This delicious treat is traditionally prepared for new mothers after childbirth to soothe the labored muscles and inflammations.*

2 cups dark brown sugar
¼ teaspoon saffron powder
1 teaspoon ground cardamom
8 cups boiling water
½ cup oil
1 cup whole wheat flour
½ cup chopped walnuts
Pistachio slivers

In a mixing bowl, dissolve the brown sugar, saffron, and cardamom in the boiling water. Set aside.

Pour the oil into a six-quart pot and place it over medium heat. When the oil is hot, in about 2 to 3 minutes, sprinkle the flour into the oil and stir for about 2 to 3 minutes, until the flour smells roasted. Pour the prepared sugar water in gradually while stirring and cook until it is a thick drink with pea soup consistency. Add the walnuts and mix. Simmer for another 15 minutes before serving hot. This makes a delicious treat for rainy days.

Orange Marmalade / *Muraba e Narinj*

CONSERVES

Muraba

Unlike the heavy-set jams of the western world that are simply used as a spread on bread, *muraba* are chunky and aromatic and serve another purpose. These breakfast treats are enjoyed in Afghan homes as fruit compotes with freshly toasted bread and ruby-red tea, brewed to perfection, on the side.

Muraba are prepared when the fruits of the season are ripe and plentiful. The most common *muraba* are made out of sour cherries in the Spring, apples in the Summer, quinces in the Fall, and oranges in the Winter. Some *muraba* are prepared with slivered pistachios or almonds for a crunchier texture. Before the three decades of war, *muraba* were accessible both commercially and in private batches. Unfortunately, a record-breaking drought and the catastrophes of war have caused the production of *muraba* to decline.

Muraba are largely consumed in the metropolitan cities of Afghanistan and are considered a delicacy in the more remote areas. *Muraba* prepared with summer fruits last through the winter, especially in the higher altitudes and cooler climates such as those of the capital city and other regions north of the Hindu Kush Mountains.

Sour cherries are scarce in certain climates, but black cherries can be used as an excellent substitute with the addition of more lemon juice. Another hard-to-find fruit in tropical climates is quince (*behi*). Quince are found in Indo-European fruit markets in autumn when the fruit gets ripe. This mysterious fruit is tart to eat raw. The magic comes with heat when it starts to change color from light yellow to deep red and the tartness relaxes, as a sweet aroma wafts from it. Quinces grow in higher altitudes and snowy regions of Afghanistan and are harvested from late October to November. Like in many parts of the world the yellow, fuzzy fruit with a sweet smell is preferred to be made into *muraba* in Afghanistan. This delectable *muraba* is served in the mornings with toasted Afghan bread and tea on the side.

Cardamom and rose water give Afghan *muraba* a distinguished aroma. All varieties of the Afghan nan, when toasted, are excellent choices to be served with *muraba*.

SOUR CHERRY CONSERVE

Muraba e Alubalu

Makes 36 ounces

This sweet and sour jam (muraba) is prepared with sour cherries, sugar, and lemon juice. Cherries (alubalu) grow in higher altitudes where it snows in winter like in Kabul. The Paghman district located in the west of Kabul is known for the best quality regular and sour cherries. Sour cherries are edible and taste good with a sprinkle of salt to balance the tanginess. However, in culinary uses, sugar is added for the sweet and sour taste. This cherry conserve tastes great with toasted Afghan flat nan and cardamom-flavor tea for breakfast. Muraba e alubalu is also prepared for the fasting month of Ramadan and is served in Sahar after a meal (midnight meal before the fasting starts at the following dawn).

3 pounds sour cherries
¼ cup lemon juice
1 box pectin (2 ounces)
2 cups sugar
1 tablespoon ground cardamom

Remove the stems and pit the cherries. In a large saucepan add the cherries to 1 cup of water and the lemon juice and bring to a boil. Lower heat and simmer, covered, until cherries are soft, about 30 to 40 minutes depending on the cherry variety.

Mix the pectin with the sugar and add to the cherries. Raise the heat to medium-high. Boil the cherries uncovered until the muraba reaches the desired consistency, about 20 minutes. Muraba should be thick but still drippy. It will thicken more as it cools. Add the cardamom. Stir well and allow to cool completely in sterilized glass jars.

PEAR CONSERVE

Muraba e Nak

Makes 40 ounces

Green Anjou pears (nak) are cooked in water and sugar until syrupy for this conserve. Cardamom and rose water are added for aroma, saffron for color, and pistachios for crunch and beauty. Green pears are cultivated in all climates of Afghanistan. From Herat in the west to Maidan/Wardak in the center and Badakhshan province in the northwest, all produce the best quality pears. However, Badakhshan is known for the production of the best yakh-nak (cold/ice pears), that are presumed more tolerant to the cold climates of the North, as the name indicates.

2½ pounds firm green Anjou
  pears
2 cups sugar
1 tablespoon lemon juice
Pinch ground saffron
½ tablespoon ground
  cardamom
⅓ cup chopped pistachios
1 teaspoon rose water (optional)

Peel and quarter the pears. Core and then slice each quarter widthwise into ¼-inch thick slices.

Place the pear slices, sugar, and ¾ cup of water in a large saucepan. Add the lemon juice and saffron. Stir and cook gently for about 40 to 45 minutes or until the candy thermometer registers 220 degrees F (gel point). To test for doneness, place a tablespoon of the syrup over a cool saucer and leave it in the freezer for 1 minute. If the syrup wrinkles when pushed with a finger, it is ready.

Add the cardamom, pistachios, and rose water and stir. Simmer for about 5 more minutes. Allow to cool. Transfer to sterilized glass jars and refrigerate after each use.

APRICOT CONSERVE

Muraba e Zardalu

Makes 32 ounces

This muraba *is prepared with apricots (zardalu) cooked in sugar syrup. Afghanistan has many varieties of the best apricots in the world, of which the* amiri *and* qaisi *varieties are loved most by Afghans for their juicy texture and sweetness. Tons of this extraordinary fruit are exported to other countries in Asia and Europe and to the U.S. Apricots are pitted and dried on rooftops in the villages for winter consumption. The dried apricot varieties are called* keshta, gholeng, *and* chapa namak.

4 teaspoons fruit pectin
3 cups sugar
2 teaspoons ground cardamom
1 tablespoon lemon juice
2 pounds fresh apricots, peeled, split, pits removed, and sliced
½ teaspoon rose water
2 tablespoons slivered pistachios

In a saucepan, mix 2 cups of water and the fruit pectin, sugar, cardamom, and lemon juice. Boil over medium heat until a candy thermometer reaches 220 degrees F.

Toss in the apricots and cook for about 10 minutes or until the apricots are transparent and the syrup is thick. Skim off any foam that forms.

Set aside to cool. Mix in the rose water and pistachios. Ladle into sterilized glass jars.

QUINCE CONSERVE

Muraba e Behi

Makes 40 ounces

When quince fruit (behi) is used in conserve preparation, it is considered the delicacy of all muraba. *Quince conserve is prepared with quince slices, sugar syrup, nuts, cardamom, and rose water. Saffron adds color to the jam. Quince has heat-activated color-change properties. The longer the quince cooks the richer and darker the color becomes, from yellow to dark maroon. Quinces ripen in the fall in the cooler climates of Afghanistan. When incorporated into meat stews, the grainy pulp and the sweet aroma of the quince make the dish delectable and special.*

2 pounds firm quinces
3 cups sugar
1 tablespoon lemon juice
¼ teaspoon ground saffron
2 teaspoons cardamom seeds
1 cup boiling water
2 tablespoons chopped
  pistachios
1 tablespoon flaked almonds
½ tablespoon rose water

Peel and quarter the quinces. Core and then slice each quarter into 3 slices. Place the quince slices and 3 cups of water in a large saucepan. Cover and simmer the quince gently for about 30 minutes or until the fruit is tender and the water has evaporated.

Stir in the sugar, lemon juice, saffron, cardamom seeds, and 1 cup of boiling water. (For a darker colored *muraba* add 1 additional cup of boiling water and cook for an additional hour.) Stir the *muraba* to mix. Cook the fruit on moderate heat for about 2 more hours or until a candy thermometer reads 220 degrees F.

Stir in the nuts and rose water and cook for about 2 minutes. Allow to cool, and then stir gently. Foam will disappear gradually as the fruit turns transparent. Transfer to sterilized glass jars and refrigerate after each use.

LOQUAT CONSERVE

Muraba e Loquat

Makes 24 ounces

Loquats grows in the tropical Eastern zones of Afghanistan such as Nangar-har province. The fruit ripens during the Spring season and is exported to other provinces and the capital city. Loquat conserve is prepared after the fruit halves are skinned and the seeds are removed. Saffron adds color and cardamom and rose water are incorporated for aroma. This muraba can be consumed as a spread on toasted nan when processed into puree after cooking. Slivered pistachios and flaked almonds add to the crunchiness of the conserve.

3 pounds fresh loquats
2 cups sugar
Pinch ground saffron
Juice of ½ lemon
1 tablespoon pectin
1 teaspoon ground cardamom
1 teaspoon rose water
½ tablespoon slivered pistachios
½ tablespoon flaked almonds

Wash the loquats thoroughly and cut the fruit in half. Cut off the blossom end and discard the seeds and the sack that they're enclosed in. Peel the halves and place them in a mixing bowl. Add the sugar and mix. Leave at room temperature for 3 hours to macerate.

Transfer the fruit with juices to a pot and place on medium-low heat. Sprinkle in the saffron and stir to mix. Add the lemon juice and pectin. Cook uncovered for about 20 to 25 minutes until juice has thickened but is not sticky to touch, or until a candy thermometer registers 220 degrees F.

Remove from heat. Mix in the cardamom and rose water. Set aside to cool. Once cool, sprinkle with nuts and transfer to sterilized jars. Or puree to desired chunkiness without nuts. Serve with toasted nan.

Loquat Conserve / *Muraba e Loquat*

ORANGE MARMALADE

Muraba e Narinj

Makes 16 ounces

This aromatic marmalade is prepared with sour orange peel cooked in water and sugar to a syrup consistency. Saffron is added for color and cardamom for aroma. Roasted almonds and pistachios are added to the conserve last. The ever-green Nangarhar province, in the northeast of Afghanistan, is home to Afghan citrus and is where the annual Orange Blossom Festival is held in the spring. Poetry competitions, music, and feasts take place in an awe-inspiring atmosphere pervaded by the sweet aroma of orange blossoms.

10 medium-size firm sour oranges*
1½ cups sugar
1 teaspoon ground cardamom
Pinch ground saffron
1 tablespoon lime juice
½ pound mixture of slivered
  walnuts and pistachios

*Regular oranges can be substituted if sour oranges aren't available.

Using a potato peeler, peel the oranges, leaving a thin layer of the white pith on the oranges. Using kitchen scissors, cut the peel into 1-inch-long narrow strips. Place the peels in a saucepan and pour in enough water to cover the peels. Bring to a boil and then lower heat and simmer for about 3 minutes. Drain. Repeat boiling and draining one more time to rid the peels of their bitterness. Cover the peel a third time with water and then cover the saucepan and boil for 30 minutes or until the peels are tender. Drain.

In another saucepan, dissolve the sugar in 1 cup of water and bring to a boil on medium heat. Add the cooked orange peels, cardamom, and saffron. Boil for 6 to 8 minutes on medium heat or until the mixture is syrupy and thick. Add the lime juice and nuts. Stir to mix. Allow the *muraba* to cool and then transfer to sterilized glass jars.

APPLE CONSERVE

Muraba e Seb

Tart apples (seb) are peeled, cored, and sliced to be cooked in sugar syrup into a delectable conserve that is served with toasted Afghan nan for breakfast. This muraba *is prepared when apples are in season and plentiful. Apples are cultivated in many regions of Afghanistan, particularly in Maidan, Wardak, and Lugar provinces. Firm, tart autumn apples, called* seb tirmahi, *are perfect for making this conserve that can last through the winter.*

1½ pounds green tart apples,
  such as Granny Smith
1½ cups sugar
2 teaspoons ground cardamom
Pinch of saffron powder
1 tablespoon lemon juice
1 tablespoon rose water
  (optional)

Peel and core the apples and cut them into 1-inch chunks. Cook the apples in 1 cup of water on low heat for about 8 minutes or until the fruit is tender.

Add the sugar, cardamom, and saffron. Stir gently to dissolve the sugar. Continue to cook the apples on low heat for 30 to 40 minutes or until the fruit is translucent and the syrup has thickened (220 degrees F on candy thermometer).

Skim off any foam that forms. Stir in the lemon juice and cook for 2 to 3 more minutes. Allow to cool and then mix in the rose water. Transfer to sterilized glass jars to store.

Creamy Green Tea / *Qaimaq Chai*

BEVERAGES

Nawshaba Ha

Tea, called *chai* in Afghanistan, has been around ever since the first donkey loads of the Chinese trade carried it through Kabul to India via the Silk Road thousands of years ago. The *chai* tradition has since become the symbol of hospitality throughout Afghanistan. Let's have a cup of tea together means the beginning of a long-term friendship between strangers. There is no home without tea. Passing through the slums of Kabul, old kettles can be seen steaming on embers, ready to be served, even to the passers-by.

Tea consumption serves multiple purposes. Whether green or black, tea is traditionally a breakfast complement and is called the 'Morning Chai.' Morning is the only time most Afghans sweeten their tea—other times tea is served plain with sweets on the side. The quench of a hard day's thirst is satisfied by endless cups of ruby-red plain tea served in china teapots. The magical effects of caffeine are energizing to the tired muscles and mind. Green tea is the *chai* of the elderly while black tea is for everyone. And when sweetened tea is consumed with bread it is the feast of the poor.

A tea and milk mixture called *Qaimaq Chai* is brewed through a special process of airing (*badkash*) resulting in the magical transformation of the green tea color to peach. *Qaimaq Chai* is served at celebratory events like engagement parties or the day after a wedding.

Afghanistan is a country of snowy winters and chilly autumns. While tea is the beverage of all seasons, cold beverages are mostly prepared on warm summer days using the freshly picked fruits of the season. Cherry juice, Afghan lemonade, and orange shrub are the most popular beverages widely served to guests between meals. Raisin juice (*kishmishab*) is prepared commercially and sold at stalls in busy town areas.

The lunchtime beverage that replenishes the thirst of the scorching summer heat is *Doogh*. *Doogh* is prepared when village women, sitting on a mat under a huge shade tree, fill a clay urn with fresh yogurt and water. They know rocking that urn to-and-fro will take a considerably long time before the tangy *doogh* is separated from the butter. When the gassy beverage is then mixed with finely chopped young cucumbers and dried crushed mint, the flavor is irresistible. In this book, the modern version of *doogh* is made with sour yogurt and club soda to gain similar results.

GREEN TEA WITH WALNUTS AND SPICES

Chai Chawa

Makes 4 servings

Chai Chawa *is prepared with green tea leaves. Ginger, walnuts, and fennel seeds are simmered with the green tea for their flavor and therapeutic properties, such as soothing inflammations and soreness of muscles. This beverage is sweetened with brown sugar or* gur *and is scented by ground cardamom. There is nothing more soothing than a cup full of* Chai Chawa, *especially on rainy days or after a day of hard work or on snowy days in subfreezing temperatures. Afghans also love to prepare this tea for new mothers after childbirth or for anyone suffering from menstrual cramps or muscle pain.*

3 teaspoons green tea leaves
¾ cup dark brown sugar, or to taste
2 tablespoons fresh ginger paste
2 teaspoons fennel seeds
4 tablespoons coarsely ground walnuts
1 teaspoon ground cardamom

In a saucepan bring 4 cups of water to a rolling boil. Add tea leaves, brown sugar, ginger paste, and fennel seeds. Cover and boil on a low flame for about 10 minutes or until all tea leaves have expanded. Filter the tea through a sieve, discarding the leaves and seeds.

Transfer the tea back into the same pan. Add the walnuts and cardamom. Cover and simmer for a further 5 minutes. Transfer to a teapot. Cover with a kitchen towel and let stand for 2 to 3 minutes before serving.

MINT GREEN TEA

Chai Nanaa

Makes 4 servings

When mint is simmered with basil and saffron in green tea, it transforms into a soothing and aromatic drink with the addition of honey and lemon. Afghans love the aroma of mint (nanaa), which has versatile culinary uses in Afghan kitchens. Adding mint to a salad stimulates the appetite and for that reason mint must be chopped finely before being added to salads. Many Afghan soups are sprinkled with powdered mint, as are ashak *and* mantu *dumplings.*

1 teaspoon green tea leaves
2 cups fresh mint leaves
4 fresh basil leaves
4 strands saffron
Juice of 1 lemon
2 tablespoon honey (optional)

In a kettle bring 4 cups of water to a rolling boil. Add the tea leaves, mint leaves, basil leaves, saffron, and lemon juice. Cover and simmer for about 5 minutes, until the flavors are well blended and the water has turned into a yellowish-green color. Add the honey and stir well (optional). Filter through a tea sieve and divide among four teacups. Serve immediately.

DILL TEA

Chai Shebid

Makes 4 servings

This simple beverage is prepared by simmering green or black tea with dill (shibed) and mint. Sugar and lemon juice are added for flavor. Dill is said to have soothing effects on the digestive system. When dill is incorporated into short-grain rice dishes such as Shoulé Goshti, *it gives the* shoula *a unique flavor and aroma. Dill is used both fresh and dried in Afghan kitchens.*

**2 tablespoons dried dill or 1 cup
  fresh chopped dill**
¼ teaspoon ground cardamom
**1 teaspoon dried mint or ½ cup
  fresh mint leaves**
**1 teaspoon green or black tea
  leaves**
3 tablespoons sugar
Juice of one lemon

In a kettle bring 4 cups of water to a rolling boil. Add the dill, cardamom, mint, tea leaves, sugar, and lemon juice. Cover and simmer for about 10 minutes, until the flavors are well blended and the tea leaves have expanded. Filter through a tea sieve and divide among four teacups. Serve immediately.

GINGER AND MINT TEA

Chai Zanjabil wa Nana

Makes 4 servings

Fresh ginger (zanjabil) is used in preparing Chai Chawa and Chai Zanjabil. Ginger has soothing effects on sore muscles, inflammations, cramping, and ulcers. Mint, honey, and saffron add to the color, aroma, and freshness of the black tea. This chai is considered to be the beverage of choice for the elderly with aches and pains. Other times, it is prepared for cold, rainy days, or after a day of hard work.

2 cups fresh mint leaves
3 fresh ginger pieces
  (¼ inch each)
4 strands saffron
1 tablespoon lemon juice
1 teaspoon powdered
  black tea
2 tablespoons honey
  (optional)

In a kettle bring 4 cups of water to a rolling boil. Add the mint leaves, ginger, saffron, lemon juice, and black tea. Cover and simmer for about 5 minutes, until the flavors are well blended and the water has turned into a yellowish-green color. Add the honey and stir well (optional). Filter through a tea sieve and divide among four teacups. Serve immediately.

CREAMY GREEN TEA

Qaimaq Chai

This is a fancy green tea and milk beverage with a touch of cream (qaimaq), sugar, and cardamom. This drink goes through a color transformation from coffee-brown to peach when milk is added to the tea through a special cooling and pouring process called baad kardan *(airing).* Qaimaq Chai *is typically prepared for celebratory events such as engagement parties and is served with pastries and kabobs.*

¼ cup green tea leaves
½ teaspoon baking soda
6 cups regular whole milk
1 cup sugar
2 teaspoons ground cardamom
½ cup clotted cream or
   whipped cream

Bring 3 cups of water to a rolling boil. Add the tea leaves and baking soda. Boil gently on low heat for about 30 minutes.

Working with two bowls, place 3 ice cubes in one bowl and, holding the tea kettle about 12 inches high, pour the tea mixture over the ice until the kettle is empty. Place 3 ice cubes in the second bowl and pour in the tea mixture the same way, from the first to the second bowl. Repeat this procedure 4 times. The tea color will change to a dark coffee brown.

Filter the tea back into the kettle and discard the tea leaves. Add the milk, sugar, and cardamom. Stir to mix. Simmer for about 10 minutes, by which time the mixture's color should have turned to a rich pinkish-peach shade. Divide among 8 china teacups. Top each with a tablespoon of the clotted cream.

MILKY SPICE TEA

Sheer Chai

Makes 4 servings

This simple beverage is prepared with black tea, milk (sheer), cardamom, and sugar. Tea culture plays a large role in showing Afghan hospitality. Long-term friendship starts with "let's have a cup of tea." Afghan tribes were possibly among the first in the world outside China to be introduced to tea when the neighboring Chinese merchants traveled along the Silk Road through Afghanistan. Bread and tea are the poor man's meal. Breakfast is called "the morning tea (chai sobh)" even if egg dishes and meat are included.

2 black tea bags
2 cups boiling water
¼ cup sugar
1 cup regular whole milk
1 cup half & half
1 teaspoon ground cardamom

Place the tea bags in the 2 cups boiling water on low heat and boil for about 10 minutes. Add the sugar, milk, half & half, and cardamom. Simmer for another 5 minutes. Discard the tea bags. Divide the tea among four serving cups. *Sheer Chai* tastes great with cakes, salty cookies, or *khajur* pastry.

RAISIN WATER

Kishmish Ab

Makes 4 servings

Raisins (kishmish) are soaked in hot water (ab) overnight and sold as a nutritious beverage by vendors on hot summer days to boost energy. Afghan grapes are grown in the provinces of Kandahar, Kapisa, Herat, Ghazni, Kabul, and Parwan for both fresh consumption and production of raisins, owing to their high commercial value. Afghan grapes and raisins are sold to both local and neighboring markets and overseas countries. When they are not dried, grapes are preserved in a covered container called a kangina *(constructed of soft, wet earth dried in the sun), for up to six months.*

1 cup dark raisins
4 cups hot water
1 tablespoon split pistachios

Wash and rinse the raisins with warm water. Soak the raisins in the 4 cups of hot water overnight. Meanwhile, soak the pistachios in cool water in a separate small bowl overnight.

The next morning, drain the nuts and skin them. Then add to the raisin mixture. Mix and serve, ladling some of the raisins and nuts into each glass with the juices.

TANGY YOGURT AND CUCUMBER DRINK

Doogh   Makes 6 servings

Traditionally, doogh is obtained when butter is separated from yogurt, leaving behind a tangy, gassy white liquid. Water is added to the yogurt in a large clay vessel called a jug, and the jug is rocked on a pillow for about an hour. In some villages, a large sack made of animal skin, called a mashk, is used for making doogh. However, mechanical and electric doogh makers are replacing the old system. Doogh is usually mixed with finely chopped cucumbers and powdered mint. Afghans enjoy having doogh on warm summer days and usually take a nap afterward due to the mildly soporific properties of the drink. The addition of club soda and a pinch of salt to plain yogurt and an electric mixer can achieve a similar taste and flavor to traditional doogh.

3 cups plain yogurt
4 cups club soda, chilled
1 teaspoon salt
1 cup finely chopped cucumbers
1 teaspoon dried mint flakes

Leave the yogurt at room temperature for 24 hours to turn sour. Then chill for about 4 hours.

Beat the cold sour yogurt. Add the club soda and mix. Add the salt and mix the *doogh* with an electric mixer until foamy. Add the chopped cucumber. Crush the mint flakes into powder and add to the *doogh*. Mix with a spatula. Serve chilled, preferably on warm summer days.

Tangy Yogurt and Cucumber Drink / *Doogh*

BASIL SEED JUICE

Sharbat Raihan

Makes 4 servings

This basil seed (raihan) juice is prepared on the tenth day of Muharram, a religious holiday in Afghanistan observed in remembering the martyrdom of the grandsons of the Prophet Mohammad, peace be upon him. Since the martyrdom took place in an arid desert with no water in sight, juices and water are symbolically served to the attendees of the religious Memorial Day to this day, specifically in Shia communities. Sharbat Raihan is also served at the burial site after funerals.

1 teaspoon basil seeds
¾ cup warm water
½ cup sugar
3 cups cold water
2 tablespoons rose water
Ice cubes (optional)

Soak the basil seeds in warm water for about 10 minutes or until they expand and turn transparent around the seeds.

Meanwhile, dissolve the sugar in the cold water. Add the rose water and stir to mix. Add the basil seeds solution to the sugary cold water. Stir to mix. Chill the drink for a couple of hours. Serve.

LEMONADE WITH ORANGE AND LIME

Sharbat Limo

Makes 4 to 6 servings

This juice (sharbat) is prepared with three citrus fruits, orange, lime, and predominantly lemon (limo). It quenches the thirst on hot summer days. In Kabul and other large cities, Afghans treat their guests to a glass of fresh Sharbat Limo. *A few provinces contribute to the making of this* sharbat. *Fresh citrus fruits from Jalalabad, crystal clear water from Paghman, sugar from Baghlan, the heavenly scent of roses from Kabul, and the one-of-a-kind ice from the Salang Mountains.*

1 orange
1 cup lemon juice
¼ cup lime juice
1 tablespoon rose water
¾ cup sugar
7 cups cold water
Ice cubes (optional)

Peel the orange into thin strips and slice the peel narrowly, then measure 2 tablespoons and reserve for serving. Squeeze out the orange juices and measure to ½ cup.

Place the orange juice, lemon juice, lime juice, and rose water in a mixing bowl. Stir the sugar into the cold water until dissolved and then stir with the juices. Let chill for about 4 hours.

Divide the lemonade among serving glasses. Place ice cubes at top of lemonade in each glass. Sprinkle with reserved orange peel.

Saffron / *Zafaran*

GLOSSARY OF AFGHAN INGREDIENTS

GLOSSARY OF AFGHAN INGREDIENTS

Alu Bokhara / Dried Sour Plums *Alu Bokhara* is a tart plum that complements the strong flavor of beef stews as well as gives color and flavor to the Afghan *Dahl* appetizer (page 28).

Badenjan / Seedless Eggplants The dimples at the bottom of eggplants determine

their quality. A good quality eggplant that is young, seedless, and crisp has a small, round dimple (as shown on the right eggplant). An oblong, irregular imprint (like on the left) represents a bitter, seedy, and softer eggplant, not suitable for cooking. They are sometimes referred to as male and female eggplants with females being inferior.

Behi / Quinces The hard, grainy pulp and sweet smell of quinces make them a delicacy for all *muraba* and meat stews.

Chaka / Drained Yogurt This is a drained yogurt often mixed with herbs and spices. To make it, plain yogurt is whisked and placed in a strainer lined with cheesecloth to allow the water to drip away. The result is then mixed with a pinch of salt, ¼ teaspoon garlic paste, and ¼ teaspoon powdered mint per 1 cup of *chaka*.

Gandana / Leeks A cultivar of a wild variety of leeks, this vegetable is widely used in Afghan cooking. Persian tara, scallions, Chinese chives, or leeks are good substitutes.

Gholeng / Dried Apricot *Gholeng* is a variety of dried apricot (see also *keshta*). They are soaked whole with the seed to prepare *Haft Mewa* (page 271). Any variety of dried apricot can be substituted.

Hulba / Fenugreek Seeds *Hulba* have a bitter taste and a strong aroma. They are boiled briefly and then rinsed to rid them of the bitterness. They are used both for pickles and sweet rice dishes in Afghan cooking.

Jalghoza / Pine Nuts *Jalghoza* are the edible kernels of pine trees used in Afghan cooking due to their mild, nutty flavor.

Keshta / Dried Apricots *Keshta* is a variety of dried apricot (see also *gholeng*).These sweet fruits add flavor, color, and sweetness to *Haft Mewa* (page 271) and *Piawa Soup* (page 53).

Khurfa / Purslane Afghans traditionally harvest and carry this weed from the wild to their kitchens and cook it into a delectable *qurma* served with chalow rice or nan on the side.

Mash / Mung Beans These tiny beans are widely used in combination with short-grain rice for *shoula* cooking. The coarsely chopped version is utilized to prepare *Mashaba* (Beef and Bean Soup, page 50) and *Bolani Mash* (Mung Bean Bolani, page 18).

Munuqa / Raisins *Munuqa* are a large, dark raisin with intense sweetness and flavor. You can substitute any black raisins.

Palow Spice Blend The proportion of individual spices used in *palow* dishes (long-grain rice and meat dishes) varies by households. Below is the most popular ratio of the spices that form this spice blend. The amount used when the spice blend is combined with rice is 1 teaspoon Palow Spice Blend per 6 cups of rice.

    1½ tablespoons ground green cardamom
    1 teaspoon ground black cardamom
    1 tablespoon ground cumin
    1 teaspoon ground cloves
    ¼ teaspoon ground cinnamon
    ¼ teaspoon ground black pepper

Qurut is the tangy substance made from yogurt after the butter is separated. The paste is shaped into balls and sun-dried. It is used in a variety of Afghan dishes. *Chaka* could be substituted (see page 318).

Rawash / Rhubarb is a cold-season perennial crop grown in the foothills of Kabul and other cities. Its tart flavor balances the spiciness of certain Afghan stews (*qurma*).

Senjid / Lotus Tree Fruit *Senjid* are a dried fruit similar in size and seed to dates. In English they are also called lotus tree fruit, oleaster, and Russian olives. They are available for sale online in the US. Their pulp has a mildly sweet flavor with a dry powdery texture. The outer layer is dry and flaky. *Senjid* add color to *Haft Mewa* (page 271).

Sheep Feet These are a delicacy that cannot be substituted with lamb shank. Sheep feet are available in Mexican and Middle Eastern markets in the US.

Siah Dana / Nigella Seeds These seeds have a pungent bitter taste. Their roasted fragrance gives Afghan nan and pastries uniqueness. They also add flavor to *turshi* and chutney condiments.

Sumac (*Ghorè Angur* substitute) is a spice made from the berries of the sumac bush. The tart, lively spice adds flavor to various kabobs as an appetite stimulant.

Toot / Mulberries Mulberries are a popular fruit in Afghanistan. The provinces of Badakhshan, Kapisa, Kunar, Laghman, Nangarhar, Nimroz, Nuristan, Parwan, Panjshir, Samangan, and Takhar are the most prominent commercial producers of mulberries. The harvest season is from June to September. As you drive from Kabul, you

can find fruit stands every mile selling mulberries on the highway from Kabul to the north of the country. There are white, red, and black varieties and they are eaten fresh or dried. Black mulberries have more intense flavor and sweetness than white mulberries. In Afghanistan dried mulberries are ground with walnuts into a delicious dessert called *Chukida* (page 250) that is served with plain tea.

Zafaran / Saffron This expensive spice is used for flavor and color both in rice cookery and desserts. Saffron is grown mainly in the western area of Afghanistan.

INDEX